ILLEGAL TENDER

Counterfeiting
and the
Secret Service
in
Nineteenth-
Century
America

DAVID R. JOHNSON

Smithsonian Institution Press
Washington and London

To Peggy
For all her gifts
but especially for her love

© 1995 by David R. Johnson

Editor: Jenelle Walthour
Designer: Linda McKnight

Library of Congress Cataloging-in-Publication Data
Johnson, David Ralph, 1942-
    Illegal tender : counterfeiting and the Secret Service in
    nineteeth-century America / David R. Johnson.
       p.   cm.
    Includes bibliographical references and index.
    ISBN 1-56098-359-0
    1. Counterfeits and counterfeiting—United States—
History—19th century. 2. United States—History—Civil
War, 1861–1865—Counterfeit money. 3. United States—
Secret Service. I. Title.
HG336.U5J63   1994
364.1'33—dc20   93-40105

British Library Cataloguing-in-Publication Data is available

Manufactured in the United States of America
01 00 99 98 97 96 95 94   5 4 3 2 1

♾ The paper used in this publication meets the minimum
requirements of the American National Standard for
Permanence of Paper for Printed Library Materials
Z39.48-1984

For permission to reproduce illustrations appearing in this
book, please correspond directly with the owners of the
works, as listed in the individual captions. The Smithsonian
Institution Press does not retain reproduction rights for
these illustrations individually, or maintain a file of addresses
for photo sources.

ILLEGAL TENDER

CONTENTS

ACKNOWLEDGMENTS

ALTHOUGH I BEGAN writing this book longer ago than I care to remember, one of the pleasures of my nearly interminable journey has been the encouragement of many friends and colleagues, who have offered advice and support along the way. Woodruff Smith took valuable time from his own work to offer devastatingly helpful critiques of the book's structure and argument. Roger Lane and Roger Lotchin read the entire manuscript and offered many valuable suggestions to improve it. With their insightful comments, several scholars, including Jeffrey Adler, Daniel Czitrom, Eric Monkkonen, and Mark Haller, helped me to improve the evolving manuscript. I, of course, occasionally ignored their sound advice, placing myself in the position of accepting responsibility for the result.

Many people eased the travails of a visiting scholar. Muriel Atkin and Kenneth Jackson greatly exceeded the usual bonds of friendship by providing essential help in arranging accommodations for extended research trips to Washington, D.C., and New York. Timothy Gilfoyle introduced me to the wealth of information on counterfeiting in the New York City Municipal Archives. The staffs of various archival collections provided essential help in locating records. I especially thank Kenneth Cobb, at the New York Municipal Archives; Cindy Fox, Teresa Matchette, and James Cassedy, at the National Archives; and William Bischoff and John Kleeberg, at the American Numismatic Society, for their assistance. The staffs of the Ohio and the New Jersey historical societies also offered valuable help in locating some obscure source materials. Michael Sampson, of the Office of Public Affairs for the United States Secret Service, and Kenneth Vittitow, special agent in charge of the Secret Service's San Antonio office, provided crucial assistance in assembling the illustrations for this book.

In an era of tight budgets, I am grateful to have received financial assistance from a faculty research grant from the University of Texas at San Antonio and travel to collections grants from the National Endowment for the Humanities. Dwight Henderson, dean of the College of Social and Behavioral Sciences at University of Texas at San Antonio, gave some timely financial assistance for illustrative materials.

Every aspiring author needs a publisher who can turn his ruminations into a presentable book. I have been most fortunate that Mark Hirsch thought well enough of my manuscript to invest both his own and his staff's considerable talents in its publication. I have enjoyed working with all those at the Smithsonian Institution Press who have helped bring this project to fruition. I owe particular thanks to my editor, Jenelle Walthour.

Finally, I thank Peggy and Elizabeth (and our two cats) for enduring hot summers in distant places, and for providing me with the emotional support so essential to the completion of this scholarly endeavor. This book would not have been possible without them.

INTRODUCTION

GEORGE STANLEY was a busy man. Absorbed in his own personal search for success, he worked first as a carpenter, then as a horse dealer, and finally as a restaurateur in post–Civil War New York City. Superficially, his climb from skilled worker to small businessman represented a modest version of the familiar "rags to riches" saga, which seemed to explain the financial success of so many businessmen at the time. Stanley did indeed make a great deal of money. That, however, was the problem. Stanley literally made his own money: he was a counterfeiter.

Illegal Tender: Counterfeiting and the Secret Service in Nineteenth-century America describes what the U.S. government did to put the many George Stanleys in nineteenth-century America out of business. The government did this job well, because today Americans take the integrity of their money for granted, rarely worrying about the George Stanleys of the world. Paying cash for something is routine; neither the customer nor the clerk give more than a cursory glance at the money that is exchanged, because both trust that the money is genuine.

There was a time, however, when there was no such trust. When the Civil War erupted, perhaps as much as half of the paper notes in circulation were counterfeit. Skillful, well-organized counterfeiters working in a number of cities printed bogus notes by the thousands. Using methods surprisingly similar to legitimate businesses, counterfeiters worked as manufacturers, wholesalers, and retailers; they developed methods for advertising their products and had local, as well as regional and national, distribution networks.

In these circumstances merchants had to be careful about the money they accepted, and customers (at least the honest ones) had to be concerned about the notes they offered in payment for goods. For the merchant, failure to recognize counterfeit notes could result in substantial financial loss; for the customer, it could mean the loss of one's reputation and freedom.

By undermining people's trust in their currency, counterfeiters like George Stanley posed a serious threat to the efficient development of the nation's economy. What, however, could be done about it? The answer to that question turned out to be complicated, because the solution to a national problem like counterfeiting required the expansion of the federal government's ability to police American society. Most nineteenth-century Americans, however, were deeply suspicious of their federal government and viewed proposals to expand its powers with alarm. Any attempt to create a sound currency, which would promote economic development, clashed with the cherished belief that the federal government should have only a limited role in the nation's life.

Throughout the nineteenth century—especially prior to the Civil War—most Americans were far more devoted to their local communities than to the nation. As a result, they had built a political system that, in practice, severely limited the role of government in general and of the federal government in particular.[1]

Americans could not, however, restrict the government from their lives forever. Urban communities, trying to cope with problems arising from rapid social and economic change, initiated the accordance of greater authority to government. Despite their best intentions, urban Americans found that private solutions to public problems in such areas as health, transportation, water systems, and policing were ineffective. City and later state governments had to assume greater responsibilities for dealing with these problems, and in doing so, they aided the process of centralizing power in American society.

Thus it became a peculiarity of "the state" in the American con-

text that centralization of power began locally. Governments assumed increased control over their citizens' lives at different times,
for different reasons, and through different agencies.[2]

State building, in this generalized sense of a gradual centralization of governmental power, was well under way—though haltingly
—by the middle of the nineteenth century. Most Americans had not
had any direct experience with state building or awareness of it. Only
residents of the largest cities and states, which were experiencing
rapid change, would have had some personal understanding of this
evolving process.

At the federal level state building had not even begun. Indeed,
Jacksonian Democrats pursued policies that had collectively led to a
systematic decentralization of federal power. By midcentury they
had reduced the federal government to near impotence.

The Civil War halted and then began a reversal of the Jacksonian
legacy, not merely because winning the war required an unprecedented use of federal force, but also because the war gave the Republican party access to national power. As inheritors of the Whig traditions of government, the Republicans would promote a social and
economic agenda that encouraged the use of government power to
achieve their goals. Some of their policies did not survive the widespread efforts to reject federal state building after 1865, but the Republicans' reassertion of the national government's sovereignty over
the currency and the banking system ranks among the most important—and indeed fundamental—changes the Civil War produced.
No other wartime measures can claim so crucial a role in American
state building in the late nineteenth century as these. Money, to re-
coin a phrase, was power.

As an essential article for meeting the needs of individuals, businesses, and governments, money already had a long history of stirring
fundamental passions in American politics. Regardless of the particular form the debate over money assumed at any time—whether it was
taxes, banks, or the controversy over "sound" currency—the fundamental issue was always power.[3]

The Constitution reserved the right to coin money (and the implied power to regulate it) to the federal government. Although Congress created the U.S. Mint and the Bank of the United States to implement this authority, neither institution exerted much control over
national development in the antebellum era. The Mint's failure to pro-

duce enough coin for a rapidly expanding economy encouraged state banks to compete with it as a monetary source by issuing their own notes.[4] Antipathy toward federal power also undermined the Bank of the United States, which had performed some regulatory functions for the economy reasonably well prior to Jackson's veto of a new charter. Pursuing their ideological bias against centralized power, the Democrats succeeded in passing their subtreasury plan in 1840, thereby separating the federal government from any authority over banks. With the power to influence economic development so effectively dispersed among the states by these measures, the federal government's presumed constitutional monopoly over money seemed defunct.

The Civil War resuscitated that power with a vengeance. Faced with huge costs and scant resources, Secretary of the Treasury Salmon Chase adopted monetary policies that quickly forced the federal government to exercise its constitutional sovereignty over the currency. This was not, however, an assertion of power alien either to Chase or to his party's beliefs. Republican doctrine advocated the development of an infrastructure for a national capital market through the use of centralized state power.[5] A wartime emergency thus offered an opportunity to implement a major Republican policy goal.

Chase asked Congress for authority to issue paper notes in payment of government obligations. Congress responded with the Legal Tender Act of 1862, which historian Bray Hammond believes "recovered from desuetude the responsibility of the federal government for the monetary system and established for the first time the power of the federal sovereignty to do what had hitherto been generally considered both unconstitutional and inexpedient." This act, however, did more than simply restore a neglected authority. According to Hammond, it also "established a national monetary medium which derived its value from the will of the government. . . . as an exercise of sovereignty [greenbacks] advanced the government's powers far beyond what had ever been ascribed to it before."[6]

A second major assertion of federal authority in economic matters was the National Banking Act of 1863, which made the federal government the sole monetary source by driving state bank notes out of existence.[7] When the Supreme Court upheld the constitutionality of federal authority over the currency in the Third Legal Tender Case (1871), currency reform—unlike so many other measures adopted during the war—permanently enhanced federal power.[8]

Precisely how the federal government might have used its authority in economic matters to promote state building is not particularly clear in the current historiography, which tends to focus instead either on the political controversies surrounding monetary issues or on the general structure and operations of the new financial system after the war. In neither case have historians found much evidence connecting the federal government's assertion of sovereignty over the currency to a continual process of state building.[9]

Such connections did exist. They evolved from the unforeseen implications of the power to coerce, which was inherent in the national government's assertion of sovereignty in monetary matters. Since coercion is fundamental to, and indeed defines, state power, the power to coerce, more than anything else at the time, gave the federal government the ability to participate in state building.[10] Prior to the Civil War the federal government had lacked the authority to employ systematic coercion against its citizens in the course of their daily lives. As a consequence of the war, it acquired that authority.

Coercion, however, is merely an abstraction—particularly in a federal system—unless it assumes concrete form. A nation-state has to acquire the administrative capacity to extend its authority throughout its territory, in order to give substance to its theoretical claims. It must have the ability to penetrate its domain in a systematic manner.[11] Creating new policing agencies is one way to achieve that ability.

Policing can be crucial to the state-building process, because the effort to deal with criminals offers a national government many opportunities to affect the behavior of the entire population, not just a small group of deviants. The need to deal with crime justifies the passage of criminal laws, the creation of a central bureaucracy, the employment of agents, and the arrest, trial, and incarceration of offenders. In the process of erecting such a system, government officials in effect create standardized definitions of correct behavior for all their subjects. A policing system in this context becomes a powerful tool for socializing citizens to recognize the power of the state in their lives, as the enforcement apparatus gives the state an effective means for penetrating into the local civil fabric of society in order to enforce its version of political and social order.[12]

Considering American antipathy toward government in general and the federal government in particular, no one intended to champion federal policing as a means to expand the central government's power. Instead, that power tended to expand by accident rather than by design. When Congress passed the Legal Tender Act, the issue of the currency's integrity became inextricably bound to this assertion of sovereignty. The act, in effect, created new, crucial relationships between money, crime, and the American nation-state.

When state banks had issued notes, their value had fluctuated in accordance with public perception of each bank's worth as a privately operated corporation. Problems of sovereignty had not arisen, because the value of these notes had depended on the repute of individual banks rather than public trust in government. Since state governments had not guaranteed the value of these notes, they also had paid little attention, beyond passing a few obligatory laws against counterfeiting, to the problems of protecting the integrity of this currency. In these circumstances, the responsibility for protecting antebellum currency had devolved onto local law enforcement agencies. Their record in that endeavor, however, had been extremely poor. Despite local laws against it, counterfeiting had flourished.

In the absence of effective law enforcement, counterfeiting became a well-organized criminal activity capable of distributing its products on a national scale. Rooted in criminal social institutions that flourished in the working-class neighborhoods of America's cities, counterfeiters engaged in a multitude of complex operations that made their crime one of the nineteenth century's most successful illegal activities.

Congress paid little attention to the threat that counterfeiters posed to the new currency authorized by the Legal Tender Act. Public suspicion of paper money, however, made counterfeiting an important problem for the federal government, as the integrity of its notes became a crucial political issue. The Republican party expected the new currency to play a vital role in the evolution of the national economy and the national state. The national currency would simplify and streamline economic development by maintaining a consistent value over time and through geographical space, thereby facilitating the process of exchange in an increasingly complex economy. At the same time, the central government's control of the currency would enhance its power as a crucial participant in the creation of a modern, capitalist economy—but only if the general population willingly accepted this new currency.[13]

The new monetary arrangements rested, in other words, on

trust.[14] In an era that distrusted paper money on principle and harbored considerable hostility toward the idea of centralized power in general, the federal government's claim to sovereignty over the currency rested on shaky foundations, as long as counterfeiting remained a serious threat.

The need to create and to sustain the public's trust in the national currency required that the federal government extend the boundaries of its state-building activities by expanding its capacity to police society. Existing federal law enforcement agencies lacked the ability to meet this need. The Customs and Internal Revenue services and the Postal Inspection Service had broad administrative responsibilities that included some criminal matters. Their mandates, however, did not extend to dealing with professional criminals in the urban underworld. Federal marshals were both the largest and the most widely distributed policing agency of the era, but they were primarily officers of their courts, not detectives skilled in the pursuit of urban criminals.[15]

Since counterfeiters based their activities in their local communities, the national government's need to deal with them required new methods of federal policing in those communities. The development of such methods provided a major opportunity in state building. Federal power would be applied to a crime problem in order to protect the nation's interest in the integrity of its currency.[16]

It was not, however, an opportunity that the Republican-controlled Congress deliberately and thoughtfully considered, perhaps because its program to promote the national economy had not anticipated the need to expand federal policing. Instead of exploring the connection between those two goals—a connection that was not necessarily obvious—Congress merely created a separate fund for the suppression of counterfeiting, leaving the details to the Treasury Department. This was an unusual arrangement at a time when Congress typically scrutinized budgets closely, especially those of executive departments. By simply appropriating a sum of money dedicated to a particular purpose, Congress, in effect, assigned the problems of implementing its intentions to the Treasury Department. The state-building implications of the need to protect the currency were thus left to a small group of bureaucrats.[17] After some initial dithering, they responded by establishing the United States Secret Service in 1865.

This, then, was state building through a process shaped by the specific opportunities that occurred at specific historical moments.[18] In the context of the U.S. federal system, particularly one dominated at the time by a system of courts and parties, state building could not have occurred in any other way. Raised in a political culture that still exalted local over federal authority—despite the centralizing policies of Republicanism—the Treasury officials who created the Secret Service worked hard to make new ideas and needs conform to old precepts and procedures. Their efforts to devise a solution to the conflict between prevailing beliefs about the proper relationship between national and local authority and the need to ensure the integrity of the currency temporarily restrained the transforming power of this expansion of federal policing authority.

The Secret Service's initial development clearly illustrates the complex interaction between old beliefs and new needs, as federal responsibilities increased in response to a specific crisis—the Civil War. Once established, however, the Service displayed an ability to survive both the restraints of its creators and its own excesses to become a permanent part of the federal establishment. Its often turbulent early history demonstrates how durable a bureaucracy can be that claims a unique mission (the suppression of counterfeiting) that is related to a vital national interest (the integrity of the currency).

The federal government thus acquired a new bureaucratic entity that was unique because of the nature of its mission and its impact. The Secret Service was one of the few federal agencies that emerged from the Civil War with the capacity to use centralized power to affect the lives of *individuals* living in communities well beyond the confines of Washington, D.C.

Criminals, of course, were the first to feel the effects of this new policing system. Federal detectives represented a new and threatening phenomenon. For the first time in American history, a federal police worked hard and successfully to impose national authority on the chaotic subcultures of the urban underworld and the criminal justice system. In the process, the Secret Service ignored the norms that had governed relations between the underworld and that system. Rejecting tradition, it substituted more uniform and less forgiving standards and procedures, which contributed to a more uniform approach to criminal prosecutions in federal courts.

This campaign against counterfeiters expanded the federal presence in cities, because the key to the counterfeiters' success lay in their ability to convert the nation's urban areas into manufacturing, distribution, and communication centers for their product. Criminals learned for the first time that the federal police were different from their local brethren. Unlike local lawmen, the Secret Service developed an enviable reputation for honesty and efficiency, which made counterfeiting an extremely unprofitable business. In one of the most successful, though little noticed, campaigns in the history of law enforcement, the Service essentially destroyed counterfeiting as a major criminal activity by the end of the nineteenth century.

Urban residents, who had the most to gain from this intervention, did not initially welcome this expansion of federal authority. Although they would benefit most from efforts to ensure the reliability of the nation's currency, their fear of centralized power overrode their economic self-interest. To them, it was acceptable for the government to create a new currency and banking system; however, it was quite something else, in an era in which the local police were a source of regular controversy, to establish a federal police to protect that system. Popular distrust of centralized policing forced the Secret Service to create an enforcement system capable of overcoming that fear.

As the Service performed its task, the broader implications of its activities would become clearer. The suppression of counterfeiting would become an avenue for socializing ordinary citizens to accept the expansion of federal power in ways only tangentially related to counterfeiting.[19] State building became a process of experimenting with standards and techniques that would simultaneously win public approval and fulfill a nation-state's need for conformity to its standards. Devising the right balance took years, but the Service never deviated from its fundamental mission to obtain obedience to a national standard of respect accorded to the national currency.

The history of the Secret Service thus provides a case study of how a centralized bureaucracy developed to overcome the deficiencies of a political system that interfered with a nation-state's assertion of power. By the 1890s the Service had created something new—a policing agency that penetrated into the far corners of the nation—and it had evolved a set of bureaucratic standards for controlling that system. It had developed among its members a loyalty to its mission that transcended party politics, and had imposed national standards of behavior on the vast majority of the country's citizens. The need to protect the national currency had mandated the use of crime control to dissolve some of the cultural and institutional barriers to centralized power.

Illegal Tender analyzes how the effort to suppress counterfeiting illustrates the essential point that the Civil War had permanently enhanced the power of the central government in American federalism. Chapters 1 and 2 examine the social and economic structure of counterfeiting, in order to describe the nature of the problem confronting the Secret Service. The success and longevity of the criminal community gave its members the hubris to believe that they could challenge the federal government's assertion of sovereignty over the currency with relative impunity. Chapters 3 and 4 analyze how federal officials organized their response to that challenge. Through their efforts, the Secret Service evolved into a separate bureaucracy whose mandate and behavior served federal—not local or party—interests. Chapters 5 and 6 describe how the Service's campaign against counterfeiting penetrated local communities to establish and to enforce national standards in law enforcement. Finally, Chapter 7 examines the utility of the nation-state's power to suppress crime as a tool to shape the behavior of businessmen as well as ordinary citizens. By the 1890s the evolution of the Secret Service had illustrated the beginnings of a fundamental shift toward an increase in federal power in American life.

THE SOCIAL WORLD
OF COUNTERFEITING

TOM HALE, PROPRIETOR of the Exchange at 16 East Houston Street, offered his customers liquor, faro, and opportunity. Located between Broadway and Bowery, the Exchange attracted its clientele primarily from the Irish and German slum tenements of such notorious nearby streets as Crosby, Mulberry, Mott, and Elizabeth, but also from the wider social world of lower Manhattan. Most of these customers merely slaked their thirst and placed a small bet at the faro table run by Charlie Adams before hurrying on to other business. A smaller group, however, huddled in conversation with their friends and acquaintances and discussed the criminal business opportunities of their environment.

Although it is unlikely that Hale deliberately created a metaphor for his social world in the name he chose for his saloon, the Exchange was in fact a microcosm of that milieu, which was sustained by the presence of Hale and Adams. Hale and Adams anchored the social world of the Exchange, because their functions within the saloon required fairly constant attendance. Hale, as the proprietor, needed to be present to monitor the legitimate side of his business. As the saloon's faro dealer, Adams had a similarly legitimate reason (despite gambling's technically illegal status) for being at the saloon. Each man, therefore, had a public persona within the Exchange that simultaneously justified and facilitated his legal, quasi-legal, and illegal activities. Both were well-established entrepreneurs by the mid-1860s.

Adams's family had christened him Langdon Moore upon his birth in a small New Hampshire town in 1830. He developed a fondness for gambling while working in Boston during the 1840s. After moving to New York City in 1853, he adopted his alias and quickly immersed himself in the demimonde of lower Manhattan. His landlord introduced him to Yankee Sullivan and other major sports figures, and Adams sharpened his gambling skills at faro houses along West Broadway, where he soon knew many major gamblers. In 1856 he branched into counterfeiting. Buying the used notes of defunct state banks from a Wall Street broker, Adams altered their denominations to higher values (a technique called "raising" notes) and passed them to unsuspecting victims. In the early 1860s he became a wholesale dealer in counterfeit notes, while simultaneously pursuing his gambling interests. In 1865 he hit upon a scheme that altered his career and established his notoriety for the remainder of the century. In a variation on the theme of the prodigal son, Adams planned and executed the burglary of the bank safe of Concord, New Hampshire. The first of many such burglaries he committed, it established his reputation as one of New York's premier gambler-counterfeiter-burglars.[1]

Hale had been born in Saratoga County, New York, in 1836. In his late teens he began his criminal career by forging a check on the account of an aunt who had raised him after his parents' death. With the proceeds from that venture, Hale absconded to New York, where he quickly made the acquaintance of various thieves and gamblers. Arrested for the forgery, Hale served three years in prison in the mid-1850s, and then immediately returned to lower Manhattan to pursue his entrepreneurial opportunities. He had apparently developed a reputation for planning and executing robberies. In the late-1850s, he began patronizing the Exchange, which was at that time owned by counterfeiter Ike Webber.

Hale soon became the saloon's bartender, a job that expanded the range of his acquaintances beyond the Exchange's regular customers and involved him in various criminal opportunities. In one scheme he and John Disbrow, a commission merchant and ardent Methodist from New Jersey, organized a partnership with Webber to manufacture and distribute counterfeit postal currency. By the early sixties Webber had sold the Exchange to Hale, probably to raise cash to invest in counterfeiting. Hale would shortly follow Webber's example by selling the saloon to Sam Stewart in late 1865 or early 1866.[2]

As active members of New York's social world of entrepreneurial hustlers who routinely mixed ordinary business with crime, Adams and Hale had numerous friends and acquaintances who visited the saloon. Mingling with the transient customers from the neighborhood, they found the Exchange's legal business a convenient mask for their own presence. Hank Hall, Bill Gurney, Bill Brockway, Dave Keene, Jerry Cowsden, Jack Foster, and Sam Stewart, among others, were regulars at the saloon.[3]

Like Hale and Adams, these men pursued legitimate or quasilegitimate and criminal careers simultaneously. Hall, for example, made a living as a bounty broker during the Civil War, while Gurney worked as a cattle dealer. They continued to meet at the Exchange, however, to explore criminal business opportunities, particularly in counterfeiting. Shielded from interference by the public environment of the saloon, they negotiated deals and arranged partnership responsibilities. In 1865, for example, Hall engineered the most embarrassing breach of security in the history of the Treasury Department by persuading Edward Langton, one of the Treasury's printers, to make lead impressions of genuine one hundred dollar compound note plates. After Langton delivered the impressions, Hall had Webber print the notes while he and Bill Gurney distributed them through their networks of dealers and shovers in New York and Pennsylvania.[4]

As just one of many saloons pullulating across the city, the Exchange provided a vital physical setting for the institutional framework that nourished New York's underworld. That framework was not only a series of locations but also a society. Hale and his friends were products of counterfeiting's historical evolution and the changing opportunities for crime in the nation's largest cities. It was their activities, rooted in specific criminal traditions and urban neighborhoods, that sustained the underworld's institutional framework.

Counterfeiting's evolution for over a century and a half prior to the mid-nineteenth century created a historical memory of its practices that could be transmitted across generations of criminals, as new individuals learned its lore and techniques. It is probably one of the oldest crimes in America, dating approximately from the 1680s.

From the available evidence, the first counterfeiters were probably producing counterfeits to deal with personal monetary problems rather than for a market. Robert Fenton, for example, while employed as a servant in Philadelphia, made coins for his master and another individual in 1683. Just who suggested this venture is unclear, but there is no indication that these three men sold their products to anyone else.

Fenton's lowly status protected him from a severe sentence, but his subsequent activities indicate that he may in fact have inspired this early counterfeiting scheme. In 1691 he was convicted for forging and passing paper bills of credit in Boston. Later, in 1698, Fenton confessed to a Connecticut court that he and a partner from Long Island had made counterfeit coins; that he had another partner in Northampton, Massachusetts, who passed coins for him; that he had made counterfeiting tools for a Boston joiner; and that a Connecticut man had employed Fenton to make coins for him.[5] The extent and persistence of Fenton's activities indicates that he was either highly inventive or that he had brought his knowledge of counterfeiting with him from England. Considering that he committed his first counterfeiting offense while a servant in a colony and a town that were barely a year old at the time, it is reasonable to speculate that Fenton had some acquaintance with English criminals prior to his arrival in Philadelphia. If he had lived near or in London, it would not have been difficult for him to acquire knowledge of counterfeiting. By the end of the sixteenth century London had developed several identifiable criminal areas, including Alsatia, which had reputations as centers for counterfeiting.[6]

Coining did not, however, lend itself to elaborate organization because of its simplicity. Since the necessary skills and materials were widely available, anyone with the basic knowledge could produce coins in practically any locality. The spread of coining, therefore, both demonstrated the growing willingness among colonial criminals to engage in counterfeiting as they acquired the requisite technical knowledge, and created a rudimentary basis for future development. Whatever the origins of Fenton's knowledge, his persistent counterfeiting activities contributed to the diffusion of that knowledge, as well as to the formation of social networks that could, as in his case, cross colonial boundaries by the end of the 1690s.

The opportunity for more elaborate counterfeiting operations, particularly counterfeiting paper currency, had to await economic and political events. In the rudimentary economy of the seventeenth century, paper notes had yet to circulate as currency, and colonial merchants relied on a cumbersome barter system to conduct their businesses. As the economy became more sophisticated, the need for a convenient circulating medium created political pressures on local assemblies to issue paper notes.

When colonial legislatures bowed to these pressures and authorized various schemes for paper currencies, they unwittingly created a market for counterfeit notes. Furthermore, the bitter political struggles over whether and in what form to issue colonial currencies created shortages in availability. Notes might be plentiful in some colonies, while scarce in others. Thus, colonists who preferred the convenience of paper notes and had difficulty securing them might be inclined to look for illegal sources for their supply. The pressing need to have cash on hand appears to have overcome their scruples.

Manufacturing paper notes required greater skills, more expensive equipment and materials, more time, and more organization than making coins. Despite the difficulties, there were criminals willing to try producing paper notes. Thomas Morton, who was infamous for passing counterfeit money, probably provided in 1707 the necessary knowledge to a group of skilled Boston tradesmen who produced the first large-scale printing of counterfeit bills of credit in Massachusetts. This group had more elaborate equipment than Fenton had ever used, including a press and counterfeit plates.[7]

Demand for spurious notes from groups such as Morton's contributed to the further elaboration of the counterfeiters' social world. There is evidence from as early as 1717 of a wholesaling operation in which counterfeiters offered their customers paper money through the mail.[8] They apparently had considerable success; by the 1720s traffic in counterfeit notes had become a serious problem in New England.[9]

With sufficient demand for their products to justify more permanent organizational efforts, counterfeiters created relatively stable production centers, which they located in rural areas. The small size of deviant areas within colonial cities and their relatively underdeveloped institutional frameworks probably explains this preference. Until the 1830s, even cities in the settled areas of the east coast were not sufficiently large or developed to provide safe hiding places for manufacturing activities. Since the production of counterfeits required considerable capital investment, as well as security from disruptions, it made sense to seek the most protected sites for the expensive equipment. Counterfeiters therefore located counterfeiting "plants" in rural areas whose isolation decreased their vulnerability to interference.[10]

Rural locations did not, however, fragment counterfeiting networks into purely local operations. Criminals' interest in counterfeiting and in expanding the market for their products provided a framework for stable regional relationships. Joseph Bill, for example, participated in counterfeiting activities in New York, Massachusetts, and New Jersey during a long career that began in the 1740s and lasted until his execution in 1773. Before his execution, Bill confessed to having engraved several plates for other counterfeiters, indicating that he maintained fairly regular contacts with other criminals. Some of those contacts may have been among the many counterfeiters who operated plants stretching from New Jersey through New Hampshire and, by the early nineteenth century, into Canada. Counterfeiting had become a major business in rural New England and the mid-Atlantic states, operating with near impunity and on a large scale.[11]

The distribution system that supported these production centers linked rural and urban areas. Dealers and shovers (criminals who passed counterfeit money) operated along a North-South axis stretching from the Canadian border, through the New England states and portions of upstate New York, down to New York City and Philadelphia. The southern terminus of this distribution system is obscure, though it may have reached into portions of the upper South.[12]

Marketing these notes provided dealers and shovers with opportunities to diffuse knowledge about counterfeiting within the social world of crime. Seth Wyman, a thief who had conversed with counterfeiters while in jail but had not himself engaged in this activity, illustrates this process. In 1808 Wyman was in rural New Hampshire when he met an old acquaintance who cautiously asked if Wyman was interested in making some money. When he said yes, this man introduced Wyman to a dealer who sold him $1,200 in notes. Wyman and his wife spent several days in Boston, where they had considerable success in passing these counterfeits. Over time and with a stable production system to supply them, hundreds of ordinary criminals such as Wyman would acquire a knowledge of buying and passing counterfeits.[13]

By the early nineteenth century, then, counterfeiting had become a familiar activity among America's criminals. They had learned the practical techniques for making spurious notes, and had developed the skills for constructing social networks either to produce or to distribute their products. In effect, they had created a body of knowledge, rooted in practical experience but not confined to particular locations, that individuals and groups could draw upon whenever the opportunity arose.

Urban demographic and spatial changes in the decades after 1820 transformed the social organization of crime in the United States and provided counterfeiters with significantly expanded opportunities. For the first time, changes in the American urban milieu replicated the underworld institutions that characterized European cities.[14] While this process began in every major city in the antebellum period, it naturally was most highly developed in New York City.

As the nation's premier city, New York pioneered in the formation of this new underworld culture. The key to this process was the transformation of lower Manhattan, the area below 14th Street, from its colonial configuration of a jumble of social classes, land uses, and economic activities into an essentially working-class area that also contained the city's principal industries, entertainment districts, and exclusive shops.

Economic success and rapid population growth fueled this transformation. New York's success in dominating the nation's major markets created opportunities for the hundreds of new businesses and the thousands of new residents that poured into lower Manhattan. Their arrival created pressure for new residential developments to accommodate the mushrooming population. Responding to this pressure, the settled area at the tip of the island began its expansion north. In 1820 the densely built area had only reached Houston Street; by the 1860s it was approaching 42nd Street. Less densely settled but nevertheless significant residential and business areas stretched even farther northward along the banks of the Hudson and East rivers.[15]

Ironically, this northward march did not ease the congestion of lower Manhattan but did allow more specialized land use. The port, which had been confined to the East River, spilled over to the Hudson by the 1850s, as those West Side residents who could afford to moved north.[16] Although the port's flourishing business necessitated expansion, the spread of its facilities to both flanks of lower Manhattan greatly affected the area's social organization.

The port provided unskilled workers with thousands of jobs. The wages and the employment routines of these jobs, however, created problems for those who sought them. No job lasted more than a few days, and the businesses that handled loading and unloading ships did not have regular work crews, preferring instead to hire on a daily or even hourly basis instead. Workers constantly had to loiter around the docks, waiting for the next employment opportunity. They could not, therefore, afford to live too far from the docks, because that might jeopardize their chances of obtaining work on any given day. Since the wages were low, dock workers had to find cheap rooms.[17] Landlords responded to the problem of accommodating low-paid workers on increasingly valuable land by subdividing buildings to maximize rents, which in turn caused properties to deteriorate and contributed to the spread of slum housing.

Similar problems and consequences appeared in other industries. Businesses that required large amounts of land to accommodate their heavy, space-consuming machinery tended not to locate in lower Manhattan. Many businesses that did locate in the area, such as the clothing trades, were extremely labor-intensive. Although they provided residents with thousands of job opportunities, intense competition for these positions kept wages low, while seasonal business cycles meant that workers routinely suffered layoffs. While life for these workers was not as precarious as for dock hands, many managed to avoid outright poverty only by extraordinary effort.[18]

Immigration complicated the problems of employment and housing. New York served as the major port of entry for tens of thousands of immigrants. Most moved elsewhere, but large numbers did not. Pressed by necessity to adapt quickly to an unfamiliar cultural and economic setting, these newly minted New Yorkers usually found work in the rapidly expanding, labor-intensive businesses of lower Manhattan. Unable to earn decent wages, they joined the ranks of the burgeoning working class in a search for living quarters, which only exacerbated the area's housing problems.[19]

The transformation of lower Manhattan into a working-class district naturally affected its retail institutions. Residents with small amounts of cash, or sometimes only ambition and luck, opened a variety of stores. Junk stores and pawnshops competed with grocers, barbers, tailors, and especially saloons for the patronage of their neighbors. While neither particularly grand nor successful, they were numerous. By 1865 at least 3,823 saloons and 2,284 groceries jostled for customers below 14th Street. One grocer's lament that he barely cleared three or four dollars a week merely reflected the hard facts of economic life for these small businesses. Retailing was probably as precarious a way to earn a living as factory or dock work.[20]

By midcentury, economic and spatial changes had transformed lower Manhattan into an area of marginal existence for most of its residents and small businesses. Marginality spawned a distinctive lifestyle. With their opportunities for success constrained by the district's particular economic structure, some individuals would succeed through greater skill or luck than their neighbors, while some would redefine the concept of opportunity.[21]

The changes affecting lower Manhattan expanded the potential for crime in an environment where hustling to make a living had become a way of life. Deviant opportunities emerged from either the character and pace of economic life or the development of specialized land uses. The port, for example, provided innumerable possibilities for theft, while the presence of small businesses that dealt in used products created a ready market for stolen goods. The emergence of Broadway as an elite shopping district offered similar possibilities, from pickpocketing to burglary. For dockhands unable to find work, factory hands facing unexpected financial crises, and workers struggling through seasonal layoffs, occasional crime beckoned as a solution to short-term problems.[22]

Gambling and prostitution offered another set of opportunities. Both were officially illegal yet widely accepted and heavily concentrated in lower Manhattan. Gambling dens and brothels catering to the middle and the upper classes lined Broadway and some adjacent streets as far north as 24th Street by midcentury, while dozens of less respectable establishments scattered themselves along the more notorious streets. Each business created different possibilities for employment. The more elaborate gambling dens hired runners to canvas the hotels and to steer customers to them; they also needed dealers, waiters, and doorkeepers. On a less grandiose scale, policy shops needed runners and clerks. Brothel madams recruited fresh talent from the neighborhoods. Hundreds of young women worked in brothels for varying periods of time, either to supplement their incomes or to earn money while looking for more respectable work.[23]

Deviant work opportunities in lower Manhattan created the context for an urban underworld. Other areas of the burgeoning city also provided similar opportunities but not, at least prior to 1865, on so vast a scale. The existence of so many illegitimate opportunities drew the criminally inclined to lower Manhattan, where working-class institutions like saloons provided them with meeting places to sustain their associational networks. The sheer number of those saloons, furthermore, enhanced the anonymity of criminals by giving them an abundance of places in which to meet.[24]

Criminals did not, however, exist as a separate group within this environment. A burglar who broke into a store one evening did not necessarily retire to his favorite saloon the next day to plan his next crime. He might instead go on a spree, enjoying his earnings from the burglary as long as they lasted. Then he might hold a legitimate job for as long as it suited him, before returning to his favorite saloon to check on other criminal opportunities. So-called professional criminals, to whom society gave tidy labels as burglars, sneak thieves, or counterfeiters, typically spent their work lives hustling for opportunities along a spectrum that ranged from legal to illegal, rather than specializing in one activity.[25]

A work environment in which everyone hustled to earn their livings provided some specific opportunities to engage in counterfeiting. First, New York's printing industry concentrated in lower Manhattan. With so many firms of varying sizes engaged in a wide variety of printing tasks, a large number of supply stores clustered in the area to sell paper, type, ink, and various kinds of presses, which were also the raw materials of counterfeiting.[26]

Many printers and engravers lived in the Second Ward, where most printing firms were located, or in the northern section of the Sixth Ward, a notorious slum district in the heart of lower Manhattan. Recent technological innovations in printing undermined the value of their skills, forcing many to work for minimal wages or perhaps preventing them from finding any employment at all. Counterfeiters such as Peter LaRue could take advantage of this situation. LaRue helped manufacture $25,000 in counterfeit fives and tens in Canada. Intending to hire someone to sign the notes, he and an associate brought the notes in September 1830 to New York, where LaRue had friends at 80 Forsyth Street. This scheme went awry when LaRue gave some of the notes to his friends, who made the mistake of trying to pass them unsigned. Despite that mishap, LaRue's mission demonstrates that counterfeiters expected to find specialized help with their schemes among New York's working-classes.[27]

Some printers and engravers coped with the tight job market by setting up small independent shops, but their marginal existence meant that they might be willing to undertake illegitimate work on occasion. Edward Hulseman, for example, was an engraver living at 80 Nassau Street in the Second Ward. Claiming that he was returning to Germany to print notes for the Prussian government, Hulseman persuaded several members of a bankrupt printing firm to teach him the necessary techniques. They also sold Hulseman a press and several dies, with which he manufactured counterfeit ten dollar notes on a New York bank.[28]

Criminals contemplating a counterfeiting scheme could also count on their environment for other forms of assistance. Saloons, of course, provided convenient places to discuss plans and to make deals, while lower Manhattan's dense network of streets offered hundreds of inconspicuous delivery sites. With so many workers and small businessowners living a precarious existence, there was also a potentially large pool of customers willing to distribute or to buy counterfeit money.

The activities of Lewis King and Smith Davis illustrate these possibilities. King was a cart driver living at 134 Prince Street in 1830. Following his arrest for shoving, constables found $432 in various denominations of counterfeit notes on six different banks concealed in his stable. King confessed that he had been buying these notes from Davis. He testified that Davis, a horse dealer living at 359 Grand Street, was "in the habit of selling large quantities of spurious notes to different persons. . . ." Struggling entrepreneurs like Davis may have found counterfeiting a particularly useful way to enhance their profit margins in a fiercely competitive world, while shovers like King could make fairly decent wages passing counterfeits.[29]

In summary, lower Manhattan concentrated an unprecedented number of resources, services, and business opportunities for counterfeiting. Counterfeiters only had to apply their knowledge to these new circumstances to take advantage of the situation. Their lifestyles and needs matched the new urban environment extremely well, while the relatively ineffective apparatus of law enforcement lowered whatever risk did exist for using cities as sites for both manufacturing and distributing counterfeits.

TABLE 1.1

Counterfeiting Arrests, 1830–1860

Year	Number of Arrests (100 percent sample per year)
1830	19
1840	31
1850	13
1860	90
Total	153

Source: Indictment Papers of the District Attorney of New York City, Court of General Sessions, 1790–1879, New York City, Municipal Archives, New York.

The profile of arrested counterfeiters in Tables 1.1 to 1.4 provides an overview of counterfeiters arrested from 1830 to 1860 (see Table 1.1).[30] Table 1.2 reveals the extent of their commitment to lower Manhattan's opportunities (see Table 1.2). First, they were far from randomly distributed among the city's neighborhoods. Ninety-one percent of those in the profile who gave addresses to the police

TABLE 1.2

Addresses of Arrested Counterfeiters, 1830–1860

Area	Cases	Percent (known cases)
East Side	4	6
West Side	2	3
South of 14th Street	63	91
Unknown	84	—
Total	153	100

Source: Indictment Papers of the District Attorney of New York City, Court of General Sessions, 1790–1879, New York City, Municipal Archives, New York.

lived below 14th Street. That contrasts rather dramatically with the general distribution of population for the whole city. In 1855, for example, only two-thirds of all New Yorkers lived below 14th Street.[31] Counterfeiters were therefore significantly more concentrated in lower Manhattan than the general population.

Employment information from this profile indicates that these criminals had varied backgrounds. Although 40 percent reported that they worked at unskilled jobs at the time of their arrest, almost as many others claimed skilled occupations, and just over a fifth had business-related jobs.[32] Ordinarily, the possession of a skill or a business encourages tendencies toward legitimate behavior. Presumably, someone who has a skill or runs a business enjoys more opportunities for upward mobility than someone lacking such advantages. The marginal nature of most small businesses in mid-nineteenth-century New York and the relative lack of jobs for skilled workers in lower Manhattan, however, undermined these normal expectations. Qualifications meant little; businessowners and skilled workers had to hustle just as hard as the unskilled to maintain a living.

This occupational range also demonstrates how well counterfeiters blended into their surroundings. Unfortunately for the general public, counterfeiters evinced no preference for particular kinds of legitimate work. They could, literally, be anyone—from a seamstress or a carpenter buying food, to a gambler paying off a winner, to a shopkeeper making change.

Counterfeiters also blended into their environment because of their age. New York had a disproportionate number of young adults, primarily in the twenty to twenty-nine age group.[33] With an average age of twenty-eight, counterfeiters tended toward the upper end of that group. Although this average obscures the fact that counterfeiters' ages in this profile ranged from seventeen to fifty-eight, the typical counterfeiter conformed to the city's general age profile, adding yet another protective layer to the counterfeiter's activities.

Counterfeiters did, however, differ from New York's general population in one important respect. By 1855 the city had become ethnically diverse. Immigrants were over half the population, with particularly large numbers of Irish and Germans residing in the city.[34] Counterfeiting did not reflect this ethnic distribution. Although it was a multi-ethnic activity, second- or third-generation Americans decisively dominated it. Fifty-nine percent of the profile

TABLE 1.3

Ethnicity of Arrested Counterfeiters, 1830–1860

Nationality	Arrests	Percent
American	63	59
Irish	24	22
German	13	12
English	7	7
Unknown	46	—
Total	153	100

Source: Indictment Papers of the District Attorney of New York City, Court of General Sessions, 1790–1879, New York City, Municipal Archives, New York.

were native-born (see Table 1.3). The Irish occupied second place, followed by the Germans, with the English placing last.

Native-born dominance of counterfeiting probably arose from a knowledge of its traditions and techniques. It is noteworthy that the English, who presumably brought their criminal culture with them during the colonial period, are underrepresented in the profile. The nature of counterfeiting in England partially accounts for this laggardly position. Harsh penalties and difficulties with copying English bank notes discouraged the continuation of a strong counterfeiting tradition. English counterfeiters confined themselves almost exclusively to coining by the nineteenth century.[35] American counterfeiters, on the other hand, had vast numbers of notes to copy, and the chances for arrest were minimal. Unlike their English cousins, then, American counterfeiters had more than enough opportunity to practice the most complex aspects of their craft. As the beneficiaries of more than a century of development, native-born counterfeiters simply no longer needed to rely on the criminal knowledge of immigrants. Instead, they could tutor the newcomers.

The 1860 arrest of Sarah Chapman, Margaret Donohoe, and Margaret Moran for shoving several two-dollar notes on a Boston bank illustrates the diffusion of counterfeiting knowledge among newcomers. Since the police did not charge any of the three with dealing in counterfeit notes, it is likely that they had obtained their supply from someone else. Neither Donohoe, a seventeen-year-old milliner from England, nor Moran, a nineteen-year-old servant from Ireland, could have had the information or the experience necessary to negotiate with a dealer. They would have needed help with such a transaction. Chapman, however, was a thirty-two-year-old, American-born seamstress. She probably had sufficient knowledge of counterfeiting to introduce her younger associates to its procedures. Her willingness to plead guilty to a lesser charge indicates that she had some familiarity with the criminal justice system. Furthermore, Donohoe, who was arrested with Chapman, also pleaded guilty but received a suspended sentence, implying a judgment that she was not the primary culprit in the shoving expedition. Moran, who had been arrested some days earlier, escaped altogether when the prosecutor refused to pursue the case.[36] From the few known facts about the case, it appears that Chapman, the old hand, was showing the younger immigrant women how to shove.

It is doubtful that Chapman consciously chose to teach the techniques of a crime to immigrant volunteers. It is likely, however, that within the opportunity structure of lower Manhattan, American counterfeiters met immigrants who had, for whatever reasons, decided to participate in the illegal opportunities their environment offered. As the dominant group in counterfeiting, the Americans therefore had the chance to pass on the traditions of this crime to those recent arrivals who sought the opportunity.

The arrests of Chapman, Donohoe, and Moran reflected how antebellum law enforcement contributed to the success of counterfeiting. Ninety-one percent of the arrests in the sample were for shoving (see Table 1.4). In effect, the police dealt only with the most common kind of offender, virtually ignoring the more difficult problems of attacking the dealers and manufacturers, whose activities were essential to the success of counterfeiting.

In the absence of effective law enforcement, and surrounded by the supportive urban environment of lower Manhattan, counterfeiters could reasonably expect to enjoy long careers in the business. Joshua Minor, for example, inherited his knowledge from his father, who practiced counterfeiting for thirty years in upstate New York. Like so many others, Minor moved to New York City, where he was a successful street contractor and an important counterfeiter by the 1860s. Harry Cole, another rural New Yorker, had engaged in counterfeiting for fifteen years by the mid-1860s, and would continue to do

TABLE 1.4

Criminal Charges against Counterfeiters, 1830–1860

Charge	Case	Percent
Shoving	139	91
Dealing	4	3
Manufacturing	10	6
Total	153	100

Source: Indictment Papers of the District Attorney of New York City, Court of General Sessions, 1790–1879, New York City, Municipal Archives, New York.

so for another twenty. William English, only thirty years old in 1867, had already amassed a decade of experience with this work.[37]

Longevity promoted stability within the counterfeiters' social world. The presence of so many experienced counterfeiters sustained the institutional network, which recruited newcomers and facilitated exchanging information and arranging deals. It is thus no accident that counterfeiters could routinely be found in saloons along certain streets. The Exchange, for example, had plenty of competition as a counterfeiters' den. Other saloons catering to this business were located nearby, including those at 50 East Houston Street, Broadway at Houston, and Crosby at Houston. The area bounded by Houston, Broadway, the Bowery, and Chatham became the heart of counterfeiting for New York—and for the United States as well.[38]

The counterfeiters' social world, however, was not so small that it was possible for everyone to know each other. Although they lived in a subculture with a particular set of well-defined institutions rooted in a specific urban environment, they could each know only a part of that world. Bill Brockway, one of the most prominent coneymen (counterfeiters) of the entire century, claimed that he had never met such equally prominent men as Harry Cole and Phil Hargraves, and that he had met Joshua Minor only twice.[39] Since there is no record that Brockway ever worked with any of these men, his claim seems credible. Even familial ties did not necessarily create the basis for associations. Hank Hall, for example, was Minor's brother-in-law, but the two men never worked together, even though they shared acquaintance with individuals such as Bill Gurney, who could have linked them in business ventures.[40] Counterfeiting was therefore fragmented into many networks whose membership changed constantly in response to the opportunities of the environment.[41]

Business considerations apparently dominated criminal relationships. For example, Richard Weeks was not particularly good friends with Gurney but "[did] business for him sometimes when he [could] make anything." While Langdon Moore referred rather casually to several counterfeiters without mentioning the nature of his personal relations with them, he specifically described Jerry Cowsden as a "business acquaintance."[42]

Once entrenched in lower Manhattan, counterfeiters concentrated their activities there for the remainder of the century. Developments after 1865 reinforced their hold. The area continued to serve as the city's entrepot for immigrants, as the heart of its economic life, and the center of its entertainment activities—all of which strengthened and expanded counterfeiting's institutional structure.[43]

While continuing to patronize their usual saloons, counterfeiters also penetrated Little Germany and the Lower East Side. Coin wholesaler Martin Leonard, for example, frequented a saloon at Broadway and Chatham, lived at 29 Henry Street, and maintained a network that included men residing on City Hall Place, Spring Street, East Broadway, and Avenue B.[44] James Street, located at the edge of the Lower East Side between the East River and Chatham, also attracted counterfeiters. Phil Hargraves, who may have been among the pioneers of this movement into Little Germany and the Lower East Side, met some of his customers on James Street in the 1870s. Several other counterfeiters followed his lead, and James Street became a favorite haunt for the remainder of the century.[45]

Arrest data for the decades following the Civil War confirm the persistence of the counterfeiters' commitment to lower Manhattan (see Table 1.5). Sixty percent of the arrested counterfeiters in 610 known cases between 1865 and 1899 resided in the area below 14th Street. Manufacturers and shovers remained heavily concentrated there, indicating that counterfeiters continued to value the area's superior access to materials, networks, and opportunities (see Table 1.6). As a result, no other part of the city matched lower Manhattan's cluster of counterfeiters and their activities. Counterfeiters did not,

TABLE 1.5

Addresses of Arrested Counterfeiters, 1865–1899

Area	Cases	Percent (known cases)
East Side	176	29
West Side	71	11
South of 14th Street	363	60
Total	610	100

Sources: Register of Monthly Reports, 1865–1871, U.S. Secret Service, Record Group 206, National Archives, Washington, D.C.; Daily Reports of Agents, 1875–1899, U.S. Secret Service, Record Group 87, National Archives, Washington, D.C.
Note: 800 cases (57 percent of all cases for this period) provided no address.

however, confine their activities exclusively to lower Manhattan. By taking advantage of new circumstances, they gradually extended their operations, albeit on a reduced scale, throughout much of Manhattan.

Institutional development was the key to territorial expansion.

TABLE 1.6

Addresses of Counterfeiters by Offense, 1865–1899

Charge	East Side	West Side	South of 14th Street
Shoving	110	49	229
Dealing	30	8	38
Manufacturing	31	8	76
Total	171	65	343
Percent of cases	30	11	59

Sources: Register of Monthly Reports, 1865–1871, U.S. Secret Service, Record Group 206, National Archives, Washington, D.C.; Daily Reports of Agents, 1875–1899, U.S. Secret Service, Record Group 87, National Archives, Washington, D.C.

Counterfeiters could not safely engage in their work outside the working-class milieu, which masked their activities and supported their networks. Although that setting was most extensively developed in lower Manhattan by the 1860s, it was not confined to that district but was constantly expanding with the general movement of population.

Job opportunities drew the working-classes northward. Several of New York's more unsavory industries, such as slaughterhouses and packinghouses, fat and bone rendering factories, breweries, distilleries, swill-milk farms, and manure yards, had migrated northward along the banks of the Hudson and East Rivers. While these, as well as numerous other sorts of small factories, provided many jobs, the city government and the building trades were probably the largest employers. Rapid population growth required massive public improvements above 14th Street. Dozens of streets needed to be opened and graded; water and sewer mains had to be laid. Once the city completed its tasks, contractors rushed in to build homes, shops, and factories.

All this activity supplied work to thousands of American, Irish, and German New Yorkers, most of whom had to live within reasonable walking distance of their jobs. That need and low wages encouraged a replication of the housing problems of lower Manhattan. Shanties clustered in several areas, and tenements quickly appeared. The areas between Third Avenue and the East River, and Ninth Avenue and the Hudson River gradually emerged as major working-class tenement districts.

Working-class culture and institutions joined this northward migration. Though not as numerous as they were in lower Manhattan, groceries, used-clothing stores, and pawnshops rapidly materialized in the newer tenement areas, as did those other mainstays of these neighborhoods, saloons, and brothels.[46]

As their protective environment moved northward, so did the counterfeiters. Precisely when the migration occurred is unclear, although there were some early pioneers such as Daniel O'Connor, who in 1839 established a manufacturing plant complete with engraving equipment, several note plates, and a press at Tenth Avenue and 37th Street. Arrest data for the period prior to 1860 indicates, however, that O'Connor was not typical, since only 9 percent of all the cases in that sample had locations north of 14th Street.[47]

Nevertheless, many counterfeiters had migrated to the East

and West sides by the 1870s. Those who made this move probably accentuated the already fragmentary character of counterfeiting networks, because it would have been difficult, although not impossible, for them to maintain close ties to networks in different parts of the city.[48] The clandestine nature of their work required that counterfeiters not be strangers in saloons where they hoped to do business. They had to establish themselves as regulars with some pretense of legitimate employment, in order to use the public spaces and the meeting places of the new working-class neighborhoods. To qualify as regulars, they, like their honest neighbors, had to live in the vicinity.

Counterfeiters like Tom Congdon were probably transitional figures who helped to diffuse knowledge about counterfeiting into the newer areas. Congdon had become a fairly prominent coneyman by the 1860s, having worked with such important counterfeiters as Harry Cole. In the early 1870s Cole moved to Philadelphia, while Congdon transferred his operations to the East Side. He resided on 42nd Street between Second and Third avenues, and spent a great deal of time at a saloon at 42nd and Third. Congdon's extensive network and experience may have made him a valuable asset to the emerging counterfeiting culture of the East Side.[49]

Phil Hargraves, who manufactured both coins and notes, was another coneyman who made the trek northward. Transferring his operations first to the area around 28th Street and Broadway, and later to East 102nd, Hargraves simultaneously pursued careers as a horse dealer and counterfeiter. Within a few years, he had built a network of customers that included Rance Abrams, James McGuire, and Mat Rooney. Abrams was a wholesaler who frequented saloons at 46th Street and Eighth Avenue, and on Third Avenue above 23rd. McGuire, another horse dealer (and burglar), bought coin through Abrams that he sold to saloon keepers like Holly Bergen (a retired burglar). He patronized saloons on 16th Street near Ninth Avenue. Rooney, a saloon keeper (who had served time in Massachusetts), visited saloons on Tenth Avenue near 40th Street.[50]

By the late 1870s the expansion of counterfeiting's institutional structure and the migration of experienced counterfeiters into the East and West Sides created new income opportunities for New Yorkers with no prior record of criminal activity. Residents of the new working-class neighborhoods faced the same low wages and fierce competition for jobs as their antebellum predecessors had, and responded similarly. Most continued to eke out honest livings, by whatever legal means that were available. A few, however, sought to enhance their income through crime—such as a counterfeiter working in a butcher shop who told an informer that "there is not money enough in it [the shop] so he is going to sling out queer again."[51]

George Stanley was one of those who added counterfeiting to their list of occupations. Stanley lived on East 74th Street and had previously worked as a carpenter and a sawyer. That combination of jobs implied that he tottered on the line between skilled and unskilled labor, experiencing the attendant income uncertainties. Apparently dissatisfied with that situation, Stanley dabbled in horse dealing. His efforts to branch out may have led to an acquaintance with Hargraves, who attended horse auctions when he was inclined to pursue his legitimate career. However this first encounter occurred, Stanley had become an associate of Hargraves, McGuire, and Rooney by May 1880, and he was developing a reputation as a manufacturer and dealer in counterfeit coin.

Success encouraged Stanley to expand his legal and illegal activities simultaneously. Within three years he had become a fence for stolen property and had also opened a restaurant near his home. He also developed his own counterfeiting network, using Rooney as his distributor and seven East Side residents as shovers. The range of his activities demonstrates how counterfeiting was used by nineteenth-century individuals to enhance their entrepreneurial opportunities.[52]

None of Stanley's network, except Rooney, who had apparently quit the saloon business and was working as a car man in 1883, had any known experience with counterfeiting until recruited by Stanley. Aside from Rooney, the network consisted of two housewives, a peddler, a laborer, a porter, and a harness maker. Their willingness to become shovers illustrates how cash-poor individuals might regard petty crime as an opportunity to supplement their incomes.

Stanley and his network generally mirrored the characteristics of late nineteenth-century New York counterfeiters. At age twenty-seven, when he first began manufacturing coins, Stanley was two years older than the average age of all known manufacturers. He was, however, typical in that manufacturers were significantly older than shovers, whose average age was twenty-one.[53] Stanley's shovers ranged from nineteen to twenty-eight years of age, with twenty-two

TABLE 1.7

Occupations of Arrested Counterfeiters by Role, 1865–1899

Role	Unskilled	Skilled	Business
Shoving	151	119	203
Dealing	18	18	54
Manufacturing	25	83	43
Total	194	220	300

Sources: Register of Monthly Reports, 1865–1871, U.S. Secret Service, Record Group 206, National Archives, Washington, D.C.; Daily Reports of Agents, 1875–1899, U.S. Secret Service, Record Group 87, National Archives, Washington, D.C.

as their average—one year older than the average age of all known shovers. His group demonstrates that counterfeiting continued to be an option for young adults, which is not surprising in a city that was bursting with tens of thousands of young men and women struggling to earn a living.

The occupational range of Stanley's network also conformed to the general profile of counterfeiters (see Table 1.7). Skilled individuals were more likely than any other group to engage in manufacturing and less inclined to participate in shoving. Aside from Stanley, who had at least some knowledge of carpentry, only the harness maker could claim to have a skill. Counterfeiters with skilled occupations probably engaged in manufacturing because of their familiarity with tools, although they did not offer any explanations for this preference. If true, this would also help explain why the unskilled concentrated overwhelmingly on shoving. Four out of six of Stanley's shovers, for example, had unskilled jobs. They probably shoved because they lacked both the ability and the knowledge to engage in more complex counterfeiting tasks.

Stanley's network also reflected the role of small businessowners in counterfeiting. He himself had graduated to that status by opening his restaurant, which given its location, did not cater to the tastes of fashionable New York. It did, however, provide Stanley with a legitimate place to meet his friends. There is no evidence that he attempted to pass his homemade coins on any of his customers, but the peddler who shoved for him probably did so to his own customers. As the lowest players in the hierarchy of capitalism, peddlers operated on extremely narrow profit margins. The opportunity to bolster that margin probably provided the incentive Stanley's peddler needed to join the network. As a group, entrepreneurs/counterfeiters, like the unskilled, were far more likely to engage in shoving than in any other activity.

Finally, Stanley's network illustrated the continuing importance of the Americans and the Irish in counterfeiting. Together, they eclipsed all others in this business prior to 1880, although the Americans clearly dominated numerically (see Table 1.8). This dominance made them the leaders in the process of diffusing the knowledge of counterfeiting to Manhattan's East and West Sides. Phil Hargraves, an Irishman from lower Manhattan, and James McGuire, an Irish-American, taught Stanley, an American, the business. Stanley in turn recruited a network composed almost entirely of Americans. (The single exception, Matt Rooney, claimed American birth, but he may, more accurately, have been Irish-American.)[54]

TABLE 1.8

Distribution of Counterfeiting Arrests by Ethnicity, 1865–1899

Period	American	Italian	Irish	German	English
1865–1871	1	14	2	2	1
1876–1879	21	7	5	4	2
1880–1884	55	29	11	7	5
1885–1889	60	92	7	6	3
1890–1894	57	79	10	9	3
1895–1899	73	110	17	18	5
Total	267	331	52	46	19

Sources: Register of Monthly Reports, 1865–1871, U.S. Secret Service, Record Group 206, National Archives, Washington, D.C.; Daily Reports of Agents, 1875–1899, U.S. Secret Service, Record Group 87, National Archives, Washington, D.C.
Note: The number of arrests for the entire period (100 percent sample) was 1,410. Of that number, ethnicity was identified in 728 cases (52 percent of all cases).

TABLE 1.9

Addresses of Counterfeiters by Ethnicity

	Area	American	Italian	Irish	German	English
1865–1871						
	East Side	0	0	0	0	0
	West Side	0	0	0	0	0
	South of 14th Street	0	1	0	0	0
1876–1879						
	East Side	2	0	0	0	0
	West Side	6	0	2	0	0
	South of 14th Street	7	3	3	1	1
1880–1884						
	East Side	13	4	2	1	0
	West Side	9	2	3	1	0
	South of 14th Street	21	17	4	2	4
1885–1889						
	East Side	14	22	0	0	2
	West Side	4	4	1	0	0
	South of 14th Street	28	44	4	5	1
1890–1894						
	East Side	15	11	2	0	1
	West Side	8	9	1	0	0
	South of 14th Street	23	27	3	0	0
1895–1899						
	East Side	18	26	10	0	0
	West Side	4	6	1	0	2
	South of 14th Street	14	55	4	1	1
Total		186	231	40	11	12

Sources: Register of Monthly Reports, 1865–1871, U.S. Secret Service, Record Group 206, National Archives, Washington, D.C.; Daily Reports of Agents, 1875–1899, U.S. Secret Service, Record Group 87, National Archives, Washington, D.C.

Note: Totals differ from those in Table 1.8 due to incomplete data regarding ethnicity and addresses.

Immigration patterns would, however, soon change the prevailing composition of Manhattan's counterfeiters. The late 1870s and early 1880s apparently marked a transitional period in the ethnic origins of recruits to counterfeiting. By the mid-1880s the ethnicity of counterfeiters had changed dramatically (see Table 1.9). Part of this change may have been due to declining Irish interest in this crime. Although the actual figures are quite small, it may nevertheless be significant that the annual number of Irish arrested for counterfeiting after 1865 never exceeded and usually fell far short of the number arrested in 1860. There may have been two reasons for this decline. First, the Irish never secured reliable roles as dealers and manufacturers, despite the individual successes of people like Hargraves.[55] Thirty-four percent of all Americans engaged in counterfeiting between 1865 and 1899 worked as dealers or manufacturers, while only 22 percent of the Irish did. More importantly, the small number of Irish involved in counterfeiting on both an annual and cumulative basis, as well as their paucity of skills, probably made it difficult for them to develop and to sustain positions in the more demanding (but also more lucrative) roles.

The diversity of lower Manhattan's criminal opportunities may also have influenced Irish participation in counterfeiting. As racing and faro developed into widely popular forms of public entertainment, the Irish discovered that their knowledge of and love for horses and gambling gave them an advantage in finding work in New York City's burgeoning entertainment industry. Illegal enterprise thus beckoned powerfully to the Irish at midcentury, and they moved rapidly to seize this opportunity. They became far better known for their contributions to the development of gambling than for their work as counterfeiters.[56]

Irish counterfeiters did not, of course, disappear entirely. Instead, their relative position in this crime declined. Having ranked as the second most numerous ethnic group in counterfeiting in 1860, they dropped to third place by the end of the century. Although they enjoyed a brief resurgence in the late 1890s, the Irish always concentrated on shoving, a pattern which indicates that counterfeiting offered them limited opportunities within the criminal underworld.

Counterfeiting did not, however, depend on the support of any particular group to sustain it. With an institutional structure firmly in place, it provided individuals and groups with one possible re-

sponse to their environment. All that was required was an introduction to its operations. Native-born Americans' dominance of
counterfeiting during midcentury simply sustained counterfeiting's
institutional framework, while individuals from other ethnic groups
pondered their options.

New immigration patterns undermined this American dominance of counterfeiting by the mid-1880s, when New York's preemi-
nence as a manufacturing center and port of entry began attracting
tens of thousands of Southern and Eastern Europeans. Two groups
with very different backgrounds dominated this new migration: Italians, with practically no nonagrarian skills, and Jews, with considerable experience in handcrafts and small businesses.[57]

Most of these immigrants poured into lower Manhattan, which
continued to offer more working-class jobs than any other area of the
city.[58] The Italians, perhaps attracted by earlier settlements of their
compatriots, gravitated to the Five Points area and the nearby Four-
teenth Ward. Arranging themselves by their place of origin, they
transformed Mott, Prince, Mulberry, and Hester streets into centers
of Neapolitan, Sicilian, and Calabrian life as early as 1880. Jewish immigrants, who had no readily identifiable areas of prior settlement,
collected on the Lower East Side.[59]

With this burgeoning population of impoverished immigrants
crowding into the heart of Manhattan's counterfeiting culture, it is
not surprising that they quickly undermined American domination of
this crime. What was unusual, however, was the distinctive pattern
of ethnic participation in counterfeiting that emerged.

In 1880 New York contained almost equal numbers of Eastern
European Jews and Italians.[60] Considering the similarities in their
locations, economic plight, and exposure to the criminal opportunities of lower Manhattan, both groups hypothetically ought to
have played prominent roles in counterfeiting during the closing decades of the century. Between 1880 and 1899, however, the police and
the Secret Service arrested 310 Italians and only 13 Jews.[61]

Differences in cultural backgrounds that may predispose one
ethnic group and not another toward criminal behavior cannot explain this extraordinary disparity. Both the Italians and the Jews
contributed to New York's underworld, working in gambling, prostitution, extortion, theft, and other criminal activities.[62] Some of the
new immigrants thus replicated the behavior of Americans, Irish,
and Germans who had been operating before them on the illegal mar-

gins of economic opportunity in lower Manhattan. It is not, therefore, the fact of criminal behavior but rather the particular patterns of participation in counterfeiting that require explanation.

Italians apparently became far more prominent than Jews in counterfeiting because they had easier access to its subculture. Differences between the activities of Italian and Jewish criminals prior to 1880 created that advantage. Italians mingled more readily with counterfeiters than Jews did in the years before the massive immigration of their compatriots, thereby gaining valuable experience and knowledge that they could share with the new arrivals. Both Italians and Jews are noteworthy for their complete absence from the sample of antebellum New York counterfeiters. Neither group had then been large. Their members had committed little crime, and serious offenses among them had been practically nonexistent.[63] In these circumstances, it is impossible to trace the evolution of either group's participation in counterfeiting prior to 1860.

Nevertheless, it is Italians—not Jews—who first appear in the available records after 1860. Surprisingly, by the mid-1860s they were already active in some of the more complex counterfeiting tasks, such as dealing. Since that role required considerable knowledge and extensive contacts for success, their participation as dealers indicates that they had already become trusted members of the counterfeiting community, an achievement which created further opportunities for them. Joe Coppini, for example, had enough connections to engage in the highly arcane business of buying and selling used plates.[64]

The activities of Italians like Coppini permitted them to become integrated into the criminal milieu of lower Manhattan. They joined interethnic groups that taught them the traditions and the practices of American counterfeiting. Coppini frequented a saloon at 119 East Houston Street, where he arranged deals for coins and notes with such counterfeiters as Joe Gordon and James Miller. Barto Lombardo (alias Harry Philips) became a partner with Jack Gill, a coin manufacturer, in a shoving group that operated from a saloon at 294 Bowery. The Gill-Lombardo network included six Americans and six Italians. Like other criminals, these Italians did not confine themselves to a single activity. Coppini dabbled in burglary and invested in a saloon; Lombardo was a barber. Other Italians engaged in small businesses, highway robbery, and con games.[65]

Although interethnic cooperation would always remain characteristic of counterfeiting, the influx of so many Italians after 1880 helped change the character of its institutional setting. Italian-owned gambling houses, brothels, saloons, and groceries sprouted throughout lower Manhattan. These businesses did not necessarily drive out their competition but did establish additional, alternative meeting places for counterfeiters. Eventually, the increase in the Italian population, as well as the simultaneous migration of American and Irish counterfeiters to the East and West Sides, permitted Italians to dominate the center of New York's counterfeiting culture. By the late 1880s such favorite haunts as James Street had become thoroughly Italian counterfeiter preserves.[66]

Similar changes were under way elsewhere in Manhattan, although not to the same extent as below 14th Street. By 1880 Italian immigrants also settled uptown on the East Side between 109th and 111th streets. These were new arrivals, not older residents moving up the island from Little Italy.[67] Nevertheless, they located in the same emerging working-class districts that had attracted American and Irish counterfeiters, and they may have made contact with those established criminals quite early.

This original settlement expanded rapidly with continuing immigration, and Italians became a significant part of the East Side's ethnic population. They were not quite as dominant uptown as they were in lower Manhattan, but their numbers did promote some degree of exclusivity within ethnic working-class districts. Two coin mills that operated simultaneously within two blocks of each other illustrate the rise of exclusivity. Four Italians ran the mill at 328 East 74th Street, without assistance from any other ethnic group. Six Americans worked the mill at 303 East 76th Street. Both networks drew their members almost entirely from the immediate neighborhood. Italian and American counterfeiters thus lived in close proximity, engaged in the same activity, but organized along ethnic lines.[68]

Trends in the arrest data show that American counterfeiters retained their dominant position during the first half of the 1880s, and that the Italians replaced them as the principal group beginning in the second half of that decade. Information on the locations of Italian and American counterfeiters demonstrate that this case of ethnic succession occurred first in lower Manhattan. During the late 1870s and early 1880s the Americans were dispersed throughout Manhattan, although they remained concentrated south of 14th Street. The

Italians made their first appearance in lower Manhattan prior to 1880, and dramatically increased their presence there during the early 1880s. After 1885 they were clearly the dominant group in that area.

Ethnic uptown settlement preferences help to explain the East Side's development into the second most important site for counterfeiters late in the century. The Irish tended to move into the West Side, while the Italians preferred the East Side. Since the Irish importance in counterfeiting declined even more than that of Americans, the West Side had relatively less ability to sustain the institutional framework of counterfeiting. It therefore became the least prominent of the three counterfeiting areas in New York.

Italian succession to the lead role in counterfeiting did not rest merely on immigration patterns. Other developments also contributed to this shift. For example, some Italian entrepreneurs engaged in counterfeiting more aggressively than the Americans. Italian peddlers and barbers particularly active. Their small profit margins may have spurred them to look for shortcuts to success, but the nature of their businesses also helped. Both dealt primarily with other Italian immigrants, whose unfamiliarity with the coins and notes of their new homeland made them easy victims, and whose increasing numbers provided expanding opportunities to distribute counterfeit money. American counterfeiters, on the other hand, were far less likely to be peddlers or barbers. Their relative lack of participation in those businesses limited their access to the growing opportunities that the Italians could so easily exploit, which helps to explain their declining importance in counterfeiting.

The Americans also found their access to the more lucrative aspects of counterfeiting restricted as well. Italian counterfeiters apparently used their profits to invest in note manufacturing, dealing, and shoving, all of which tended to be more profitable than coining. They had a major advantage over the Americans in the note business, because almost all of their notes came from overseas production centers. Although the Italians occasionally employed Italian immigrants living in England and France to make their notes, they relied most heavily on printers in their homeland for this service.[69]

Overseas production thus made it possible for one ethnic group to dominate a major aspect of counterfeiting. Italian manufacturing plants were obviously immune to interference, since American authorities had no practical way to conduct overseas investigations. Overseas production also gave Italians other, equally important advantages. Production costs were probably lower overseas, giving New York Italians a greater profit margin. They also had exclusive access to these notes and absolute control of their distribution in the United States. Other groups not only had to wait for these notes but also had to obtain them through Italian contacts.

Americans, then, slipped into second place among counterfeiters by the mid-1880s. They apparently retained that position through their continuing role in coining. Coin manufacturing did not depend on overseas plants; indeed, the materials were so readily available that it was a highly decentralized activity, incapable of promoting ethnic exclusivity. Even there, however, Americans lost pride of place, as the Italians took control of dealing (see Table 1.10). More importantly, as long as Italians dominated the business of counterfeit notes, no other ethnic group could effectively challenge their primacy.

Increasing Italian involvement in counterfeiting changed more than its ethnic composition and business nature. The Italians also made it *seem* a more dangerous occupation. Non-Italian counterfeiters occasionally carried weapons but rarely used them. Indeed,

TABLE 1.10

Comparison of American and Italian Roles in Counterfeiting in New York City, 1865–1899 (100 Percent Sample)

Role	Americans	Italians
Shoving coins	85	80
Shoving notes	32	116
Dealing coins	6	28
Dealing notes	0	46
Manufacturing coins	20	20
Manufacturing notes	3	2

Sources: Register of Monthly Reports, 1865–1871, U.S. Secret Service, Record Group 206, National Archives, Washington, D.C.; Daily Reports of Agents, 1875–1899, U.S. Secret Service, Record Group 87, National Archives, Washington, D.C.

weapons seem to have had a ritualistic quality in confrontations among thieves. Knives and guns lent seriousness to an argument, but a thief with a weapon usually restrained himself or allowed his friends to prevent him from using it. In 1881 one Paddy Crowley, for example, threatened to stab Martin Leonard in a dispute over contributions to a defense fund for a colleague. When the shouting reached an appropriate level, two of Crowley's friends held him back, and Leonard escaped without a scratch. Similarly, in 1897 a thief named Dunphy threatened to shoot Jeff Davis for informing on a mutual friend. Instead, Dunphy dissolved into tears and announced he would tell everyone he knew of Davis's perfidy. Both confrontations demonstrate that criminals of this era usually sought to enforce "honor among thieves" through a combination of bluster and public exposure.[70]

There is no evidence that Italians made counterfeiting more violent in any absolute sense. Nevertheless, they did have a reputation for violence, which developed from a combination of actual incidents, their sense of ethnic solidarity, and popular perceptions that the Mafia had come to New York.

Men like Gaetano Russo, a Sicilian from Palermo, certainly contributed to the sense of danger when dealing with counterfeiters. Russo enjoyed an extraordinarily long career. In 1860 he was convicted of arson in New Orleans. He gained his freedom by informing on some prisoners who were planning a jailbreak, and then headed for Chicago. While in Chicago, he murdered an Italian barber but won acquittal in a second trial. Arriving in New York in the early 1880s, Russo quickly joined the ranks of local counterfeiters. In 1885 he slashed the face of a partner in a dispute over their business arrangements, escaped conviction for counterfeiting, and promptly left for Boston. His subsequent career included at least one conviction for counterfeiting in New York and another murder, this time in San Francisco. Russo finally returned to New Orleans, where he passed into obscurity following one last arrest in 1913 for counterfeiting.[71]

Other Italians also killed men in disputes over counterfeiting.[72] These killings may have alarmed a public willing to believe the worst of the new immigrants, but in the absence of any systematic evidence that Italians were more prone to violence than other ethnic groups in New York, it is impossible to conclude that they in fact substantially increased the physical dangers of counterfeiting. Nevertheless, violent men such as Russo made counterfeiting *seem* more dangerous.

Group solidarity and ethnic prejudice helped to reinforce this impression. Counterfeiters frequently attended court to learn the identity of informers and other matters of interest to them. They usually tried to remain inconspicuous, but Italians seem to have adopted a more boisterous approach. Secret Service operative Andrew Drummond once commented disapprovingly on their demeanor, saying that "During the recent Italian trials here this term of court, there was from 30 to 50 of the most villainous looking low browed Bandits in the courtroom every day." According to Drummond, upon the acquittal of one of their friends, "they broke out by clapping of hands and calling 'Bravo' 'Bravo,' and when another was convicted they passed the corridor among our witnesses muttering curses."[73]

Such behavior naturally encouraged a feeling among spectators that Italian criminals were both clannish and dangerous. Drummond, for example, readily concluded that "they are banded together for the common cause of cftng [sic], Robbery & Murder."[74] Since much the same thing could be said of American and Irish criminals, who had been active far longer than the Italians, Drummond's remark indicates a willingness to stereotype the newest arrivals as particularly evil-minded.

There was no evidence that Italian counterfeiters had significantly greater organizational cohesion than other ethnic criminals. That, however, did not prevent the authorities from attributing it to them. In late 1885 James Brooks, chief of the Secret Service, wrote to his operatives to warn that "there exists a large gang of Sicilian counterfeiters in this country with members in all the large cities." Brooks refrained from giving this group a title, but Drummond did not. He responded to Brooks's warning by saying that

> it has long been known to me that the Italian cftrs [sic] in the Country from Palermo and all parts of Sicily are banded together and that to betray one of their members is death at the hands of some chosen member. This order is called the 'Maffa' [sic]."[75]

Drummond got more than the spelling of Mafia wrong. Sicilian (and Neapolitan) counterfeiters like Russo had certainly become fairly common in New York by the 1880s, but there is no evidence that they had actually belonged to the Mafia or the Camorra prior to emigrating. There is also no evidence that they attempted to recreate the organizational structure of the Mafia or the Camorra in New York or elsewhere prior to 1900.[76]

The Italians did, however, bring their own conceptions of underworld norms, which they naturally attempted to apply to their new environment. Applying those concepts to new circumstances proved to be difficult, as the activities of one group of Italian shovers unwittingly demonstrated. Salvatore Brancatto, a Sicilian tailor and thief who dealt in counterfeit notes, supplied this group of approximately seventeen men, apparently with the assistance of two other Sicilians, Angelo Lamano and Salvatore Lafarino. Beginning in early November 1898, a series of crises erupted within this group that various individuals attempted to resolve. They did so by applying normative solutions rooted in Italian criminal customs.

The first crisis occurred when Brancatto and Lamano mistakenly discussed their plans for distributing a new counterfeit note in Lafarino's presence. Lafarino had been serving as the network's "boodle carrier" (a courier who delivered counterfeit notes from the dealer to the shovers), and he had decided to change his role to earn more money. Accordingly, Lafarino demanded that Brancatto and Lamano make him a partner in the distribution of the new note. He threatened that if they did not, he would kill them. After initially assuring him that he could participate, Brancatto and Lamano demonstrated their good faith by arranging a second meeting with Lafarino at which they all pledged to "unite together by oath in the new company."[77]

American counterfeiters routinely struck new bargains and created new alliances with their associates, but they did not engage in solemn ceremonies or make oaths to bind themselves to one another —nor did Italian criminals in the United States. Brancatto and Lamano were borrowing an idea from a shared Sicilian heritage to solve a particular problem. Lafarino would recognize the gesture and accept its sincerity, because he understood its origins.

That same urge to rely on mutual understandings to solve particular problems occurred again, when Brancatto's arrest precipitated another crisis for his network. His arrest provoked a series of meetings. First, Lamano and Lafarino assembled all the members of their group at Lamano's restaurant on Mott Street. Concerned that there had been a security leak, they collected everyone into a single room, arranged them in a circle, and administered an oath "to swear at [the] point of a stiletto that they would not reveal anything." They also announced that the penalty for betrayal of this group oath was death.[78]

Four days later the group met again to elect a new "leader." They chose Joseph Marino to succeed Brancatto, making Lamano treasurer and Frank Greco secretary. They also selected Francesco Gioiosa (a Neapolitan, the only non-Sicilian in this group) to administer a defense fund for Brancatto. Finally, they announced that they would solicit money for the defense fund from other "leaders" in Hoboken, uptown Manhattan, and Baltimore.[79]

These efforts to create a hierarchical organization bound by oath to secrecy and cooperation quickly disintegrated. For example, electing Marino as leader apparently did not bind him with any obligations to the group. Brancatto's associates elected him simply because he had been their only contact with the wholesaler who provided their notes. No one else in the group knew or had the confidence of that dealer; to continue operations, they had to have a leader who could buy from that wholesaler. Marino was the wholesaler's cousin.[80] There is no evidence that Marino did anything for this network except sell them notes when they had money to buy.

As treasurer, Lamano merely bought notes from Marino, which he then offered to resell to other network members. When Lamano had no money, Marino had no obligation to sell to him on credit. Indeed, within two weeks of the meeting that created this hierarchical structure, Lamano was broke and was begging Greco for capital to buy notes. By January 1899 the entire network had collapsed, and Lamano was trying to arrange new partnerships with some of his former associates.[81]

Leadership roles thus derived from access to a source of notes, a situation similar to that of other, non-Italian counterfeit networks. Leaders who had neither money to buy notes from wholesalers nor notes to sell to their network had no means to control their shovers, who tended to drift away in search of other opportunities. Furthermore, neither the leaders nor the group had the ability to enforce the oaths of secrecy. The Italian criminals of the city displayed rather contradictory behavior in dealing with the Mafia's image and its supposedly inviolate codes of conduct. A few clearly feared its reputation but still responded by informing the Secret Service about its presumed activities.

Italian informers were rather easy to find, because they shared

with other counterfeiters the same urges for revenge against enemies, the desire to destroy their competition, or the need for living
expenses. Frank Greco, for example, continually informed on his fellow Sicilians, while gaining sufficient trust to be elected secretary.
Even Gaetano Russo informed on his business partner. One convicted Italian counterfeiter provided the information that caused the
demise of a long-standing coin mill operation, because he was incensed that his associates had escaped punishment. Contrary to the
legend of death for informers, only Frank Managra came close to
dying for providing information to the Service. Managra, however,
came out of the fray unscathed, killing one of the four men who attacked him.[82]

Although Italian criminals had achieved a predominant role in
counterfeiting, New York's underworld was too ethnically and cul-
turally diverse, and the business of counterfeiting too rooted in the
general opportunity structure of working-class neighborhoods, to
sustain the sporadic efforts of some Italians to recreate the organizational traditions of the Mafia. Ignoring such considerations, contemporary American observers found the "Mafia" label a convenient way
to conceptualize their own understanding of Italian criminality.

The counterfeiters' social world was a complex subculture that depended on a symbiotic relationship with working-class neighborhoods for its survival. Counterfeiters typically held legitimate jobs
whose pay scales, seasonality, and instability prompted them to supplement their incomes with illegal activities. To participate in such
activities, however, potential counterfeiters had to be socialized into
the specialized world of crime. They achieved that socialization
through chance meetings with practicing criminals in the saloons,
groceries, and other institutions of their neighborhoods.

Experienced counterfeiters transmitted the knowledge and the
traditions of their work to those whose behavior elicited their trust.
Entree into the counterfeiters' social circle was determined by a common background in the peculiar stresses of working-class life, and a
mutual interest in illegal income—not a shared ethnic background.

Like a craft guild, counterfeiting relied on certain traditional
mechanisms to preserve its continuities. Counterfeiters did not acquire their craft through formal instruction or institutions; knowledge and techniques had to be transmitted orally and perfected by

practical experience. The social institutions employed to transmit and to preserve this practice had to consist of places such as working-class saloons, which combined anonymity with open access. In saloons, personal relations that depended on informal, oral arrangements prevailed.

Counterfeiters derived a significant advantage over law enforcement from the structure of their social world. Its reliance on an oral culture and on personal relationships effectively shielded them from the police. One had to learn the social conventions and traditions of that culture to understand the business of counterfeiting. Few police officers had the time or the ability to develop that knowledge. Until the Secret Service committed itself to the systematic penetration of this criminal culture, governmental power of any sort had little practical meaning in this social world, particularly during an era in which local detectives usually treated crimes such as counterfeiting as opportunities for personal profit. In the absence of a serious threat to their livelihoods, counterfeiters were free to develop markets for their products well beyond the boundaries of their own communities.

THE MONEY
MARKET

THE FIGURES were alarming. According to the *New York Times*, nearly 80 percent of all bank notes in circulation in 1862 were counterfeit. With 1,389 state banks to choose among, counterfeiters had ignored the notes of only 253, probably because the notorious instability of those banks had undermined public willingness to accept their currency. Equating a sound currency with public virtue, the *Times* gravely concluded that counterfeiting "is not only productive of great loss in time and money, of irreparable damage to the poor and innocent victims of these numberless frauds, but is undermining our morality as a nation."[1]

However great a threat it posed to the nation's morality, counterfeiting had become a flourishing business by midcentury. Preferring instead to regard counterfeiting as a symptom of social decay, the *Times* ignored the economic context that encouraged professional criminals to devote so much of their energies and resources to it. That was a critical oversight, because counterfeit money was a manufactured commodity serving a market that displayed surprisingly rational, albeit illegal, economic behavior. Like the manufacturers of legal merchandise, criminals needed to evaluate such basic considerations as opportunity, risk, demand, price, and quality in determining whether to invest their capital, time, skills, and organizational talent in the business.

As the *Times*'s survey indicated, many professional criminals had obviously decided at midcentury that the opportunities for profit far outweighed the risks. The nation's currency problems prior to 1860 created such opportunities. Money was scarce, or perhaps more accurately, Americans perceived that the currency supply did not match their needs. With the limited financial data available, it is impossible to determine precisely how much cash the economy needed at any particular time or how well the financial system responded to that need. Moreover, national, regional, and local economic development did not proceed uniformly, which further complicates any effort to determine capital demand.[2]

Although the Constitution reserved the power to issue currency to the central government, federal monetary policies failed to satisfy the nation's real or perceived needs. The United States Mint, perhaps reflecting the widespread aversion to paper money that had developed during the late colonial era, issued only gold and silver coin. Inadequate supplies of either metal, however, severely limited the amount of coin the Mint could place in circulation. In effect, the federal government's restrictive currency policy prevented the Mint from meeting the nation's monetary needs.

State governments sought to remedy this situation through a subterfuge. They chartered privately owned banks and granted them the right to issue currency backed by each bank's capital reserves. Since the states neither directly issued these bank notes nor supported them with their credit, they could claim that state bank notes did not violate the federal government's constitutional monopoly over the currency. This bizarre logic was upheld by the Supreme Court.

The development and proliferation of state banks was a great boon to counterfeiters, who without paper money to copy probably could not have perpetuated the lessons of their colonial heritage into the nineteenth century. Coining would have remained an option, but it was a laborious and time-consuming technique, which had limited potential for profit and required little organizational talent. Indeed, it was such an undesirable option that only 1 percent of all silver coins and 2 percent of all gold coins in circulation in 1860 were counterfeit.[3] Producing and distributing counterfeit notes was a more profitable and a more elaborate undertaking. Thus, the public's willingness to accept state bank notes, despite their distrust of paper money, created an enormous opportunity for counterfeiters to apply their collective knowledge to new circumstances.

Another boon to counterfeiters was the relatively low risk of arrest. Local efforts to suppress counterfeiting were sporadic and unsuccessful. Despite the many state laws against counterfeiting, no city or county police force ever organized an effective campaign against it.

The evolution and structure of policing during the antebellum era contributed to this failure. Effective action against counterfeiters depended upon good detective work, but local governments did not design their law enforcement agencies to encourage detection of criminals. Prior to the introduction of preventive policing in the 1840s, the antiquated watches worked only at night and merely arrested the thieves that they caught inadvertently while on patrol. Since they usually had other jobs during the day, watchmen had neither the opportunities to develop knowledge of the underworld nor the time or incentive to engage in detective work.

As full-time, salaried officers, constables could presumably address the problem of counterfeiting, since local governments expected them to deal with criminals as part of their routine duties. The constables' sources of income, however, discouraged any systematic attention to suppressing crime. They supplemented their meager salaries with lucrative fees for serving court papers. Any time-consuming detective work they might perform detracted from their ability to collect those fees. Confronted with a choice between unremunerative public detective work and profitable fees, constables typically did the obvious.

Constables did work for rewards that private citizens offered for detecting thieves; however, such incentives for capturing counterfeiters were rare. Rather than offering rewards, victims of crime concentrated overwhelmingly on the problem of recovering their property. That concern had a peculiar effect on early detective work: Constables typically allowed criminals to escape prosecution if they restored the stolen goods. By the late 1830s these bargains had evolved into corrupt relations between criminals and constables that benefited both.

The introduction of preventive policing did little to change this situation. However useful the new police became in patrolling the streets and maintaining public order, they were not an appropriate instrument for pursuing counterfeiters. For example, a uniformed officer who entered a saloon full of criminals hardly created an atmosphere for open exchanges of information about the counterfeiting business. Patrolmen could and did arrest individuals who passed counterfeits when store owners made complaints. Arresting shovers, however, had no effect on the elaborate criminal enterprises that sustained counterfeiting.

Police detectives had replaced constables in most cities by the 1850s. These officers, however, continued the tradition of expending their energies only for rewards, while maintaining the convenient corrupt arrangements that had previously evolved between constables and thieves.[4]

The deficiencies in law enforcement prevented local policing agencies from dealing effectively with counterfeiting. Concerned private citizens had few alternatives to remedy this situation. They could, for example, accept prevailing norms and offer rewards for detecting counterfeiters. A group of New England bankers adopted this approach in 1853, organizing an association that offered rewards for the arrest of counterfeiters. Over the next dozen years this association paid rewards for approximately forty convictions annually, without noticeably hindering the operations of counterfeiters.[5]

Concerned citizens could also appeal to the federal government for help. The irony in this tactic was that business owners sought federal assistance to protect the integrity of bank notes whose existence mocked the central government's constitutional monopoly over the currency. Nevertheless, some retailers, disgusted with the lack of effective measures against counterfeiters, occasionally petitioned both the Treasury and Interior departments for relief, urging the secretaries to appoint private detectives and other citizens as federal agents. The secretaries usually agreed to do so, but only as a temporary expedient.[6] Although these agents made some arrests, federal officials did not permit such ad hoc appointments to evolve into a formal system for suppressing counterfeiting. However capable these temporary agents might have been, they were also expensive, which made the secretaries reluctant to authorize their operations. Private federal detectives, therefore, remained a rarity.

Indeed, prior to the Civil War the federal government largely ignored its constitutional authority to deal with counterfeiting. Congress had dutifully passed the necessary laws but had neglected the practical matters of enforcement. U.S. marshals were the only federal officers available to enforce these laws, and their efforts hardly inspired confidence. Like local constables, marshals earned most of their incomes from various fees, which meant that their time spent detecting counterfeiters would detract from their ability to earn those fees. Federal parsimony and the absence of an urgent central state interest in antebellum counterfeiting encouraged a disinterest in crime detection. Lacking a national currency to defend, the secretaries usually refused to compensate marshals and their assistants for the time-consuming task of investigating and assembling evidence for detecting this crime. Most marshals, therefore, were unconcerned with counterfeiters.[7]

In an apparent effort to deal with these problems, some marshals petitioned Congress in 1860 for funding specifically dedicated to detecting counterfeiters. Their petition prompted Congress to pass the first appropriation for that purpose.[8] In acceding to their request, however, Congress accepted the prevailing ethos among law enforcement officers that detection was an extraordinary, not ordinary, part of their work, deserving financial rewards beyond regular pay. Rather than marking the beginnings of a concerted effort to pursue counterfeiters, this appropriation simply gave federal officers an opportunity to earn discretionary income through detective work, just as their local brethren had done.

The Civil War intervened before the marshals could test the efficacy of this new arrangement. Nevertheless, the belated attempt to create incentives to pursue counterfeiters only emphasized the futility of law enforcement efforts to suppress them prior to 1860. Counterfeiters, particularly the manufacturers and distributors, operated in a virtually risk-free environment.

Counterfeiters used this freedom, as well as the opportunities that the state banking system created, to supply the demand for their products from two consumer groups: other thieves and merchants.[9] Thieves bought counterfeits to pass on unsuspecting merchants, which was simply one low-risk way for them to earn their livings. Their efforts provided a ready market for the sale of new counterfeits. Some merchants, however, were not so unsuspecting. Peddlers, saloon owners, hoteliers, country merchants, and even factory owners created an eager pool of customers for counterfeiters. In fact, there were many entrepreneurs willing to cheat their customers or employees by giving them counterfeit money in change. Their profits were enhanced by every spurious dollar they had bought at a discount from its face value and managed to pass on the public. Some of these dishonest merchants belonged to the deviant criminal sub-culture of working-class neighborhoods. Others lived and worked outside of that subculture, operating businesses that enjoyed the respect and the trust of their neighbors and limiting their criminal activities to acquiring counterfeit money for their own use.[10]

It is impossible to determine whether merchants or thieves provided the larger market for counterfeit money. The demand for this product is also difficult to estimate. An intriguing ancillary crime, however, suggests that there was a persistent, significant demand for counterfeit currency. During the 1850s some unknown genius, who was probably a counterfeiter, created the green-goods game, a confidence scheme predicated upon the dishonesty of small business owners who bought counterfeit notes.[11] The game, which required a mailing list of businesses (possibly compiled from city directories) and an advertisement with a price list, was simple. For example, William Foss, a Massachusetts criminal in the mid-1860s, sent merchants a genuine five-dollar note and a price list for counterfeit denominations. Impressed by the quality of his "product," victims from Michigan, Illinois, Missouri, and Iowa sent Moss their money and orders. He kept the money and ignored the orders.[12]

In 1865 Minnie Price, a major Philadelphia counterfeiter, refused to risk good money as samples. Instead, he printed 5,000 circulars addressed to "Merchants, Farmers, and Mechanics desirous of making money, fast and easy," offering first-class counterfeit notes at discount rates. Although the Secret Service arrested Price before he could mail his circulars, the size of his operation indicates that thieves had come to expect great things from the green-goods game.[13]

Gullible merchants responded so often and so generously to these circulars from thieves that the green-goods swindle became a standard ploy for the next forty years. Since the essence of any successful confidence game is a combination of plausibility and greed, the fact that this game lasted so long is testimony to a widespread demand for counterfeit money. The amount of business these criminals did is also evidence of a sizable market for bogus notes. Two New York con men collected $30,000 in forty-seven days in returns from a circular they had mailed in late 1870. Another of these operations was receiving hundreds of letters a day when the authorities raided it in 1874. A decade later a half-dozen con men used 136 separate names and addresses to handle the volume of their correspondence. In 1893 the records of a major green-goods operation showed a profit of $40,185 for a single month.[14] The persistence and size of these operations provide some of the best evidence of an extensive illegal market for counterfeiting between 1860 and 1900.

Capitalizing on changes within the nation's urban communications system after 1820, counterfeiters created new production and distribution centers to meet the demand for their products. By midcentury Canadian and rural productions sites lost their primacy, as counterfeiters exploited the resources of their social world to create a national counterfeiting network that was firmly rooted in cities.

First, two principal counterfeiting centers emerged. On the East Coast, New York City and Philadelphia merged their individual advantages within the nation's urban system to create a unified manufacturing and distribution center. New York's greater resources, however, made it the dominant partner. As the nation's premier city, it pioneered in the formation of a new urban culture, including the development of working-class neighborhoods and amusement districts and their attendant subcultures. Local criminals were, therefore, well placed to seize upon the economic opportunities that those changes had created.

As the two largest cities in America, New York and Philadelphia offered counterfeiters superior technical resources. Together they controlled a combined 70 percent of the engraving, lithographic, and printing firms in the United States.[15] In addition, the three largest firms manufacturing state bank notes—the American, National, and Continental Bank Note Companies—were headquartered in New York.[16]

Dramatic changes in the printing trades in these cities also helped the cause of counterfeiting. As shop owners adopted new machine technologies, hundreds of apprentices and journeyman printers faced economic uncertainties and became potential participants in counterfeiting operations. It is probably no accident that the area bounded by Broadway, Houston, Bowery, and Chatham in New York was not only the center of printing in the United States but also the heart of counterfeiting.[17]

Counterfeiters could, therefore, expect to find among the nearly ten thousand employees of all these printing businesses a few skilled engravers willing to sell their talents. New York, with twice as many of these workers as Philadelphia, apparently provided the majority of the underworld's engravers. William L. Ormsby, an engraver at the National Bank Note Company, had cut plates for fourteen different banks (twenty-two different notes) for Joshua Minor by 1866. Robert S. Jones, an employee of the Continental Bank Company, engraved several plates for Jerry Cowsden. Charles Smith began working for counterfeiters in 1838, and eventually included such luminaries as Bill Brockway among his customers. Ormsby, Jones, and Smith were only some of the many New York engravers who supplemented their legitimate work with income from counterfeiting.[18]

New York and Philadelphia also dominated counterfeiting because of their superior communications with each other and their hinterlands. By the 1840s thieves could travel from one city to the other in less than half a day, greatly facilitating their ability to arrange and to maintain contacts. Frequent mail deliveries supplemented easy travel connections. Although communication with the hinterlands was slower and less frequent, no other seaboard cities could match the relative ease with which New Yorkers and Philadelphians did business with the rest of the country. The New York–Albany–Buffalo corridor was particularly important in directing the flow of travelers westward, and gave New York counterfeiters access to the Old Northwest. Philadelphia gained entry to the same area via its slower but still important canal and rail route to Pittsburgh. Sea routes from both cities were the principal means of traveling to the South.[19]

This ease of communication affected counterfeiting in ways analogous to legitimate business. Superior communications between thieves and their customers encouraged mutual cooperation among criminals in the two cities, and enhanced their business by offering easier access to larger numbers of customers than any other cities could match.

St. Louis and Nauvoo, Illinois, combined to create the second major production center in the nation. This peculiar pairing may have reflected the evolving character of the Old Northwest's urban system, whose immaturity would affect the social structure and the opportunities of the region's local underworlds.

Although the Midwest enjoyed rapid population growth from the beginning of the century, urban development suffered from inadequate trade connections prior to the opening of the Erie Canal and the introduction of river steamboats. Cities such as Pittsburgh, Cincinnati, Louisville, and St. Louis lacked the size and the social diversity to match the fully developed criminal subcultures of New York and Philadelphia. Large infusions of canal and then railroad workers into the region during the late 1820s probably changed that situation. These transients created a demand for housing and amusements, which generated working-class neighborhoods where criminal institutions could begin to develop.[20]

Counterfeiting was thus a highly localized activity in the West until the late 1840s. Replicating the experiences of colonial counterfeiters, thieves operated primarily from rural locations. Counterfeiters worked at such sites as Cave-in-Rock (on the Ohio River in southern Illinois), where they made coin sporadically over a forty-year period from the 1790s to the 1830s. A federal marshal's investigation in Ohio revealed that as late as 1847 counterfeiters overwhelmingly preferred rural over urban locations.[21]

That preference began to change in the 1840s. As the urban system matured, so did counterfeiting. Migration fostered this maturation process. Experienced counterfeiters with more sophisticated techniques and knowledge, as well as contacts with the more developed criminal subcultures of New York and Philadelphia, began moving into the Old Northwest. Edward R. Graham was one of these early migrants. Bringing plates for counterfeiting four different bank notes, Graham moved from Rochester, New York, to Cincinnati in 1848. Further north, in that same year, a group of German counterfeiters extended their operations westward from Buffalo to Cleveland.[22]

Others joined this migration in subsequent decades. By the 1860s, relocations to the Midwest had become fairly common. In 1866, for example, a group of approximately ten New York City counterfeiters moved to Chicago. Archibald McGregor, Clinton Barns, and Thomas Jones—all from the Rochester area—resettled in Elkhart, Indiana, and continued buying their spurious notes in the Bowery.[23]

Although a maturing urban system and the migration of experienced thieves contributed to the development of counterfeiting in the Old Northwest, as late as the Civil War the region still lacked certain essentials. The absence of a sufficiently large printing industry in the area was significant. None of the region's rising cities had enough firms to provide reliable support for counterfeiting. Cincinnati and Chicago had more printing businesses than any of their rivals, yet their combined 55 firms paled in comparison to the 520 located in New York and Philadelphia.[24]

St. Louis, with only nine printing firms in 1860, offered even less potential assistance to counterfeiters. It did, however, have other advantages that may account for its emergence as the dominant partner in the region's St. Louis-Nauvoo production center. As one of the oldest cities in the Mississippi-Ohio River system, St. Louis benefited enormously from the expanding national economy after 1815. By 1860 it was the dominant city in the region. Its location astride the region's two largest water routes made it relatively more attractive as a production site, because counterfeiters had greater access to more customers than in the other river cities.

Size and location, however, were not the only factors that made St. Louis a production center. Public antipathy toward banks also helped. Missourians enjoyed the peculiar distinction of having refused to charter a single state bank prior to 1836. When the legislature finally did authorize a bank, it imposed so many restrictions that the city and the state remained chronically short of currency throughout the antebellum period.[25] Local businesses, therefore, had to rely on currencies from state banks outside Missouri to sustain their activities. This dependence made them more vulnerable to counterfeits, because they had to use currency from banks whose reputations and notes were unfamiliar to them. Most Americans had similar problems, but the combination of the state's greater need and greater ignorance created a relatively more attractive market for counterfeits in St. Louis.

Finally, the fortuitous presence of counterfeiters with sufficient capital to back production schemes may have tipped the scales in favor of St. Louis. The city retained a rough-hewn character longer than the other major river towns. Its critical location attracted such significant criminals as Frederick Biebusch, who may have helped the development of St. Louis's underworld. Biebusch, a Prussian-born immigrant, arrived in St. Louis in 1844. He quickly became involved in the local underworld as a fence for stolen goods and a wholesaler-dealer in counterfeit notes. By the 1860s he owned a saloon and was financing several counterfeiting production projects. He was also lending large sums of money to many prominent citizens, a practice that made him virtually immune to prosecution.[26] Biebusch was only the most prominent of a group of counterfeiters that included William Stanley and Peter McCartney. Their presence was sufficient to create a preference for St. Louis among counterfeiters interested in printing new issues.

Nauvoo's role as the other half of this western production center probably reflects the evolving nature of counterfeiting in the region. As a very small but strategically located settlement, it may have developed its peculiar function after the Mormons' departure in the 1840s. The town's decline into obscurity may have attracted the attention of counterfeiters, particularly at a time when they had not entirely abandoned their early preference for rural or isolated locations. Under ordinary circumstances, the gradual shift to larger towns might have undermined Nauvoo's printing function, but its location on the Mississippi River permitted easy communication with St. Louis. Nauvoo's combination of obscurity and accessibility seems to have satisfied the needs of St. Louis's counterfeiters, who continued to use it through the 1860s.[27]

The emergence of this western production center did not mean, however, that the region's counterfeiters enjoyed the same advantages as their eastern cousins. Engravers were particularly scarce; those who did succumb to the blandishments of thieves had to serve many masters and lived rather hectic lives. Nathaniel Kinsey, Jr., a native of Cincinnati, engraved plates for counterfeiters in Pittsburgh, St. Louis, Nauvoo, Cincinnati, and London, Ohio. His prized apprentice, Benjamin Boyd, filled orders from many criminals, while scurrying from one small town to another. He lived first in Cincinnati, then in Mattoon, Decatur, La Clair, Clinton, and Fulton, Illinois, and Des Moines, Iowa. Boyd's perambulations through the Midwest testify to these engravers' need to find safety in obscurity, at a time when the region's cities were too small to provide sufficient protection for this vital part of the process of producing counterfeit notes.[28]

New York–Philadelphia and St. Louis–Nauvoo were the only production centers for counterfeiting in the United States at midcentury. No Southern city challenged their dominance. The absence of printing firms (New Orleans had only two in 1860); the lack of adequate communication links between the coastal cities and the Southern interior; travel difficulties; and the absence of significant white working-class populations combined to make Southern criminals dependent on Northern production and distribution for counterfeit notes.[29]

The two major production centers developed market areas com-

mensurate with their manufacturing capabilities and geographical locations.[30] At midcentury the New York–Philadelphia center served
New England, the mid-Atlantic states (including Maryland), and
most of the Old Northwest. The principal distribution route within
this area followed New York City's water communications to the
West via the Hudson River and the Erie Canal, while a secondary
route followed Philadelphia's Main Line to Pittsburgh. The St.
Louis–Nauvoo center served customers within the Ohio, Mississippi,
and Missouri river systems. California—which meant essentially
San Francisco at this time—received counterfeit money from St.
Louis but apparently only on a sporadic basis. Parts of this market
area were not secure. The migration of eastern counterfeiters into
the Midwest created competition between dealers from the two production centers for customers in Wisconsin and Illinois.

After the Civil War, the South rejoined the national market for
counterfeits by dividing its business between the two major centers.
Counterfeiters used the New York–Philadelphia center's superior
sea communications to reopen a brisk commerce with Charleston, Sa-
vannah, and New Orleans. St. Louis's position astride the western
water routes gave it the edge in serving the upper South—at least
that portion west of the Appalachians. The city also competed with
New Yorkers for the business of New Orleans and Texas.

Within the national market, some cities had specialized functions. Troy, New York, and Cincinnati, Ohio, served as the principal
wholesale distribution centers. Troy supplied the New England market and acted as a major transshipment point for counterfeit money
destined for customers further west. Cincinnati, located at the junc-
tion of the two major markets, performed wholesaling for both of the
national centers. Finally, Lafayette, Indiana, seems to have been a
secondary printing center, because it was the hometown of the Johnson family, one of the nation's counterfeiting dynasties.

Criminal networks tied the national markets together. Simply
defined, a network—whose size varied according to an individual's
personal initiative—was the sum of one's personal acquaintances
(which included noncriminals). These networks had both local and national spatial connotations. As urbanization promoted the development of working-class neighborhoods in cities throughout the country, migrant thieves could transmit the criminal subculture of places
such as New York to other locations. By rooting their associational

activities in these emerging neighborhoods as they moved from place to place, criminals created a decentralized underworld structure that transcended community boundaries. As professional thieves traveled from city to city, they established connections that linked individuals together in an intricate web of national, but highly idiosyncratic, fragmented associations based on personal acquaintances.[31] In addition to providing the underlying structure for the national market, these networks also provided the personnel and the resources for manufacturing and distributing counterfeit money. Criminals relied on their associates to help them to organize the businesses that satisfied the demand for counterfeits.

The degree of organization that occurred in producing counterfeits depended upon the product being produced. Some firms had relatively simple obstacles to overcome; others had far more complex problems. As the difficulties increased, so did the level of organization.

Coin manufacturing was easy. The counterfeiter made a mold from a genuine coin, poured melted base alloy into the mold, and filed the rough edges of the resulting coin, which was then plated by using a battery. None of these production materials cost much, and the work could be done at home. Coin counterfeiters preferred to produce nickels and trade dollars. A skilled manufacturer could produce anywhere from fifty to several hundred dollars a week, depending on the coin denomination that was being copied. Partners were not needed to help with the manufacturing process, because the capital and the skills involved were minimal. Acquiring knowledge of plating technique appears to have been the only barrier to engaging in coining. Counterfeiters, however, always seemed ready to share their expertise among their friends and acquaintances within their networks.

The simplicity of the coin mills meant practically anyone so inclined could establish a business. Mills run by individuals were thus fairly common. Occasionally, a backer with capital to invest would set up a mill. The fragmentary evidence of these more elaborate organizations indicates that the investor, attempting to create a steady supply of coin by hiring a coin maker, probably had been having trouble supplying his numerous customers.[32]

Paper notes presented far more challenging problems and, therefore, encouraged more complex organization. The effort, time, and money (several thousand dollars) needed to produce an issue put the manufacturing of counterfeit notes beyond the resources of a single individual. An operation of this scope required a more complex organization than the production of coin did. Counterfeiters resolved these challenges by drawing upon their networks to form partnerships. These partnerships were generally temporary, small firms, although individual counterfeiters might invest in several such businesses over the course of their careers. Each partner made a specific contribution—such as capital, supplies, potential customers, or some skill—and received a predetermined part of the issue as his or her return on investment.

The partners might all reside in the same city or in several different cities. In the latter situation, the continuing participation in the business of counterfeiting and in the various partnerships gave the impression that these criminals belonged to permanent, intercity criminal organizations—thereby provoking contemporary news reporters and the police to postulate a "national conspiracy" among counterfeiters. On the contrary, intercity partnerships were task-specific organizations that lasted only as long as they served the interests of the participants.

Nelson Driggs's career illustrates some of these characteristics. A Scot by birth, Driggs originally worked on the canal boats sailing between New York City and Buffalo. In the early 1840s he appeared in Freeport, Ohio, where he established a general store. Although his store prospered, Driggs gained a reputation for passing counterfeits on his customers and eventually turned the business over to a relative. He then became a major dealer in counterfeits. In 1854 he was arrested in Chicago with $30,000 in spurious notes. Sentenced to ten years in the Illinois penitentiary, Driggs received a pardon from the governor in less than a year.

Late in 1856 Driggs began investing in manufacturing schemes. He first formed a partnership with Louis Sleight, John Frisbie, and the engraver Nathaniel Kinsey, Jr., to print notes in Nauvoo. The fortunes of this alliance are unknown, but Driggs next surfaced as a partner with John Roe in St. Louis. Working from Roe's house, the two men produced notes on thirty-nine different banks. The St. Louis police confiscated $285,000 in these notes during a raid on their plant in 1861. Driggs drew another ten-year sentence and served seven years before receiving his second pardon.

Once free, Driggs briefly lived a legitimate life as a merchant in

Louisville. Then he organized another partnership with Benjamin Boyd (who was then living in St. Louis) and Louis Sleight (still working in Nauvoo) to produce notes in Nauvoo. This group prospered for several years between 1871 and 1876, when the Secret Service arrested Driggs with over $117,000 and fifteen plates in his possession. By this point Driggs was seventy-six years old, and had enjoyed a long and prosperous career as a counterfeit manufacturer.[33]

Unlike Driggs, Joshua Minor did not have to migrate to find partners. After moving to New York City from his birthplace in Steuben County, Minor remained there. At some point before 1860, he became a street contractor for the city and used his profits from that business to fund partnerships in counterfeiting. In 1862 he formed an alliance with Thomas Ballard, a brilliant engraver and chemist who worked for one of the city's state-bank note manufacturers. Ballard engraved several counterfeit plates of the new national currency. Late in the decade he scored his greatest coup, discovering a way to duplicate the special paper the federal government used in printing its notes. Minor and Ballard printed their own notes for approximately nine years at a plant at 49th Street and Sixth Avenue.[34]

The longevity of this partnership was unusual, because most of these alliances did not last nearly as long. Minor even diversified his investments. In the mid-1860s he formed a second partnership with Val Gleason, an engraver who divided his time between Philadelphia and New York. This was a brief alliance that was formed only to print a single issue from a plate Gleason had made. Once the principals completed this project, Minor continued working with Ballard, while Gleason organized another partnership with new participants.[35]

Harry Cole's manufacturing career resembled Driggs's more than Minor's. Born in Batavia, New York, in 1821, Cole began his counterfeiting career working on the nearby Erie canal boats. Despite a conviction for counterfeiting in the mid-1850s, Cole became a successful criminal by moving to the New York–Philadelphia production and distribution center in 1859. Traveling regularly between the two cities, Cole developed an extensive network of associates, which he drew upon to form partnerships. In 1865, for example, he joined Rensselaer Abrams of Philadelphia in a scheme to print fractional currency. Abrams contributed a set of plates to this partnership. They apparently needed some further work, which Cole arranged to have done by an engraver in New York. Abrams's arrest and conviction for counterfeiting in 1866 aborted this scheme. Four years later Cole established a second production partnership, in which he paid for engraving the plate of a twenty-dollar note, while his associates apparently contributed the costs of printing this issue.[36]

Cole's greatest coup occurred several years later. In 1877, when living in Philadelphia, he organized a partnership with Effie Cole, his wife, and Joseph Gordon, Phil Hargraves, Jacob Ott, and Charles Ulrich. The Coles knew Hargraves from mutual ventures in the 1860s. Gordon had risen from his humble beginnings as a shover in Philadelphia to become a major dealer, saloon owner, and fence. Like many other counterfeiters, he frequently traveled to New York on business, where he knew a large number of fellow criminals.[37] Ulrich was a German immigrant engraver who arrived in New York in the early 1860s. He quickly became acquainted with James Colbert, a major counterfeiter and burglar who kept a saloon at the corner of Crosby and East Houston. Colbert asked Ulrich to engrave a plate for him, inadvertently launching one of the most prolific careers in criminal engraving. Word of his skill spread rapidly. By the mid-1860s he had made plates for Hank Hall and Langdon Moore. Then James Burdell persuaded Ulrich to engrave a plate for a hundred-dollar note and to move with him to Cincinnati to set up a plant to produce it. Ulrich, a bigamist, was betrayed by one of his several wives in 1867, and was sentenced to twelve years in the Ohio penitentiary. His pardon in 1876 may have prompted Cole to organize his partnership.[38]

Each of these criminals made a specific contribution to the partnership. The Coles apparently agreed to find a suitable location for the plant and, with Hargraves, provided the capital to purchase supplies and equipment. Gordon bought the supplies and convinced Ulrich to come to Philadelphia to engrave several plates. Ott supervised the printing. The Coles', Ott's, and Hargraves's respective shares in this venture are unknown, but Gordon was supposed to receive $25,000 of the issue for his contributions.

The partnership had great success. Ulrich engraved the plates for some of the most famous counterfeits of the period, including two fifty-dollar notes and two fives. Ott printed at least $100,000 from one fifty dollar plate; quantities for the others are unknown, but were reputedly quite large due to the partners' evasion of arrest for over a year, which gave them many months in which to operate their plant.[39]

Ott's efforts compare favorably to the output of other plants. Counterfeiters did not of course keep systematic records of their productivity, but they presumably had a vested interest in maximizing their output. Scattered production figures suggest that a firm could print between ten thousand and twelve thousand dollars a month. A few firms may have been even more prolific. Ulrich confessed that he had made $200,000 in one-hundred-dollar notes at his plant in Cincinnati. Mile Ogle, another major counterfeiter, surrendered $165,000 in tens and twenties when he was arrested in 1885.[40]

A firm was, therefore, a lucrative source of income, and counterfeiters were interested in creating and maintaining them as often as possible; however, they often lacked the ability to establish or to sustain as many of these firms as they desired.

Economic problems and personal behavior account for the inability to create a stable manufacturing base for counterfeiting. Production firms could obtain high prices for new counterfeits only as long as the general public did not know of their product. When the existence of counterfeit became public knowledge, the price plummeted, because the risk of handling the issue increased. Public discovery, therefore, undermined long-term profitability, contributing to the short life span of each plant.

The partners in a firm could compensate for this problem by simply switching to a new product line. Many firms had several note plates, especially during the era of state banks. But this strategy had its limits. Counterfeiting was still a cottage industry in the nineteenth century. Since counterfeiters did not have access to the new technologies for engraving, a new note plate took considerable time and expense to produce. Engravers earned between twenty to forty dollars a week and worked nearly a year to finish a set of plates.[41]

The critical importance of plates created a resale market for them. Considering the investment that plates represented, it might seem wiser for a firm to have kept them and reuse them as often as possible. Counterfeiters, however, did not treat plates as an asset of the partnership. Instead, plates belonged to one partner—either because he had provided the money to have them made or because he took them as part of his share in the proceedings. Once the original firm dissolved, the partner who controlled this asset could either hold the plates while he sought a new partnership arrangement or sell them.

Such options gave counterfeiters who could not afford the time and the expense of commissioning new plates an alternative means to engage in production. Firms could save considerable time and money by purchasing used plates that they could later alter. Resales must have been tempting to the owners of plates, since they commanded rather impressive prices. A good set of plates could be sold for between several hundred and two thousand dollars.[42]

The number of different plates a firm had in its inventory depended upon its capital resources, which probably varied considerably among firms but seems to have been limited. Once all its notes had been publicly identified, a firm typically had no choice but to fold, because in such these circumstances continuous production was impossible to sustain.

Capital resources to sustain or to create firms were also scarce, because of the criminals' lifestyles. Though frequently married, counterfeiters participated in the rough-and-tumble bachelor subculture of nineteenth-century cities, whose values were antithetical to the behavior essential to long-term business commitments. Sobriety was a particular problem. For example, Tom Foster, who ran a firm with William English in 1865, drank so heavily that English suspended their printing operations. In 1877 Joe Gordon went on a sustained binge that interfered with his participation in the Cole-Hargraves firm.

Spendthrift habits also undermined counterfeiters' ability to accumulate capital. Although a few men like Bill Brockway and Joshua Minor displayed sound business sense, manufacturers were frequently an improvident lot. They quickly spent whatever they made, sometimes to the point of having little money for simple necessities such as food and rent. As a group they were not interested in or capable of long-term investment schemes, creating a further restraint on the longevity of firms.[43]

The men who organized partnerships did not, therefore, represent a permanent group of capitalists who constantly invested in one firm after another. Most investors had too little capital or were too improvident to participate on a regular basis. Neither Driggs, Minor, nor Cole managed to organize more than two or three partnerships during their careers, and their various associates did no better. In general, production partnerships appeared only when enough potential partners had sufficient cash available to create them, making the manufacture of notes a haphazard affair, which helps to account for the vagaries of supply and the hustling lifestyles of these criminals. They lived in hope of making more notes, but they could not eat hope.

Once a firm was in production, distribution became the next important task. Erratic supplies of counterfeits intensified demand. Wholesalers could thus disseminate their products rapidly and usually at a good price. The standard price for new counterfeit notes or coins fluctuated between sixteen and thirty-five cents on the dollar, depending on quality and market conditions.[44]

The wholesaler was the key figure in the distribution process. Wholesaling, however, could be complicated. If the wholesaler was a member of the production firm, he obtained direct access to the product without any additional costs beyond his original investment in the partnership. Harry Cole and Joshua Minor were in this fortunate position. They supplied customers directly in Troy, Amboy, and Schenectady, New York; and Cleveland, Cincinnati, Chicago, and Milwaukee.[45]

Most wholesalers, however, rarely belonged to a production firm. Instead, they constituted a separate group that competed among themselves to obtain new counterfeits. Although there is insufficient information to determine exactly how many wholesalers participated in this illegal market, the career of Charles Young indicates that they were rather numerous. As a young farm laborer in Washington County, New York, Young in 1858 met an old criminal named Smith who was shoving counterfeits. Smith persuaded Young to join him in crime, but then died within a year. Before his death, Smith apparently told Young where to buy his stocks, because Young moved to Troy, New York, where he quickly became acquainted with several counterfeit wholesalers. He worked for a time for saloon keeper James Garfield—one of the largest of these dealers in the area—selling to Garfield's customers around Troy. Having gained both knowledge and experience, Young decided to move to New York City, where he became a wholesaler for a partnership run by Ike Webber and Jerry Cowsden. He prospered, saving enough money to return to Troy and buy a saloon in 1864. Young continued his wholesaling, competing with others in upstate New York for customers. He personally knew at least thirty-six dealers in New York (most of whom lived between Troy and Buffalo), Connecticut, and New Hampshire.[46]

Although data on wholesalers who served the South are less complete than those in the North, the available information implies an interesting division of this market based on ethnicity. At midcentury Italians apparently dominated the distribution route from New York to the major Southern ports—particularly New Orleans. Antebellum migration patterns probably explain this dominance. Prior to 1860 New Orleans's climate and economic opportunities made it the preferred destination of Italians, particularly Sicilians. This preference gave Louisiana the largest Italian community in the United States, with New York City placing second.[47]

Strategically situated at both ends of a major trade route linking the two cities, Italian criminals developed an extensive business in counterfeiting. New York Italians rarely organized ethnically distinct production firms until the mid- or late 1880s. Instead, they acted as wholesale agents for their Southern cousins. Sicilians who worked in New Orleans produce markets and docks participated in this business as retailers.[48]

Italian wholesalers also worked in St. Louis's market area, perhaps because it included New Orleans. Their ethnicity, however, probably limited their effectiveness in dealing with potential customers living in the upper South. They would be much more noticeable in Southern country towns and farming regions than in urban centers such as Cincinnati. Native-born white Southerners, therefore, dominated wholesale operations in this area. One North Carolina–Tennessee network enjoyed the services of three such wholesalers, who provided for the needs of its forty-four members.[49]

Some dealers did more business than others. James Garfield and his partner, Joseph McNeil, had excellent connections in New York City and boasted that they "did not retail at all, that their business was to take the stuff from the manufacturers & wholesale all they could of it."[50] When he had them available, Garfield claimed to sell as much as $1,500 in counterfeits notes a day. He also had enough customers in Wisconsin and Iowa to justify visiting them personally with his goods. It is impossible to determine how much Garfield earned from his business. Some of his neighbors, however, did quite well. The postmaster of Canandaigua, New York, had $10,000 in the bank and owned a hotel. Archibald McGregor of Rochester, New York, cleared between $5,000 and $10,000 a year. Whether or not these individuals were typical, their self-reported incomes suggest why Young knew so many wholesalers. It was a popular profession, because it provided a good living.[51]

Wholesaling was profitable only if wholesalers could obtain their supplies, and various problems could undermine their access to new notes. The members of a firm naturally had an interest in obtaining the highest price possible for their products. To drive up the price by increasing demand, they might send a representative on a circuit through several cities to advertise a new issue among the various wholesalers. Wholesalers who had insufficient cash to compete in this market lost an opportunity to participate in the distribution of the new notes.[52]

Wholesalers faced other problems. Their regular customers might also be short of cash when a new issue appeared, forcing them to adopt a variety of marketing strategies. They could conceivably extend credit to their retail customers, but this practice required record keeping and raised problems with collections. Credit was consequently almost never employed as a business practice. Instead wholesalers sought to maintain a cash-and-carry policy. To do so, they might commission agents—either locally or in other cities—to find buyers.[53]

Price competition was yet another problem. If a production firm sold its product to several wholesalers, customers might compare prices, forcing wholesalers to lower their rates in order to make a sale. Wholesalers tried to cope with this problem by obtaining exclusive distribution rights in their territories. Such rights were difficult to enforce, because the partners in a production firm were anxious to sell as large an amount of their product as quickly as possible. Normally that meant that the producers contacted a number of wholesalers in a market area to arrange purchase agreements prior to actual production. A bid for exclusive rights, therefore, required the wholesaler to buy in sufficient quantities to offset the reduction in the producers' customer base in any particular locality. Few wholesalers had the financial resources to acquire exclusive rights, making competition the order of the day.[54]

Retailing was similarly decentralized and suffered from many of the same difficulties as production and wholesaling. Money, appropriately enough, was the greatest headache. Credit was extremely scarce; even membership in a criminal network that had some members engaged in producing counterfeits did not obviate the need for hard cash when the product was ready for market.

Faced with the need to supply customers or lose them to others, a retailer should, in theory, have saved some proceeds for future investments. As with wholesalers, however, the notion of saving apparently did not occur to retailers. Thus, when a new issue did appear, some retailers invariably engaged in frantic efforts to raise cash. Borrowing was difficult, since associates and friends were equally improvident. Retailers resolved their cash flow problems in various ways. Some committed property crimes; others found a legitimate job, pawned some valuables, or mortgaged their homes to raise money. If none of these efforts succeeded, the retailer had to wait for the next opportunity.[55]

Even with cash on hand, a retailer was not necessarily in a position to buy. The illegal character of the production system inhibited access to information about the availability of a firm's products. Retailers (and wholesalers, for that matter) sometimes missed hearing about a new issue until it was too late. Accurate knowledge about new counterfeits was absolutely essential, but market information was difficult to obtain. Production partnerships worked in as much secrecy as they could create; wholesalers jockeying for shares in the new issue said as little as possible until they had confirmed their positions.

Retailers sought to resolve this problem by relying on rumors. Criminals roamed their networks listening for clues. This behavior placed a premium on extensive contacts within the social world of counterfeiting. Since access to accurate but quasi-secret information was so critical to success, this search became one of the major costs of operating in an illegal market.[56]

The vagaries of access to information helped to fashion another subsidiary market within counterfeiting. Wholesalers and retailers had to meet their customers' demands somehow, and the erratic flow of new issues forced them to turn on occasion to the discount and resale markets.

Discount notes came from various sources. Some members of production partnerships may have failed, for some reason, to sell their entire share of an issue. In other cases, the quality of a new issue might be so poor that few wholesalers or retailers would risk purchasing it immediately. Law enforcement agencies also contributed to the discount market by publishing warnings and descriptions of new issues before they had been widely disseminated. The enhanced risk attached to such notes, whether real or not, forced them off the regular market—at least temporarily—and damaged their prices. Whatever their source, discounted notes provided an alternative supply in the market, though there is no way to determine what amounts were available at any given time. They typically sold for between eighteen and twenty-two cents on the dollar.[57]

Those retailers who obtained some part of an issue made their profit by selling to the shovers. Either as criminals or legitimate business owners, shovers created the market for counterfeit money. Retailers used two different strategies to distribute their product to each group. First, they might themselves employ shovers to pass their counterfeits on the public. This tactic required that the retailer either share his profits with his employees or pay them a commission, which avoided the problem of finding shovers able to buy counterfeits. Since this strategy did not require a shover to invest any of his or her own money, it tended to attract ordinary criminals who wanted to participate in counterfeiting but had only their freedom to risk. Joe Gordon used shovers to circulate some of the notes he had received as his share of the Cole-Hargraves firm. Coin retailers relied on this technique more frequently than note dealers, perhaps because their shovers usually were the least able to raise cash on their own.[58]

The second, and probably preferred tactic, was outright sale. Although this strategy produced the quickest profit, it also placed the retailer in a competition for shovers on the basis of quality and price. Shovers were dependent on the retailer, but as the final distributors they were sensitive to the problems of cost and risk (lower quality increased risk by making a counterfeit more noticeable). They could and did refuse to buy from retailers offering products whose price exceeded their quality.[59]

Furthermore, since shovers were in constant need of fresh supplies, they worked with or bought from any retailer who could supply them. Retailers therefore had to judge supply and demand carefully in setting prices that would attract buyers. Such considerations probably account for the wide range in retail prices, which varied from as little as thirty cents on the dollar to as much as seventy cents.[60]

To sell to criminals and legitimate business owners, retailers had to first find them. Finding local criminals and vice operators, of course, posed few problems. Counterfeiters maintained links to those groups through their mutual location and participation in urban working-class and entertainment districts. More legitimate business owners who might be willing to purchase counterfeit money were harder to identify. Retailers, however, may have built a clientele among local merchants who frequented the bright-light districts. Since the emerging business districts and the vice areas occupied roughly the same central city areas, chance meetings between retailers and potential customers were possible. Out-of-town businesspeople, who would be likely to visit the entertainment districts, would have provided another opportunity to build a network of customers in the urban hinterlands.

Finally, an advertising campaign through the mail might also attract customers, as the example of the green-goods game demonstrates. Whatever the precise techniques retailers used, they did create customer lists, which they jealously guarded from their competitors. Their customers regularly wrote to retailers or left messages at the saloons that retailers habituated.[61]

As with wholesalers, the number of a retailer's customers determined his success and varied according to his ability to provide a reliable supply of counterfeits to his shovers. For example, John Simms of Amboy, New York, bought his notes from New York wholesalers and made monthly trips into northern Pennsylvania, where he sold to at least four regular customers, including an attorney, a doctor, and a hotelier. The three unidentified wholesalers who served North Carolina and Tennessee in the early 1870s had a moderate-sized network, which included a former Tennessee attorney general, a county commissioner, a deputy U.S. marshal, a county sheriff, eleven merchants, and twelve successful farmers.

Some networks were extremely large. James Brown of Cleveland knew five New York–Philadelphia manufacturers, nine wholesalers in Buffalo, and 148 dealers or shovers in Ohio. His network included saloon keepers, boatmen, farmers, and store keepers. It is not clear how many of those shovers bought from Brown, but the extent of his knowledge and the size of his network probably gave him superior access to information about counterfeiting and ample opportunity to peddle his goods.[62]

Shoving, the last step in disseminating counterfeits, could also involve casual organizations drawn from social networks. These criminals usually operated in small groups of two or three. One shover entered a shop, made a small purchase, and received genuine money in change. While the shover was transacting business, a companion remained outside to watch for the police and to make sure that the shover was not followed by the store keeper, who might have discovered the counterfeit. If all went well, the shoving group moved on, repeating the process as long as their supplies and luck held out. Some shovers used a rudimentary accounting system to keep track of these exchanges. After each transaction, they placed the proceeds in a separate pocket or envelope, so that their associates would be able to trace the precise amounts each shover collected. After each expedition, the group returned to their meeting place and divided the proceeds.[63]

Shoving groups from the major production and distribution centers also moved about the hinterlands regularly, passing their counterfeits on farmers, small-town merchants, and store keepers in the larger cities along major trade routes. In the meantime, rural shovers, such as John Simms's customers, used simpler methods. As local merchants, they could pass counterfeits in change without much trouble.[64]

Fragmentary evidence on the earnings of criminals reveals, not surprisingly, that shoving provided a good income, particularly to those individuals who had difficulty finding steady legitimate work at decent wages. Even those shovers who worked on commission did rather well. In the fall of 1886, Maggie Casey earned between fifty cents and a dollar a night by passing coins. That probably represented a considerable supplement to her regular earnings. Independent shovers were more successful. In the summer of 1893, a New York lemon peddler who shoved five dollar notes was depositing between twenty-six and thirty-six dollars a *day* in his savings account. Given the vagaries of supply, he probably did not save that much money every day of the year; however, the opportunity to do so no doubt motivated him to keep buying counterfeits when they were available.[65]

Traveling shovers apparently had opportunities to earn even more money. They could distribute small amounts of counterfeits among many towns and cities, hopefully reducing the risk of discovery by moving rapidly from place to place while accumulating more for their efforts as they proceeded. A group of New Orleans shovers, for example, started their tour of rural Louisiana in 1866 with $23,000 in counterfeit greenbacks. Mike Cunningham, a New York shover, had less grandiose ambitions but used the same approach in 1878. He took three hundred five-dollar notes to Cleveland and traveled to Boston, stopping at several places along the way to pass nearly all of his notes. Barring arrest, the proceeds from such expeditions could be substantial.[66]

Viewed from outside, the world of the counterfeiters seemed to exhibit a coherent structure and a permanence of impressive dimensions. Secret partnerships—whose influence extended beyond the boundaries of individual cities and across state lines—produced coins and notes that flowed into the public's coffers through a regular system of wholesalers, retailers, and shovers. There were even famous counterfeiters who provided colorful stories for the local press; their wealth and political connections seemed to insulate them from any attempt to halt their activities.

The fact that the criminals who served the counterfeit market had to engage in fairly sophisticated organizational behavior does not, however, necessarily mean that they constituted a permanent, separate group within the underworld, nor that their organizational activities elevated them to a higher status among their peers. Not every criminal engaged in counterfeiting; for those who did, it was just one of their activities. They were essentially professional criminals who participated in this market when an opportunity presented itself. Some may have preferred to earn their living by counterfeiting, but the circumstances of their social world dictated that they had to be ready to pursue whatever opportunities arose. Thus, seizing upon whatever opportunity coincided with their need to earn some money, the members of any particular criminal network engaged individually or with their associates in a variety of enterprises—including robbery, burglary, pimping, green-goods swindles, fencing stolen goods, and even legitimate business.[67]

Problems inherent to the relationship between the business of counterfeiting and the character of criminal networks contributed to this behavioral pattern. The networks consisted of individuals bound to each other by ties of acquaintance, mutual interest, and a common life-style. Social bonds did not necessarily translate into cooperative economic activities, because individual and group needs did not always coincide. Professional thieving produced an unpredictable income, and criminals maintained life-styles that did not encourage thrift.

Since counterfeiting required investment capital, the conflict between the social behavior of the criminals and the economic requirements of counterfeiting inhibited their ability to create or to maintain a steady flow of bogus money. In the absence of any disciplined approach to their activities, professional thieves had to hustle constantly. (Hustling probably encouraged inventiveness. For example, the green-goods game was, in one sense, a way to make money from counterfeit money when none was available.) They could produce the ready cash for investment in counterfeiting only on an episodic rather than a systematic basis.

Counterfeiters created ephemeral structures that met the needs of an illegal market but generally failed to escape the limitations of their life-styles. They were incapable of creating permanent, hierarchical organizations that could regulate production or distribution of their products. These constraints made counterfeiting potentially vulnerable to effective police intervention at critical points in its organization. Professional criminals could not easily recover from the seizure of a production firm or an issue, nor could wholesalers who lost their "boodle" (the notes they bought from a firm).

But counterfeiters never had to deal with the challenge of effective law enforcement prior to the Civil War, because there was an extraordinary disparity between the organization of counterfeiting and the organization of law enforcement. Despite the ephemeral character of counterfeiters' firms, counterfeiting transcended the boundaries of particular communities. It was a crime geared for a national market in an era of localized policing. Furthermore, counterfeiters created that market at a time when there was no compelling state or federal interest in protecting the currency. Since state governments did not guarantee the notes of state banks with either their faith or their credit, they had no incentive to protect it. Federal coinage played little role in either the national economy or in the schemes of counterfeiters, because the economics of counterfeiting heavily favored notes rather than coins.

This situation left the problem of protecting an essentially privatized national currency to the owners of the banks and to the ordinary citizens who received counterfeit money, both of whom could only complain to their local police or, more rarely, petition the federal government for temporary relief. In essence, the enforcement of the laws against counterfeiting depended upon private responses from victims living in local communities, but episodic local efforts to suppress counterfeiting within a particular community could not prevail against a criminal activity that flourished in a national market.

Suppressing counterfeiting thus required a coordinated, proactive effort organized on a national scale. A national policing effort, however, was inconceivable on the eve of the Civil War, when the political will to define a public interest in the currency and to create an effective policing agency to defend that interest simply did not exist. That would soon change.

LOCALISM VERSUS SOVEREIGNTY

The Origins of the Secret Service, 1863–1875

THE SPECTACULAR COLLAPSE of the nation's political system, the descent into the Civil War, and the imbroglio of Reconstruction have tended to obscure an important aspect of the American polity at midcentury: city and state governments' continued expansion into public affairs. Economic and social change did not cease in deference to the national crisis, and through the remainder of the century, city and state governments responded by continuing to increase their authority over such public services as health, welfare, and education. These issues increasingly concerned the public, and both the voters and the political parties had to adjust their beliefs and practices to deal with the implications of greater governmental centralization.[1]

State building at the local level, however, had the advantage of proximity. Still profoundly attached to their local communities, Americans could tolerate incremental centralization by governments that were familiar and, presumably, more responsive to them. Federal state building, however, was an entirely different matter. Nothing in their history had prepared Americans for the massive expansion of federal power during the Civil War or had dictated that they must accept it once the emergency of the war had ended. The weight of tradition and interest seemingly forced a quick return to an approximation of antebellum political norms, but the Civil War and Reconstruction had created the opportunity for the federal government to join the general trend toward centralization. A national state emerged from these crisis years with "vastly expanded authority and a new set of purposes."[2]

A key element in the expanded federal authority, which is also one of the defining characteristics of a nation state, was the increased capacity to police society. Although not an intentional outcome of the chaotic Civil War era, the enhanced ability to police became one its enduring legacies. The exigencies of war and the importunings of evangelical reformers within the Republican party led Congress to expand federal law enforcement, which would have been avoided in more tranquil days. For example, in 1863 Congress created the Internal Revenue Service to enforce the Revenue Laws; in 1873 it passed the Comstock Law, authorizing federal Postal Inspectors to suppress obscene mail. Both these police forces would extend federal power into local communities in unprecedented ways.[3]

Unlike the Internal Revenue Service and the Postal Inspectors, the Secret Service's authority to police society evolved without Congress's formal blessing. When Congress passed the Legal Tender Act, it neglected to stipulate an enforcement mechanism for protecting the integrity of the new currency. Although the Constitution explicitly gave Congress the power to punish counterfeiters, there were no practical precedents to create effective measures to suppress counterfeiting. Federal marshals—who were both the most numerous and most widely dispersed force available—had already demonstrated that they had neither the experience nor the incentive to acquaint themselves with the social milieu of the urban underworld.

Federal officials, therefore, had to create an effective police force to deal with urban criminals, whose activities—for the first time in American history—challenged the central government's sovereignty. Having asserted its constitutional rights, the federal government had to defend itself or jeopardize its role in national economic development.

Lacking any congressional directive, the Service had a particularly tangled evolution. There were three principal difficulties. First, the Treasury officials who would establish the Service had little if any knowledge of how to create an effective police force and had to learn by experience. Second, the creation of the Service required careful attention to the problem of forging new relations between the federal and local governments, particularly in the cities. In a political system that still adhered to traditional notions of federalism, Treasury officials had to take care that they took local sensitivities into account. Finally, the first Secret Service agents lacked personal integrity, and thus provided no more than a shaky foundation for building public trust in the government's ability to protect the currency. All these difficulties took nearly twelve years—from 1863 to 1875—to resolve.

The freewheeling environment of the war inevitably exerted considerable influence over the Service's initial development. Several executive departments engaged in various wartime policing activities that affected the Service. Early in the war official concern over disloyal activities prompted Lincoln to grant his subordinates permission to "arrest and detain without the ordinary process of law such individuals as they might deem dangerous to the public safety."[4] Secretary of State William Seward eagerly seized this authority in order to create a large menagerie of informers, Pinkerton agents, U.S. marshals, and city policemen, who censored mail and telegrams, and followed and arrested suspicious persons.[5]

Two other executive departments also developed an interest in police experiments. In the War Department, Secretary of War Edwin Stanton gave Peter H. Watson, his assistant secretary, the responsibility for supervising a wide range of confidential assignments, including the creation of a "National Detective Police" force composed of army provost marshals. Watson employed this force to pursue Confederate spies, fraudulent contractors, and bounty jumpers, and to raid gambling dens, brothels, and saloons.[6] In the meantime the secretary of the Interior impinged more directly on the Treasury's future bailiwick. In 1863 Congress authorized the secretary to pay $1,184 to a detective force "employed by a former head of the [Interior] Department" for its expenses and services in pursuing coin counterfeiters in Washington and Philadelphia.[7] This appears to have been an interesting case of a federal subsidy to private detectives to supplement the inadequate efforts of the U.S. marshals.

Congress also appropriated $25,000 for the suppression of counterfeiting in the same legislation that authorized payment to the secretary of the interior's private police. This appropriation began the process of establishing the Secret Service; there is no evidence, however, that Congress had any specific idea of how to protect the greenbacks being issued under the Legal Tender Act. There is also no indication that Secretary of the Treasury Salmon Portland Chase sought this appropriation through any desire to create a permanent Treasury police force. The exigencies of the war temporarily justified both the Legal Tender Act and the appropriation to suppress counterfeiting, and Chase apparently gave little consideration to the enforcement issue.

The form of this appropriation created the opportunity for inadvertent state-building activities by executive action. In the absence of congressional guidance or restrictions, Chase had the broadest possible administrative discretion for implementing congressional intent. In December 1863 he delegated responsibility to a subordinate, ordering that "all measures of this Department for the suppression of offenses respecting the coin and securities of this Government . . . shall be under the supervision and direction of the solicitor of the Treasury."[8]

Chase's order did not specify the precise organizational structure for suppressing counterfeiting; he merely stipulated that all "detectives and other persons in the employ of the Department and engaged in the prosecution of these measures" should report to the solicitor, Edward Jordan, who thus became the crucial figure in the initial development of the Secret Service.[9]

Little information about Jordan's career or his personal views has survived. Born in New York in 1820, Jordan had received a rudimentary education that had enabled him to become a schoolteacher. In 1844, however, he had moved to Portsmouth, Ohio, to study law and had been admitted to the bar in 1846. During the next ten years Jordan had built a career as a successful local Democratic politician in a Whig stronghold. He had also helped found a short-lived Democratic newspaper, and had served in succession as town clerk, county prosecutor, and city clerk. In 1856 his antislavery views had precipitated a switch to the Republican party, which had turned out to be a shrewd career decision. Jordan had then moved to another county, where he had won yet another term as a county prosecutor, had attracted the attention and the friendship of Ohio's most prominent antislavery politician, Salmon Portland Chase, and had campaigned actively for Lincoln. Chase had rewarded Jordan's contributions to the Republican cause by appointing him solicitor in 1861. After serving eight years as solicitor, Jordan briefly practiced law in New York City, before retiring in 1872 to live with one of his daughters. [10]

Jordan thus appears to have been a relatively minor politician with modest legal skills. His remarkably early retirement from his law practice in New York at the age of fifty-two implies that he found the shift from county prosecutor to big city lawyer difficult even with the intervening years as solicitor. (Health could not have affected his decision; he lived until 1899.) There is nothing in his career that suggests an innovative mind at ease in dealing with significant issues of public policy.

Chase did not simply abandon Jordan to his task. Either on his own initiative or at Jordan's request, Chase asked Secretary Stanton to assign Col. Lafayette C. Baker, head of the War Department's National Detective Police, to the Treasury. [11] Baker, a bureaucratic entrepreneur who had a penchant for dubious adventures and self-aggrandizement, had parlayed strident patriotism and his participation in the 1856 San Francisco Vigilance Committee into an appointment as a spy for Seward's State Department in 1861. A year later Seward had transferred him to the War Department, where Assistant Secretary Watson had made Baker a provost marshal and had placed him in charge of the National Detective Police. (Baker preferred to call his operation the Secret Service, although Allan Pinkerton also laid claim to that title to describe his force of spies.) Baker found an outlet for his sense of drama, intrigue, and moral indignation in his new position. [12]

Baker's force conducted a typically grandiose and well-publicized raid against counterfeiters throughout the Midwest in the summer of 1864. He emerged from that adventure as one of the few federal agents with practical experience in coping with counterfeiters on a national scale. He also continued to work for the War Department. After his major sweep in the summer, Baker's assistance in pursuing counterfeiters became much more sporadic. [13]

Subsequently, William P. Wood attempted to fill the void left by Baker. Wood was another of those curious bureaucratic entrepreneurs spawned by the war. He had begun life as a model maker, working in Washington, D.C., where he had been born in 1819. At the age of twenty-seven he had joined a volunteer company and had fought in the Mexican American War, where he had earned a reputation for rash aggressiveness. In 1854 Peter H. Watson, then one of Washington's ablest patent attorneys, had hired Wood as a technical assistant in a patent infringement suit. Watson had won the case, and Wood's role may have impressed not only Watson but also Edwin Stanton, a junior member of Watson's legal team.[14]

In 1862, when Watson assumed control of confidential activities in the War Department, he discovered that he needed a secure place to keep individuals accused of federal crimes, and to hire someone trustworthy to supervise such prisoners. Watson decided to incarcerate them in Washington's Old Capitol Prison and to appoint Wood as superintendent.

As superintendent Wood enthusiastically prowled the boundaries between legitimate and deviant society. He had already developed a taste for dubious ventures. For example, there is a persistent tale that he had helped Watson win the 1854 patent lawsuit with doctored evidence; and sometime after the trial he had participated in one of William Walker's Nicaraguan expeditions.[15] Now, surrounded by spies, criminals, and government detectives, and lacking both scruples and good judgment, Wood plunged into a variety of intrigues. He conducted unauthorized negotiations with the Confederate government on prisoner exchanges; sent counterfeit money to Union prisoners of war for buying supplies from their guards; dabbled in espionage with Colonel Baker; and accompanied Baker on his 1864 sweep of counterfeiters.[16]

By the fall of 1864 Wood had begun to devote his energy and enthusiasm to capturing counterfeiters, a job that was suited to his personality and circumstances. His other adventures had attracted the army's wrath and had earned him unfavorable notice with his political mentors.[17] Tracking down counterfeiters was bound to improve rather than to threaten his position. Furthermore, Wood's job as superintendent fortuitously provided him with valuable access to counterfeiters. Working simultaneously as superintendent and as Baker's assistant, Wood had incarcerated captives in the Old Capitol Prison, where he had kept them without the benefit of bail or counsel. He became an expert on the nature and the extent of counterfeiting by pumping prisoners for information, gaining knowledge that apparently impressed Solicitor Jordan enough to make Wood a Treasury agent in December 1864.[18] Wood prudently retained his position as superintendent, possibly because Jordan had not yet decided whether to create a separate detective organization within the Treasury. Jordan seems to have taken Chase's 1863 directive literally, because he personally supervised the campaign against counterfeiters from his office.

In 1864, when Congress increased the appropriation to suppress counterfeiting to $100,000, Jordan displayed no inclination to establish a distinct police force with these funds. Instead, he used this appropriation in conformity with traditional local law enforcement practices, issuing a circular that advertised the existence of a "large sum" to pay rewards for information about or arrests of counterfeiters.[19] That move stimulated some activity by local police but did nothing to advance the evolution of the Secret Service.

Jordan dithered until 5 July 1865, when Wood visited his office to receive an official appointment as chief of the United States Secret Service in a quiet, obscure ceremony.[20] Considering Jordan's recorded behavior to this point, this was a surprising event—because it was so bold. Congress had not sanctioned the creation of the Secret Service, as it had the Customs Service, the postal inspectors, and the Internal Revenue Service. The Secret Service, therefore, began with no statutory identity as a congressionally authorized federal agency. Jordan had apparently made an executive decision to create the Service.[21]

Why he did so poses an intriguing riddle. Hugh McCulloch, then secretary of the Treasury, supposedly obtained Lincoln's permission to establish the Secret Service at a cabinet meeting held the day of Lincoln's assassination. If that had been the case, why had McCulloch waited nearly three months to create the Service, and why had he neglected to obtain President Johnson's consent to such a project? McCulloch's own memoirs make no reference to this rumor.[22]

The circumstances surrounding Jordan's decision suggest that Wood persuaded him to create the Service. Wood had easy access to Jordan throughout the spring of 1865, which allowed him to carve out a position as a de facto bureaucrat by gradually accumulating agents who reported to him. In December 1864 he had hired two men; by June 1865 he was supervising nine agents.[23] His aggressive personality and his self-important reports about his work against counterfeiters may have convinced Jordan that Wood was talented. Some evidence suggests that Jordan had become an admirer of Wood.[24] Thus, Wood may well have talked Jordan into founding a separate detective bureau under his command. Jordan's decision to create this new federal policing agency, however, represented a fortuitous exercise of executive authority just at the point when such decisions were losing their rationale. The Service, therefore, owed its existence to a combination of events, administrative decisions, and inferences made by various executive officers and their subordinates during and immediately after the war.

Neither Jordan nor Wood had adequately assessed the policy implications of creating a new federal police organization. Following the Civil War, the central government's monopoly over the money supply enjoyed wide popularity and became a major element in the development of a national economy dominated by urban centers.[25] The amount of money in circulation increased significantly but not enough to meet increasing demand.[26] The need to protect the currency's integrity thus intensified. Counterfeit notes represented a potentially serious threat to the stability of complex emerging relationships between federal power, economic development, and urban growth.[27] As the only federal policing agency designed to deal with counterfeiting, the Service's fundamental mission was to protect the trust underlying those evolving relationships by effectively organizing and projecting federal authority. Jordan and Wood, therefore, had to initiate a peacetime expansion of federal policing authority to localities, institutions, and individuals hitherto unaccustomed to that influence. To succeed, they had to avoid the appearance of subverting the power of federal marshals and local police departments, or challenging settled assumptions about the legitimate role of the national government in public life.

Jordan sought to finesse these issues by acting as if nothing of importance had happened. In his circular announcing the creation of the Secret Service, Jordan reiterated his authority over anticounterfeiting activities, but chose not to mention the Service or Wood by name, or to list the Service's duties, procedures, and powers. Instead he referred to "a Division, under the direction of a competent head." He also discussed rewards, and requested that individuals working for existing law enforcement agencies send all their counterfeiting intelligence to his office.[28]

Jordan thus reserved a large and important role for himself in his circular. He stressed that all the information about counterfeiters should be routed directly to him, not to the unnamed chief of the Service.[29] Jordan clearly intended to supervise the Service's activities through a monopoly over information; he also intended to disperse his agents throughout the nation, by creating districts with offices located primarily in major cities. This administrative structure suggested an unprecedented nationally coordinated effort to deal with counterfeiters. Although the agents numbered fewer than thirty, this structure concretely projected the federal government's authority into cities and their underworlds.

Jordan's decisions about other key aspects of the Service demonstrated how heavily the past weighed on bureaucratic creativity. He knew about existing mechanisms for dealing with counterfeiting, and his adherence to established routines significantly weakened the authority of the Service. Since he had not sought a congressional statute to create the Service—which meant that he could not obtain congressional consent to grant the Service ordinary police powers— Wood's agents did not have the authority to make arrests as federal detectives. They also could not obtain search warrants to seize evidence in the course of their investigations. Wood's agents could make an arrest only after a federal marshal had deputized them. The marshals, however, were not obligated to do so. Since marshals received fees for making arrests, they were more likely to make the arrests themselves, thereby relegating the new government detectives to the role of informants.

As originally conceived by Jordan, the Service began operations as a federal agency clearly subordinate to local policing institutions. Officially, it could only search for evidence and arrest criminals at the sufferance of those agencies. This arrangement avoided raising awkward jurisdictional challenges to the authority of local law enforcement agencies, which could potentially arouse intense political hostility to the Service, by requiring the Service to rely upon them for the power to arrest. Jordan, in fact, stressed that there was no need for "jealousy between those connected with this office and the local officers; but on the contrary, there is the strongest reason for mutual confidence and co-operation."[30]

In summary, Jordan balanced his bold creation of a federal police agency with a conservative design. The Service lacked the prerequisites of bureaucratic independence. Its subordinate position in the solicitor's office deprived it of organizational integrity, while its lack of police powers inhibited its ability to fulfill its mission independently.

This muddled situation did not bode well for the Service's corporate identity or survival. The Service's mere existence and its novel mission, however, represented an opportunity for Wood, who was determined to make the most of it. He had already displayed an indifference to rules and a talent for self-promotion during the war. Those were not the most ideal traits for a subordinate, but Jordan overlooked them when he made Wood the first chief of the Service. Wood took advantage of two key administrative errors of Jordan's and some bureaucratic loopholes to create a far stronger corporate identity for the Service than the solicitor may have intended.

Jordan made his first mistake by not defining Wood's role. Since he intended to supervise the Service's operations, Jordan decided not to employ Wood as a resident bureau administrator. Instead, he ordered Wood to participate personally in investigations.[31] Wood did so enthusiastically, especially in important cases, which would enhance his reputation. His frequent travel and personal supervision of cases around the nation enhanced his authority over his subordinates, and gave him far more intimate knowledge of the Service's work than Jordan had.

Wood used that knowledge to inveigle a separate headquarters for the Service in New York City. The volume of work occasioned by New York's central role in counterfeiting provided ample justification for a separate office. Jordan, making his second major mistake, apparently raised no objection to the evolution of an unofficial but nonetheless distinct office for the Service.[32] He should have been more concerned, however, because the New York office quickly became the record center and, therefore, the institutional locus of the Service. Wood, in effect, had improvised an independent organizational identity for the Service and had given himself a powerful administrative role.

Although there is no evidence to suggest that he had maneuvered to acquire that position for any motive other than self-aggrandizement, Wood had nevertheless taken the first significant steps to make the Service a distinct entity capable of making contributions to the process of state building. He had thus escaped the restrictions that Jordan had imposed, by giving the Service a separate bureaucratic identity that justified future institutional expansion.

A rather curious title was chosen for the agents by either Wood or Jordan that also contributed to a sense of organizational distinctiveness. Since by the 1860s the public had come to detest detectives for their corruption and deviousness, it was in the Service's interests not to associate itself with that despised group.[33] Within the federal government, various departments had for some time hired individuals to perform detective work as "special agents," which also became the preferred title for those hired to pursue counterfeiters in the antebellum era.[34] Rejecting that term, either Jordan or Wood settled on "operative" as the official title of the Service's employees.[35] In contemporary usage, operative usually referred to a factory worker. Allan Pinkerton, who had worked briefly for the Treasury at the close of the war, also began calling his employees operatives at about this same time, possibly for similar reasons.[36] This nomenclature set the Service apart from most other policing agencies in the nation.

Ironically, Wood's operatives had decidedly varied credentials, which sometimes fueled incipient public suspicion of the Service. Recruits with law enforcement experience as private detectives, police officers, or federal agents constituted nearly a third of those whose backgrounds can be identified.[37] Most of these individuals had either disgraceful or undistinguished careers prior to 1865. William Hartman, for example, had worked for a private detective firm in Chicago. Wood hired him in July 1865 and had to fire him that same month because of his "notorious character."[38]

Abner B. Newcomb and Ichabod C. Nettleship were among the more promising early recruits. Newcomb had begun his career as a newspaper editor, and in 1861 he had become a private secretary to the U.S. marshal in New York. The marshal put Newcomb in charge of the office's detective work, which had given Newcomb the opportunity to engage in extensive espionage activities during the war. Hired by Wood in November 1865, Newcomb served two years before resigning to take a position as a special agent in the Treasury Department.[39] Nettleship had emigrated from his native England in 1851 at the age of eighteen. He had settled in Newark, New Jersey, where he had worked in the saddlery business until joining a volunteer regiment in 1861. He had experienced little if any combat in the war. Instead, he had held a series of army administrative posts, including acting commissary and "secret detective" in Washington, D.C. While holding those positions, he had accidentally stumbled onto and broken up a counterfeiting scheme. This achievement subsequently led to an appointment to the Treasury, where Nettleship spent the remainder of the war working with Jordan. Wood had probably become acquainted with Nettleship during that period, because Nettleship had been was one of the original force Wood assembled in July 1865.[40]

Nearly half of the early recruits, however, had criminal backgrounds. Henry O. Wright, Wood's first recruit, was typical. Wood had hired him in December 1864, prior to the creation of the Service, and Wright remained on the government's payroll through the end of 1865. He undoubtedly knew a great deal about counterfeiters. Indeed, Wright had been in a Chicago jail when Wood found him and arranged for his release.[41] Wood also hired George Hyer, who worked more briefly for the Service. Hyer had been accused of murdering five men, had served a prison term for counterfeiting, and had been arrested for forgery prior to joining the Service.[42] Another recruit, Virgil Barlow, had earned his living manufacturing counterfeit money in New Jersey before Wood hired him.[43] It was not unusual to find such individuals associated with a policing agency; detectives typically used criminals as informers in their work. Wood, however, had *hired* them as operatives and assistant operatives for a federal policing agency.

Wood's recruits did produce results, arresting more than two hundred counterfeiters and seizing large quantities of bogus notes and counterfeiting paraphernalia in their first year of operations.[44] This impressive record further exemplifies the way in which Wood expanded the power of his agency despite the limitations Jordan had imposed. His operatives followed correct arrest and search procedures on occasion, but frequently ignored them by employing a large loophole—citizen's arrest. An ordinary citizen could arrest a criminal for an act committed in his or her presence; an officer could arrest a criminal on the complaint of a citizen.

Using these criteria for arrests, Wood's operatives could thus bypass local law enforcement entirely. They could, for example, arrange to have an operative with a criminal record buy some counterfeit money. (This may indeed explain why Wood hired so many criminals.) Other operatives could then watch the transaction and arrest the counterfeiter on the strength of having observed the crime. There were numerous variations on this basic ploy. Essentially, common-law practices gave the Service the power of arrest without congressional approval. That power fundamentally enhanced the Service's authority, giving it the capacity to fulfill its mission independent of the federal marshals with whom it was supposed to cooperate.[45]

If this use of common-law practices revealed a clever ability to manipulate legal traditions to expand the power of a federal agency, other activities demonstrated how easily such inventiveness could go awry. Wood did not establish any code of conduct to guide the operatives in their work. Aside from general admonitions to be frugal, diligent, and honest, Wood offered no specific guidelines for accomplishing the Service's task. He was, after all, a detective himself; it had probably never occurred to him that he needed to define the boundaries of appropriate behavior. As a result, his detectives' reports revealed not merely a wide range of competence but also a great deal about their ethics and tactics in the Service's formative years.

Given the backgrounds of many operatives, their tactics, not surprisingly, reflected the ethics of the urban underworld. They promised immunity from prosecution to suspects in return for cooperation; provided money and equipment to manufacture counterfeit notes; offered protection to criminals in return for fees; accepted gifts; read suspects' mail; sold confiscated counterfeit notes for personal profit; ignored basic procedures for making arrests and searches; and testified for the defense at the trials of counterfeiters.[46]

Such flamboyant behavior inevitably attracted unfavorable attention. Public distaste for detective methods, Wood's indifference to appropriate hiring criteria, and the character of his agents combined to threaten the Service's long-term effectiveness. After three years of this freewheeling behavior, Jordan finally became sufficiently alarmed to order changes—or perhaps was ordered to do so.

At Jordan's direction, Wood issued the Service's first handbook of rules and regulations on 1 August 1868. Severe in tone, the guide condemned certain past practices and attempted to centralize administrative control over each agent's work routine. The provisions read like a catalog of past negligence and malfeasance. They prohibited drunkenness and any other generally discreditable behavior, proscribed using one's official position to contract debts or to borrow money, and forbade accepting gifts or gratuities to perform or to forgo official duties. Agents could not deliver or give permission to use counterfeit money to any unauthorized person, and they had to make all arrests in strict conformity to civil law.[47]

Although prompted by specific problems, the guide also represented the first serious attempt to codify bureaucratically correct, uniform procedures and standards of behavior. Each operative received a copy, but not everyone read these rules with sufficient attention or comprehension, and some of the regulations proved ineffective or unworkable. Furthermore, the Service's problems essentially emanated from its leadership. The character and behavior of its first operatives accurately reflected Wood's flamboyant style and lack of interest in personal or professional standards. Wood's pamphlet could not, in these circumstances, magically resolve all of the Service's problems.

There is no evidence that Wood made much progress toward implementing these new rules prior to the spring of 1869, when the incoming Grant administration cleaned house. George C. Boutwell became Treasury secretary, and Edward C. Banfield replaced Jordan as solicitor. Wood could not have reasonably expected to survive this reshuffling of patronage appointments. In addition to being allied with the wrong faction of Republicans, he was also under indictment in New York for false imprisonment.[48] When Banfield promptly fired him, Wood, dumbfounded, published an open letter to Secretary Boutwell full of bitter recriminations.[49] The letter failed to have any effect, and Wood returned to private life. In the meantime, Banfield appointed Hiram C. Whitley as chief of the Secret Service in May 1869.

Wood had had roots in the cultural milieu of urban detectives and criminals; Whitley did not. Both, however, had brash, egocentric personalities. Originally a businessman of varied experiences and only partial success, Whitley had happened to be in New Orleans at the time of its occupation by federal troops in 1862, when he had convinced Gen. Benjamin Butler to employ him as a spy. He quickly moved over to the local provost marshal's office as a detective. That experience had enabled him to wheedle an appointment to the Internal Revenue Service following the war, where he had spent approximately three years successfully pursuing whiskey defrauders in various sections of the nation. An investigation of a Ku Klux Klan murder in Atlanta had brought Whitley to Grant's attention in 1868, probably accounting for his appointment as chief in the following year.[50]

Although Whitley introduced significant changes in the Service's procedures, he retained Wood's contributions to its bureaucratic autonomy. Whitley maintained the dual headquarters and, like Wood, spent most of his time in New York. By this point the New York office had become a major records center for the Service and seemed on the verge of becoming its permanent headquarters.

Perhaps recognizing that his burgeoning bureaucracy needed a more formal hierarchy, Whitley refined Wood's simple arrangement in which operatives and their assistants were in almost perpetual motion around the nation. First, Whitley developed the concept of "chief operative." He informed Solicitor Banfield that he wanted to assign his "first-class men" to the division's major districts. Each chief operative would have assistant operatives working under his direction, and would be responsible for all administrative and investigative activities within his district.[51] This arrangement permitted Whitley to reward good work in two ways. Assistant operatives could look forward to promotion to chief operative; and chief operatives could anticipate moving from less to more prestigious districts, with New York having the highest status.

In 1871 Whitley also created the position of assistant chief to manage the New York office, and gave this job to Ichabod C. Nettleship. This freed him to supervise the activities of his operatives, while Nettleship looked after the bureaucratic minutiae of record keeping.[52]

Since the behavior of Wood's recruits had been a major problem, Whitley sought to improve the quality of the operatives. While acknowledging the need to hire individuals who came well recommended by important politicians, he also sought agents whose experiences paralleled his own. The new operatives tended to be from middle-class backgrounds, already having achieved some success in life. Their occupational history also indicated a certain restlessness, perhaps a dissatisfaction with their accomplishments, which inclined them to try something new.

William W. Applegate and Thomas E. Lonergan exemplified this pattern. Applegate had been born in New Jersey in 1824, had been educated in public schools, and had inherited his father's carriage-making business. In 1857 he had abandoned that business to become first a merchant and then a real estate broker. A chance meeting with Nettleship had led to a brief stint as his assistant in 1867. Two years later Whitley hired him again, as chief operative for New England. Applegate held that post for five years.[53]

Lonergan had had an even more peripatetic career. A native of Illinois, Lonergan had been attending the University of Notre Dame, when the Civil War had begun. Enlisting in a volunteer regiment at the age of seventeen, he had displayed enough leadership to be recommended for an appointment to West Point. A severe wound at Missionary Ridge had forced his discharge from the army in early 1864. Lonergan had returned to Chicago, had served briefly as a postal clerk, and then had joined the Pinkerton National Detective Agency, where he had enjoyed considerable success. During his three years with the agency, he had served as superintendent of the Chicago, Philadelphia, and New York offices. In 1867 Lonergan had resigned to become editor of the *New York Era* and professor of military tactics at a small New York college. A year later he had returned to Chicago to join on the editorial staff of another newspaper. Two years later Lonergan became chief operative of the Secret Service's Chicago office, a position he held until 1873, when he resigned to establish his own private detective business.[54]

Individuals such as Applegate and Lonergan had not had their personal codes of conduct molded by the values of the underworld. Instead, their ethical standards derived from the more stable world of legitimate businesspeople and professionals. To them, criminals were not personal acquaintances but enemies to social order. Such operatives were more inclined to consort with criminals out of a sense of duty rather than from personal preference. This situation encouraged an "us versus them" attitude, which was useful in fulfilling the Service's mission.

In addition to sharing a different perspective on criminals, these new recruits had, because of their civilian and military experiences, adapted their behavior to bureaucratic routine, to following orders, and to obeying rules. They were thus better suited to implement the Service's contribution to state building than Wood's recruits had been. Whitley could therefore expect them to understand and to support centralized administrative controls over their activities more easily than Wood's recruits had.

Although not a majority of the operatives, Whitley's middle-class recruits in the years from 1869 to 1871 were the largest group (42 percent) within the Service.[55] This represented an important change in the Service's recruiting patterns. Whitley had, in effect, brought an unprecedented number of people with respectable backgrounds into the Service. He had not, however, solved the character issue entirely. A second group of recruits (30 percent) had mixed records. Whitley retained a handful of Wood's operatives who had policing experience rather than criminal careers, and who had been relatively untainted by scandal. Informers, usually with criminal records, numbered slightly more than 27 percent of the total force overall. However, few of the holdovers—except Nettleship—lasted long, and Whitley's new approach to the informers relegated them to a far less prominent role in divisional affairs than they had played under Wood.

Whitley also sought to improve organizational pride and procedural guidelines in a new handbook for operatives issued in 1873. Parts of this *Circular of Instructions* simply elaborated upon Wood's booklet by repeating the admonitions to avoid any appearance of impropriety or disgraceful behavior. Whitley, however, added several significant sections of his own. He began the handbook with a rationale for the Service's work:

> The detection of crime, when entered upon with an honest purpose to discover the haunts of criminals and protect society from their depredations by bringing them to justice, is held to be an honorable calling and worthy of the commendation of all good men.

Whitley also stressed the uniqueness of his department's mission: "There is no branch of the Government service where so many qualifications are necessary, and none in which the field of operations is so varied." Seeking to flatter the operatives, Whitley asserted that "To meet and thwart [crime] requires the most subtle ingenuity, incessant vigilance, and unflagging energy upon the part of the officers of the law." Finally, he tried to transform the more unsavory aspects of their work with an argument for the nobility of its effects:

> Having detected the criminal it may be found expedient in the interest of public justice to use him against other offenders of the law of far greater magnitude than himself. I am aware that such a measure is open to some objection, but in certain classes of crime, especially that of counterfeiting, experience has demonstrated that a confederate may be used with very great moral and legal effect.[56]

Although nothing more than departmental bombast at one level, these general assertions of uniqueness and moral rectitude served a useful purpose in promoting group identity. By defining the Service's institutional mandate and tactics in such positive terms, Whitley sought to instill in the operatives a sense of pride in their work. "Great moral and legal effect" was a phrase pregnant with meaning for middle-class urban Americans, as well as for federal officers who defined their self-worth by the standards of that group. Associating such virtues with the heretofore unsavory practice of colluding with criminals marked a turning point in the intellectual justification for the Secret Service's existence.

When he addressed the particulars of regulating his recruit's activities, Whitley promulgated more numerous and precise rules than Wood had. He sought to standardize procedures for such duties as preparing inventories of counterfeiting equipment seized by operatives; submitting descriptions of suspects (including photographs for the first time); dealing with informers; recording an operative's expenses and activities (on a weekly basis); and routing all divisional communications through the chief's office. In addition, Whitley issued official badges to operatives.[57]

During the course of his tenure, Whitley permanently altered the Service's general administrative structure and recruiting patterns. His policies, which may have been derived from his observations of other federal departments, were making the Service comparable to mainstream federal bureaucracies, which were becoming more hierarchical and prone to using regulations to define and to enforce appropriate behavior.[58]

However much Whitley's reforms may have affected his operatives, his administrative style impressed his superiors, who steadily expanded the Service's functions throughout his tenure. Within four short years Whitley had shaped the Service into a general policing force for the federal government. His recruits investigated swindling, frauds (involving veterans' pensions, revenue, and the New York Customs House), and smuggling. They also participated in suppressing the Ku Klux Klan, pursued mail robbers, and inquired into illegal voting practices.[59] The Service's mandate soon became so broad that Whitley advised his officers that its

> ramifications . . . extend everywhere throughout the country; its officers taking cognizance, not only of counterfeiting and other frauds upon the Treasury, but of all crimes coming within the jurisdiction of the Department of Justice. Hence you will make a careful note of, and

report, cases of crime against the United States, of any character whatever, that may come to your knowledge.[60]

Considering that Whitley had carved out such a large mandate for his agency in an era deeply suspicious of federal policing, this was an impressive achievement. He had even achieved a most extraordinary coup by crossing the boundaries between two major agencies— Treasury and Justice—to serve both. If expanding power is the mark of bureaucratic success, Whitley had shown evidence of imperial ambitions.

Whitley's ambitions, however, rested on a flawed character. Just as his empire seemed secure, he plunged the Service into its most severe crisis. Whitley had many virtues as an administrator, but he, like Wood, had an unscrupulous side, which he did not bother to conceal. In his autobiography he relates with evident satisfaction an incident that occurred in New Orleans during the Civil War. He had seized a schooner loaded with contraband but had then received a request to release the ship: "Of course I was not ordered to let the schooner go, but I accepted a hint, especially when it came from headquarters."[61]

Early in the spring of 1874 Whitley took another hint. In February a group of Washingtonians, whose petitions to Congress had earned them the nickname the Memorialists, convinced the House Committee on the District to launch a new investigation into their allegations of mismanagement and corruption by the District's Board of Public Works, which "Boss" Alexander Shepherd dominated. These accusations held potentially damaging political ramifications for the Grant administration, which was already staggering from revelations of widespread corruption in the construction of the Union Pacific transcontinental railroad; in the collection of federal excise taxes on liquor; and in the ways several cabinet officers were operating their departments. Grant had appointed Shepherd to the Board, and Orville Babcock, the President's private secretary, was commissioner of public buildings and grounds under the Board of Public Works. In an administration plagued by scandal, the Memorialists' accusations were another headache that Grant's minions did not need.[62]

Led by Richard Harrington, some of Shepherd's supporters decided to undermine the House committee's investigation by plotting to frame Columbus Alexander, a Memorialist. Harrington was the secretary to the Board of Public Works and, during these hearings, Shepherd's counsel. Also, as a U.S. district attorney for the District, he knew both Whitley and Nettleship. Harrington and Whitley assumed operational control of a frame-up, which involved making it appear that Alexander had accepted stolen property. In the process the conspirators revealed the political uses and dangers of centralized policing powers.

Working from his New York office, Whitley recruited two criminals, Gustav Zeruth and Michael Hayes, to burglarize Harrington's office safe, where Harrington had placed the business records of a contractor who did work for the Board of Public Works. Assuming false identities and pretending to know the location of the contractor's records (which would presumably reveal illegal behavior in the Board's contracting methods), Zeruth and Hayes offered to turn them over to Alexander without telling him how they would fulfill their offer. When Alexander agreed to receive the records, Hayes hired a third criminal to assist him in a burglary of the safe in Harrington's Washington office. In the meantime, Harrington arranged to have an anonymous letter delivered to him warning of the impending burglary, and showed the letter to the local chief of police.

On the night of 25 April Harrington and several detectives surrounded his office and watched patiently while the burglars turned on the lights, opened the windows, and took two hours to blow the safe. When the burglars finally emerged, half a dozen men walked pell-mell down the street after them, "losing" Hayes in the dark but unerringly following Hayes's hireling. Some confusion ensued, when the hired burglar got lost and had to ask directions to Alexander's house from one of the detectives. Finally arriving at his destination, the burglar rang the doorbell and waited for Alexander to accept delivery of the stolen goods.

Alexander failed to answer the doorbell (it was 2 A.M.), forcing Harrington to arrest the lone burglar on Alexander's doorstep. Harrington immediately charged that Alexander and the Memorialists had attempted to steal valuable records, which they had mistakenly believed contained proof of corruption. His accusation prompted the congressional committee investigating the Board of Public Works to focus their attention on the burglary.[63] The result, however, was not what Harrington had hoped. The committee quickly found all sorts of suspicious behavior in Harrington's ludicrous account and launched an exhaustive probe of the whole affair. By the end of their inquiry the committee had uncovered evidence of Whitley's and Nettleship's roles in the frame-up. The committee's final report in June 1874 exonerated Alexander, pointed out the evidence implicating Whitley and Nettleship, and recommended that the secretary of the Treasury and the attorney general investigate the situation.[64]

The committee's report might not have had much impact, except that other Treasury scandals forced Grant, also in June, to fire the incumbent secretary and to replace him with Benjamin Bristow. Solicitor Banfield also resigned, and Bristow brought in Bluford Wilson to fill that post. Bristow and Wilson were notable exceptions to the usual qualities of many of Grant's appointees, because they had ability and integrity and believed that a public office was a public trust.[65]

Acting on Bristow's orders, Wilson subjected the Service to a thorough critical review. He inspected some of the district offices; interviewed several officers, including Whitley; and wrote to U.S. attorneys and marshals around the country, asking their opinion of the Service.

Wilson's letters to U.S. attorneys and marshals reveal that the Service was in serious jeopardy. Inquiring "whether or not in your judgment that [the] Service can be dispensed with without detriment to the public interest,"[66] he received a torrent of attacks on the Service rooted in animosity against the bureaucratic autonomy that Wood and Whitley had established over the previous nine years. In his report to Bristow, Wilson summarized the responses, concluding that "all concur in the expression of doubts as to its efficiency and claim not to have received from it any special or very notable assistance for some time past."[67]

The marshals whom Wilson surveyed showed the greatest hostility to the Service. Although their letters focused on issues such as competence and effectiveness, they had a more practical basis for their complaints. In the past their deputies had earned rewards for arresting counterfeiters, while the marshals themselves had been able to obtain expenses for pursuing counterfeiters. Solicitor Jordan's original circular announcing the creation of the Service had dwelled in great detail on open access to rewards for information from any source, and he had particularly stressed his hope for close cooperation with the marshals. Whitley, however, had stopped disbursing

rewards, in effect monopolizing the entire congressional appropriation for the Service itself to suppress counterfeiting.[68] This bureaucratic fiat had earned the Service the enmity of practically every federal marshal and U.S. attorney in the nation. Whitley's empire
building had thus accelerated the centralized federal policing beyond
acceptable limits. He was no longer cooperating with a general distribution of federal largesse, but rather using his appropriation to promote the interests of his national policing agency. His idiotic participation in the safe burglary provided an opportunity for his enemies to
exact retribution by attacking the very existence of the Service.

In effect, Whitley's corrupt behavior had given the champions of
local community control of law enforcement the opportunity to undermine his campaign to centralize federal power over counterfeiting.
Seizing upon Wilson's invitation to complain and to offer remedies,
the marshals and their political allies proposed a return to the old system of using the congressional appropriation almost, if not entirely,
as a source of reward money for local law enforcement.[69] Given the
abysmal record of those officers in suppressing counterfeiting prior
to the Civil War, this idea represented a direct threat to the federal
government's symbolic and practical need to maintain the public's
trust in the currency. It also threatened to make the Service yet another example of the demise of state-building initiatives spawned by
the Civil War and buried by the resurgent system of courts and parties during Reconstruction.

In a comment expressing his opposition to the idea of federal
policing, Wilson, though not a spoilsman, reflected the Republican
party's drift away from centralization: "Upon principle I am radically
opposed to any organized system of espionage in connection with our
free government."[70] Throughout his inquiry he remained unconvinced of the necessity of the Service. He was, however, fair-minded
enough to ask Whitley (who he had erroneously concluded was innocent of any complicity in the safe burglary) to submit a rejoinder
to the Service's critics, specifically asking why Whitley opposed
rewards.

Flawed though he was, Whitley displayed a much better grasp of
the uses of federal policing than did his critics. He castigated the entire concept of rewards, referring to them as "blood money" that
encouraged a wide range of abuses, not the least of which was the re-
luctance of judges and juries to believe the testimony of individuals

whose livelihood depended upon rewards. He then launched into a passionate defense of the Service. Stressing the value of a centralized approach to suppressing counterfeiting, Whitley argued that the Service's organization encouraged effective coordination of information; permitted manpower assignments based on need; eliminated jurisdictional boundaries, which encouraged competition instead of cooperation; and reduced costs while producing "larger results."[71] Whitley thus argued for the greater efficacy of relying on federal rather than local law enforcement to protect the nation's currency.

Wilson remained unconvinced. In his final report to Bristow he criticized the behavior and the competence of Whitley's operatives, but leveled his most pointed criticism at the Service's autonomy. Claiming that local police and deputy marshals had been as effective as the Service in suppressing counterfeiting but had been excluded from receiving rewards, Wilson advocated abolishing the division. Should, however, Bristow decide to continue it, Wilson insisted that all law enforcement personnel, both local and federal, have access to rewards drawn from the congressional appropriation. He also placed great stress on the need for the division's chief to cultivate "mutual cooperation" with local police departments and U.S. deputy marshals in order to make the system of suppressing counterfeiting more effective.

Wilson's recommendations required the Service to end its surreptitious experiment in autonomous federal policing, and to conform to the prevailing belief in the predominance of local law enforcement. Wilson then struck at the heart of the division's bureaucratic autonomy, the New York office. Observing that the existence of a separate headquarters prevented the solicitor from exercising "a proper and adequate check upon the operations of the division," Wilson recommended that the division's records be transferred to Washington and that the chief of the Service be required to live there.[72]

Bristow decided to keep the Service, but he endorsed all of Wilson's other recommendations. He also ordered Wilson to terminate all of the division's current employees, including Whitley. New evidence of Whitley's involvement in the safe burglary forced Bristow to demand his resignation, despite Babcock's intervention on his behalf. Whitley submitted his resignation in early September, and Bristow made it effective for the end of October.[73]

Wilson, therefore, had the opportunity to rebuild the entire division according to his own model. He began with a new chief, selecting Elmer Washburn from a small pool of applicants.[74] Details about Washburn's life are sketchy. He had been was born in Plymouth County, Massachusetts, in 1834, and may have had some formal training as a civil or mechanical engineer. Prior to the 1870s he had been a division superintendent for the Illinois Central Railroad, and following his tenure as chief he became the senior partner of an engineering consulting firm, which did work on urban water and transit systems.

In between those jobs, he had attempted a career in public service. Sometime after the Civil War he had become warden of Illinois' Joliet Prison. While warden, Washburn had sold some surplus state property at a profit and placed the money in the prison's treasury. At a time when public officials had routinely found ways to line their own pockets, Washburn's act had illustrated his personal honesty. In 1872 Chicago's reform mayor, Joseph Medill, had appointed Washburn as chief of police. This had been an odd choice, because Washburn had not been a Chicago resident and had lacked experience for the job.[75]

Controversy had plagued Washburn's brief tenure as Chicago's police chief, partly because of the bitter political battle between the reform mayor and the police commissioners, who wanted to choose their own chief. Washburn, however, was also unpopular with his subordinates, because of his administrative style. According to a contemporary account:

> There was no longer any interchange of opinion between the chief and his captains. He would listen to no suggestions, simply waving his subordinates off, and telling them that they would hear from him officially. He employed a corps of clerks who were kept busily engaged in preparing orders. Written orders were a weakness with him. A question which might have been answered by a nod of the head, was replied to with ponderous verbosity and a bombardment of officialisms over the length and breadth of a sheet of legal cap.[76]

Washburn had also earned the enmity of literally thousands of Chicagoans when he had seriously attempted to implement Mayor Medill's order to enforce Sunday closing laws in 1873. The uproar that had ensued cost Medill the next election and Washburn his job.[77]

Yet it was probably Washburn's unbending character that attracted Wilson to him. Wilson wanted someone with impeccable integrity, a devotion to bureaucratic procedure, and a capacity to enforce rules rigorously. Washburn's career indicated that he possessed those traits. He was a technocrat with a passion for rules, and his values were rooted in the emerging culture of professionalism rather than in the milieu of partisan politics.

Beginning work in late September 1874, Washburn first busied himself with moving the division's records from New York and selecting the members of his new force. Wilson wanted to keep the force small, and Washburn initially hired only eighteen recruits.[78] In light of the Service's previous record, the quality of these individuals was an important issue. Wilson was on record as wanting people of "the highest standard of detective ability and character."[79] Neither Wood nor Whitley had paid sufficient attention to this issue, but there was now a genuine opportunity to implement this ideal, because Wilson and Washburn had the personal integrity and the determination to make it a practical reality. Unfortunately, there is little information about the individuals they hired. The surviving evidence indicates that Washburn continued Whitley's general policy of hiring recruits with middle-class backgrounds and attitudes and varying amounts of practical experience in detective work.[80]

Washburn also took steps to implement Wilson's desire to reassert the dominance of local law enforcement in the suppression of counterfeiting. One of Washburn's most effective devices for achieving that goal appeared in his first General Order, issued on 31 October 1874. He directed that "neither the name of the operative, nor the manner of working any case, will be made public, either before or after an arrest or capture."[81] The Service was indeed to be secret. With its activities concealed from public view by official edict, it presumably would be unable to use favorable public opinion as a basis for rebuilding bureaucratic autonomy. Denied access to the press, the Service could not compete with local police for publicity.

Washburn also returned to the practice of issuing rewards for information.[82] This move implemented Wilson's intent to distribute the congressional appropriation more widely. It also struck at the Service's autonomy by requiring it to share its budget with local law enforcement agencies.

Wilson and Washburn apparently achieved what Jordan and Wood had failed to do. The 1874 reforms created a formal bureaucratic structure mirroring contemporary commitments to localism. Prior to these reforms, the chief of the Service had led his operatives from the field, in effect performing as principal detective. Washburn eschewed that role, adopting instead the guise of principal administrator. His new rules schooled the operatives to bureaucratic routines, which emphasized deference to the new hierarchy and to the prerogatives of local law enforcement.[83] Deprived of a separate headquarters, ordered to silence, and subordinated to the solicitor, the Service had to cultivate cooperation with, not separation from, local authorities.

These changes, however, were insufficient to subvert the Service's ability to reassert its autonomy at some later date. It continued to exist as a general national policing agency. For example, Wilson used the Service to investigate two of the most notorious scandals of the Grant era, the Whiskey Ring and the corruption in the New York Customs House in 1875.[84] Washburn did not hire local police to investigate local counterfeiting on an ad hoc basis. He maintained a separate force, which in itself provided a national rather than a local focus for the energies and the loyalties of his operatives. That in turn perpetuated the Service's identity within the federal government.

Operatives also retained the practical ability to distinguish and to distance themselves from local police. They could still make arrests at common law (even though Washburn would try to discourage them from doing so).[85] By building personal records as effective investigators, they could fulfill their own ambitions while simultaneously providing a justification for the Service's continued existence.

Despite Wilson's reassertion of localism in law enforcement, the Service survived the 1874 crisis as a distinct federal agency, in part through its general policing role within the federal government. Whether intentionally or not, Whitley had carved out a domain for investigative work that only the Service could perform. He had, in effect, created a unique role for the Service, ensuring its bureaucratic survival and its potential to contribute to federal state building. Having survived, it could now turn to the complex process of resurrecting its autonomy and projecting federal authority into the urban centers of the developing national economy.

FROM DISGRACE
TO AUTONOMY

The Secret Service's
Resurrection

EMERGING FROM THE 1874 CRISIS battered, abused, and diminished, the Secret Service possessed few apparent resources for becoming an autonomous policing agency. The Service's critics had forced it to share its budget and mission with local police officers and U.S. marshals; the Service still lacked independent powers of search and arrest; its public image had suffered considerably from the legacy of William P. Wood's and Hiram C. Whitley's egregious behavior; and its new chief lacked both experience with and political influence within the federal bureaucracy. The Service thus seemed to have few prospects for expanding its influence within the federal government or projecting its power into the haunts of urban criminals. Nevertheless the division achieved both goals by the end of the century, by first reestablishing its credibility within the federal bureaucracy. The Service's resurrection was a testament to a bureaucracy's capacity to expand its influence and power—no matter how starved it may have been of resources. Breaking the bonds imposed by the 1874 reforms involved three interrelated developments. First, the chief's role in the division was redefined. Second, the chiefs, using their newly acquired power, began to exploit the federal environment to protect the Service. Third, the nature of the Service's mission to suppress counterfeiting ultimately gave it the means to escape its subordination to local interests. In effect, the division recreated itself from the ashes of its disgrace by demonstrating that it provided valuable services that no other federal agency of the era could perform.

Focusing on its uniqueness gave the Service an opportunity to demonstrate how state building could proceed even in an environment that was fundamentally hostile to the centralization of federal power. The federal government of the late nineteenth century is today more widely known for its scandals, partisan politics, and poor handling of such issues as civil service reform and railroad regulation than for efficient delivery of vital public services by well-regulated, professionalized bureaucracies. Its failings, however, did not halt the centralization process. State-building opportunities derived from the personal efforts of a few bureaucrats who were committed to protecting and to projecting federal sovereignty within the otherwise hostile environment. Heartily embracing partisanship while simultaneously insisting on honesty, integrity, and dedication to their agencies' missions, this small band of bureaucrats demonstrated that partisanship and professionalism were not incompatible values. For example, Green B. Raum, commissioner of the Internal Revenue Service (IRS) from 1877 to 1883, transformed the IRS into an effective policing agency. He created a centralized administration that carefully deployed its resources in a largely successful campaign against moonshiners in Appalachia. Raum's reforms were so useful that his successors adopted them, transforming an individual's contributions to bureaucratic effectiveness into a permanent system for asserting federal sovereignty.[1]

The Secret Service had its own versions of Commissioner Raum. For example, Solicitor Bluford Wilson, who insisted that Washington, D.C.—not New York City—be the Service's bureaucratic headquarters and that the chief live there, created the basic conditions for the transformation of the Service's administration into an effective bureaucracy. With Wilson's reforms, the character of the chief's position was fundamentally altered.

Wood and Whitley had defined their roles as that of chief detectives. Both had reveled in the pursuit of counterfeiters, constantly traveling around the nation to participate directly in their operatives' work. They also had spent much time in New York, not necessarily because it had been their administrative headquarters but rather because it had been at the heart of the action. Both individuals, however, had given minimal attention to administrative details. Whitley in fact had created the post of assistant chief to avoid the burdens of administration.

Solicitor Wilson's new arrangements permanently redefined the chief's role from that of principal detective to principal administrator. Although Elmer Washburn participated in a few arrests, he acted primarily as an administrator during his brief tenure. Beginning with James Brooks, the chiefs became full-time administrators. This change had several important consequences. First, it fundamentally altered the chief's relations with his subordinates. Wood and Whitley had supervised their personnel through frequent personal contact with them during their travels. After Wilson's reforms, however, the chiefs had to manage their operatives through more formal means than those that had been employed by Wood and Whitley. Their movement was now considerably restricted, and they could no longer rely on casual supervision as the basis of their administrative technique.

The chiefs' transformation into administrative managers created a dilemma. Solicitors, department secretaries, and agency executives existed in an environment of legal constructs and assumptions that stressed accountability, rules, and routine. Their world bore little relation to the realities of work in criminal detection, which was uninhibited by bureaucratic norms. How then could the chiefs bridge the gap between the dual and opposing realities of what federal administrators expected and the Service's operatives had to do in order to perform their task successfully?

Service chiefs had little control over the relevant groups in this complex matrix of dual realities. Their superiors would not alter their demands that the Service conform to normative bureaucratic behavior, and criminals would not change their behavior to conform to abstract administrative niceties. The chiefs, however, could affect their operatives' behavior. Effectively managing their operatives' conduct, therefore, became the key to satisfying the demands of their superiors and fulfilling their agency's mission.

Achieving effective managerial control involved four administrative tasks: defining a behavioral standard for the division; creating a system for procuring accurate information from operatives about their work; comparing that information with the division's guidelines; and ensuring that operatives altered their behavior to conform a standard.[2]

Wood, and particularly Whitley, had made some progress in each of these areas. Both, for instance, had proscribed certain kinds of behavior; both had required regular reports from operatives; and both had admonished or fired operatives for various deficiencies. Neither, however, had been fully committed to managing the division, which, when combined with their personal failings, prevented any systematic attention to the development of a workable administrative structure.

Although he served only two years as chief, Washburn created the division's basic administrative framework for resolving fundamental organizational issues. Shortly after his appointment in October 1874 Washburn made his first essential contribution by defining the standard against which he and his successors would judge operatives: "Employees will be judged by the character they sustain, by the results they accomplish, and by the manner in which they accomplish them."[3] Although this was a broad guideline, it was also the first directive formulated by a division chief that explicitly integrated three key elements of detective work—personal integrity, methods, and results—into a unified standard for evaluating an operative's performance.

Next, Washburn addressed to the problem of accurate and complete information. In late December 1874 he issued a series of orders that created verifiable controls over operatives' methods. He began by expanding the requirements for reporting financial transactions to include those with criminals. Neither Wood nor Whitley had ever implemented any clear regulations requiring the operatives to record the details of such deals. Operatives now had to report what they paid for counterfeit money, from whom they purchased it, where they made the deal, what kind of bogus money they bought, and how much they obtained. Washburn subsequently required them to record "all charges for information and assistance," including the names and residences of each person receiving these sums. Finally, he placed the first restrictions on the amount of counterfeit notes that could be purchased, by requiring that such transactions "be made, in the discretion of the operative, for the smallest practicable amount."[4]

Washburn also significantly modified a long-standing informal procedure dating back to Wood's tenure when he directed that:

> Authority must be had from this Office before any bargain is made for information or assistance, unless the operative can clearly make it ap-

pear that the interest of the service would have suffered materially
by the delay necessary, in order to obtain such authority.[5]

Previously operatives had only been required to obtain permission to
engage in financial negotiations leading to employing someone as an
assistant. They now also had to follow the same process in negotiating
for information.

Although Washburn's directives were flexible, they nevertheless imposed bureaucratic controls over the daily routines of the Service's operatives. Operatives now had to create and to maintain paper
trails for review by headquarters of the most important and sensitive
aspects of their detective work. That would subtly shift the dynamics
of their negotiations with potential informers. Operatives, knowing that Washburn was scrutinizing their decisions, became more
cautious.

Washburn, however, clearly did not intend to impose undue restrictions on his agents' activities. Recognizing the vital role of discretion in effective detective work, he simply wanted to make sure
that the operatives knew he was watching them:

> When operatives act upon their own discretion, the rule will be, that
> they must be able to show clearly that the object they aimed to accom-
> plish was necessary, and that they took the cheapest practicable
> method to accomplish the same.[6]

Enforcing these rules proved more difficult than issuing them. Washburn sought to resolve the enforcement problem by changing another
of his operatives' reporting requirements. Weekly reports had been a
standard part of every agent's duties even prior to the formal organization of the division. These reports had taken little time to prepare,
and gave operatives considerable leeway to choose which facts to report and which to suppress. Washburn abolished the weekly summaries and ordered daily, detailed reports of everything each agent did.[7]
Inevitably, there would be delays in preparing these reports and in
Washburn's reading of them. Every agent, however, did begin to provide a written account of his daily activities, and Washburn (and his
successors) did read them.

For Washburn's system to work, he needed operatives who were
talented detectives and highly tolerant of paperwork, as well as com-

mitted to organizational rather than individual goals. Such traits were rare among urban detectives at the time; and even though Whitley had made some important progress in resolving personnel problems, the Service's chiefs still had to be careful about whom they hired. Washburn's regulations and the modifications his successors introduced would make little impact upon the division's quest for autonomy if its chiefs could not recruit and retain individuals willing to submit to the new administrative system.

Between 1875 and 1910 the division never employed more than forty-seven operatives and chief operatives at one time. In fact, the average for that period was only twenty-five, and for sixteen years, 1878–1893, the number of employees classified as operatives remained well below that average.[8] Budgetary considerations, rather than estimates of the amount of counterfeiting activity, dictated this small size. Throughout the late nineteenth century Congress authorized funding levels that reflected the era's generally penurious attitude toward expenditures from the public treasury. This explains why for most of that period the size of the division's budget made monetary discipline an obsession with the chiefs.

Despite these restraints, the Service could offer qualified individuals a decent career in government. The pay scale, ranging from $4 to $7 a day, provided a comfortable annual income. (Four dollars a day was equivalent to the salary of most urban police officers; $7 a day made operatives members of the middle class by nineteenth-century standards.) A promotion system offered the possibility of advancement, and regular employees received some paid-vacation time each year. While time consuming, the work was not particularly dangerous (no Service employee was seriously hurt in the line of duty until the murder of an operative in 1908).

Such inducements were not trivial for the time. Although the personnel records for the years after 1875 are scant,[9] what is available indicates that the chiefs looked for individuals with generally middle-class backgrounds and some practical experience in detective work. This is hardly surprising, since operatives had to be literate and familiar with simple accounting methods, and to possess some skills at managing people in order to perform their jobs.

Although James Brooks and Andrew Drummond may have been atypical of Washburn's appointments—particularly since both would serve as chiefs of the Service—their careers illustrate many of the qualities Washburn had sought. Born in England in 1825, Brooks had emigrated to America in his youth and had established his own business as a carriage manufacturer in Newark, New Jersey. He had apparently served as a cavalry captain during the Civil War. In 1866 he had used political connections to obtain an appointment as an IRS agent. Brooks's zeal for his work had made him the bane of dishonest distillers. Unable to bribe him, the members of a whiskey ring in Philadelphia had tried to assassinate him in September 1869. Although shot four times, Brooks had survived and had become a public hero. He remained with the IRS until 1874, when he joined the Secret Service.[10]

Brooks's account of his IRS adventures (drolly titled *Whiskey Drips*) indicates that he was a well-educated man with conventional middle-class values regarding the connections between the law and morality. For example, he believed that "there could not . . . be two opinions as to the necessity for their [illegal whiskey stills] suppression. Violated law called for it; the morals and health of the community demanded it."[11] In summarizing his experiences with IRS frauds, he argued that "the inspiring cause of all this wickedness is found in the terrible lust for riches, which is fast dragging our people down to perdition."[12] The religious overtones of his analysis reflected his committed membership in one of Washington's most prominent Baptist churches. He was also a Republican.[13]

Brooks's credentials impressed Washburn, who needed a mature, experienced detective to help him to reorganize the division. Brooks proved to be effective in doing so. Hired in October 1874, he was assistant chief by December.[14] Early in 1875 Washburn gave him the plum assignment as chief operative for the New York District and in the summer transferred him to Chicago, where Brooks played an important role in investigating the Whiskey Ring scandal during Grant's last administration.[15]

Drummond had been born in Pennsylvania in 1845, and had received enough education to obtain employment as a ship's purser on a steamship line in the late 1860s. That position gave him knowledge of smuggling operations. He is first mentioned in the Service's records in early 1871 offering Ichabod C. Nettleship information about illegal imports of cigars and bay oil. Nettleship had allowed him to work on other cases on a trial basis, and by September 1871 Drummond had found his life's calling. He had arrested several important counterfeiters before the 1874 debacle. That record impressed Washburn sufficiently enough for him to appoint Drummond in 1875 as an assistant operative for the Philadelphia District. Drummond became chief operative of that district when Brooks succeeded Washburn as chief.[16]

Twenty years younger than Brooks, Drummond shared Brooks's morality, honesty, and devotion to the division, all of which were reflected periodically in his daily reports. At one point, irritated by the charge that the Service used questionable methods, Drummond reacted strongly:

> I profess to be somewhat of a Christian, and there is nothing more revolting to me than the thought of inducing an innocent or hitherto honest man or woman to commit a crime that he or she might be punished for it, and I for one stand ready to put upon trial for his liberty any person who would do such a thing whether he be an agent of this Division, a cabinet minister, the poorest wretch, or the wealthiest man in our land, but we do not do such things.[17]

Despite the paucity of background information on the agents hired after 1875, the evidence suggests that Brooks and Drummond may have been exemplary but not unique. The division consistently recruited individuals with business or policing experience, above-average educations, and high standards of personal integrity. George O. Barker, for example, had run his own business for twenty years before joining the Service. Joseph A. Walker had graduated from high school, had studied shorthand, and had served as a secretary to the assistant secretary of the Treasury Department before joining the division in 1888. Elmer Gorman, whose father was police chief of a small Indiana town, had attended Purdue University for a year and had held jobs as a bookkeeper and an insurance agent before becoming an operative in 1900. George W. Hazen came from a family of Cincinnati detectives and had accumulated a record of arrests of important local criminals before joining the Service in 1894.[18]

Such competent individuals eased the burden of the chief's administrative oversight of operatives' activities. Shared backgrounds and commitments bound the Service's employees together, creating a willingness to support the division's mission as well as its distinct administrative style.[19] The operatives' reactions to the division's habitual budget problems provides perhaps the best, though indirect, evidence of their support for its mission. From the mid-1870s to the mid-1890s, the average pay of chief operatives hovered at $6 a day while assistants made even less. Even though that provided a decent middle-class income, operatives routinely worked twelve- and fourteen-hour days, six days a week, and frequently half days on Sundays. Twenty years is a long time to stay with an organization without a pay raise under those conditions, yet several individuals made the division their life's work. Edward Abbott stayed with the Service for twenty-five years (1877–1902); Michael Bauer served twenty-three years (1875–1898); and Joseph A. Walker's twenty-year career (1888–1908) only ended when he was murdered in Colorado while investigating land frauds.

Reducing an employee's pay was often insufficient to change his commitment. When the salary of James Scanlon, whose experience as a skilled machinist prior to joining the division gave him other employment options, was reduced, he responded by thanking Brooks for retaining him at a time when the division's budget problems were forcing layoffs; Scanlon conveyed his hope that he would prove worthy of the chief's consideration for him.[20]

The fact that many operatives sustained long careers through several presidential administrations creates an interesting and important exception to the presumed turmoil that patronage politics inflicted upon federal employment at the time. Despite its small size, the Service did not escape the attentions of congressmen eager to place favored constituents.[21] The nature of its work and its small budget, however, probably made congressional interference in hiring a relatively minor problem. The chiefs also had two arguments against such political pressure. First, they could argue that they did not have the money to hire more operatives, which was true for most of the late nineteenth century. For the Service to be useful in patronage politics, Congress either had to increase the Service's budget, which seemed unlikely, or to recognize the Service's limited ability as a convenient depository for patronage appointees. Second, given the importance of the Service's mandate, the chiefs could reasonably argue against candidates who lacked competence for detective work, which would encourage a congressman to look elsewhere to repay his political debts.[22]

Hiram C. Whitley began the policy of insisting that operatives have an aptitude for detective work.[23] That requirement gave Whitley and his successors a valuable screening device that mitigated the importunings of congressmen. Political endorsements were necessary to obtain an appointment to the Service but not sufficient to allow individuals who lacked the requisite talent for the work to retain their positions. The specialized character of the Service's work thus enabled the chiefs to assemble a force of political appointees whose abilities as detectives became the basis for their long careers.

Indeed, a fascination with detective work seems to have been one of the principal characteristics of the operatives. Surviving evidence indicates consistently that many operatives had a lifelong commitment to detective work. For example, James Brooks retired as chief to take a position in a private detective firm established by a former operative. Drummond, forced out of the division temporarily in 1888 by a change of administration, founded the Drummond Detective Agency in New York City. Others who followed similar paths included Ray Bagg, Benjamin Lyman, William Hirshfield, E. G. Rathbone, and L. W. Gammon.[24]

The operatives' commitment to detective work would play an important role in the Service's ability to project federal power into local communities. Working on a problem and in an environment where partisan issues rarely intruded, the operatives practiced a unity of purpose that transcended political loyalties and focused instead on their mandate to protect the currency's integrity. For the Service, the interests of the nation superseded the interests of a particular political party.

Bureaucratic unity had an important influence on the types of administrative and disciplinary problems that the chiefs encountered in the years after 1874. Each chief scrutinized the operatives' daily reports; and correspondence addressing various issues poured out of headquarters. The content—not the volume—of these missives was a stark contrast to the earlier era. Wood, for example, had hired so many criminals and incompetent or dishonest detectives that corruption had been rife during his tenure. The character of his operatives and their lack of a common background or common commitment had created enormous, if not insoluble, management problems. Beginning with Washburn, divisional management focused on mostly minor deviations from rules rather than on problems of personal and organizational integrity. Economy became a continual bone of contention because of the Service's low budgets. The operatives' financial reports received close review, and any excessive charges prompted an immediate rebuke. In December 1875, for example, Washburn demanded that Drummond obtain a refund from a Philadelphia telegraph operator who had overcharged him. Drummond dutifully visited the offending operator and collected the refund— one cent.[25] Such frugality became characteristic of headquarters throughout the post-1874 period.[26]

The chiefs also took seriously the rule that the Division's activities should remain covert. In 1878 Brooks tightened this regulation in a circular stipulating that "the Chief assumes the sole responsibility of determining what is proper for the public to know concerning matters connected with the work of this Division, and no other officer must seek to share that responsibility."[27] This rule was strictly enforced. Real or presumed violations provoked instant wrath from chiefs and abject apologies and woeful explanations from offenders.[28] Constant review and prompt reprimand not only reinforced obedience to rules, but also conveyed that the chief was watching everyone's behavior for other, more serious problems. Outright corruption, which given the Service's history must have figured prominently among the chiefs' concerns, was extremely rare. The most spectacular corruption case involved Chief Operative Charles Anchisi. In 1877 Chief Brooks uncovered evidence of fraudulent behavior by Anchisi, who had gained an impressive record with the Service under Whitley and Washburn. When Brooks had a warrant issued for his arrest, Anchisi fled New York City. He reappeared four years later in San Francisco, where he was convicted of counterfeiting.[29] Less newsworthy cases, such as two involving attempts to extort money from relatives of people under arrest, were extremely rare.[30]

The rarity of corruption may have been due to both the backgrounds of the employees and the fact that the division had begun to police itself vigorously. While Anchisi's disgrace demonstrates that social background was no guarantee of integrity, a work force containing large numbers of criminals is more prone to problems than one drawn overwhelmingly from the middle class. The chiefs' continuous review of their subordinates' activities served as an internal policing system, which protected the Service from any unforeseen frailties in its middle-class employees.

Chief operatives supplemented this review process by cross-checking their subordinates' reports, and by recommending disciplinary action (including transfers or dismissals) for such lapses as submitting inaccurate reports, borrowing money, excessive drinking, and allowing prisoners to escape.[31] In sum, the division's disciplinary procedures attended to minor as well as potentially major problems far more effectively than before. Effective management from a central headquarters helped to restore the division's integrity after the 1874 debacle and made a significant contribution to its resurrection.

Transferring the division's headquarters from New York to Washington also helped to rebuild the Service. By residing in Washington, the chief became a permanent member of the federal bureaucracy's informal sociopolitical environment. The new location allowed easy access to resident bureaucrats, which created mutual bonds of cooperation and political support. During congressional sessions, the chief had the opportunity to develop and to expand informal ties to key legislators.

Wood, perhaps relying too heavily on his ties to Secretary Edwin Stanton, had not recognized the value of the Washington environment as a source of support. His disregard for middle-class proprieties, which had shaped his hiring practices and tactics, was ill-suited to the capital's budding bureaucratic society. Whitley, as evidenced by the range of additional activities his operatives had performed for the Treasury and Justice departments, had seen the advantages of Washington. By continuing to use New York as his base, however, he had lost the opportunity to exploit more fully the benefits of cooperating with other federal agencies. His successors, however, would view their imposed residency in Washington as an opportunity to expand upon his legacy.

The Service's ability to benefit from a restriction resulted from its relationship to Washington's bureaucratic community.[32] Solicitor Wilson had objected to the Service's becoming a danger to federalism. Wilson, therefore, used the safe-burglary scandal politically to eliminate the Service's threat to the federal marshals. Within the Washington community, however, the Service was not perceived as a threat. Indeed, other agencies welcomed it for what it had to offer. For example, many departments within the Treasury and in other federal bureaus had to cope with problems of employee integrity and criminal behavior. Almost none of these agencies had the capacity to police themselves. The Post Office was the major exception, having organized the Postal Inspectors prior to the Civil War to deal with internal police matters. As the largest agency within the federal government, however, the Post Office had more than enough work for its inspectors. It either could not or would not share its limited policing ability with other agencies.

Although the Service had fewer detectives than the Postal Inspectors, it quickly established itself as a general policing agency for the federal bureaucracy. This position may have evolved from the combination of a wartime scandal and other problems in the Treasury Department. The scandal occurred when Secretary Chase had decided to hire female clerks, one of whom had promptly become embroiled in accusations of sexual misconduct.[33] With its employees' moral character at stake, Treasury officials had displayed a persistent though erratic willingness to use Service detectives to check on their workers' private lives. Beginning in December 1865 the Service became the occasional moral guardian of the Treasury.[34]

Following the war the Treasury found additional uses for the Service. Early in 1869 the IRS apparently asked for help in uncovering fraud. The Service's involvement in this case coincided with its mandate, because counterfeiters had manufactured large numbers of revenue stamps for cigar makers and liquor distillers. The division responded not only by pursuing stamp counterfeiters but also by investigating and arresting large numbers of cigar and liquor dealers.[35] In 1870, when the second auditor of the Treasury found himself inundated with claims from veterans or their relatives for pensions and bounties, he turned to the Service for help in verifying the claims. Whitley hired Abner B. Newcomb to investigate these claims, and thereafter second-auditor cases occupied much of the operatives' time.[36] Such activities established the basic trend for the Service's noncounterfeiting activities. For the remainder of the century it performed a wide range of investigations for its parent organization, including cases of embezzlement, robbery, smuggling, fraud, and illegal aliens.[37]

Assisting other agencies within the Treasury probably earned the Service a good reputation in the era's most important federal department.[38] There is no evidence that Secretary Bristow considered the value of these activities in his decision to retain the Service despite Solicitor Wilson's desire to abolish it; however, the Service's record of assistance to other Treasury agencies suggests that the heads of those bureaus recognized the division's usefulness within the department and supported its retention.

Finally, the appointment of James Brooks as chief in October 1876 contributed significantly to the division's bureaucratic evolution and good relations within the Treasury. Brooks had already spent a decade in its service. The fact that he had survived through three changes in administration (and would survive several more, including the 1884 shift from a Republican to a Democratic regime) indicated that Brooks had developed into a consummate bureaucrat possessing the skills to deflect threats to his agency.[39] For example, in 1876 Solicitor George Talbot, unenthusiastic about supervising the division, sought to rid himself of the task through bureaucratic gamesmanship. In his 1876 Annual Report, Talbot complained that supervision of the Service was "inconsistent with the general duties and functions" of his office, which had nothing to do with detecting or prosecuting counterfeiters. He therefore recommended that the Service be transferred to the Department of Justice.[40]

Talbot's complaints carried sufficient weight for Secretary of the Treasury John Sherman in late 1877 to appoint a commission composed of the solicitor, an assistant secretary, and an independent observer to study the idea of moving the Service elsewhere. The commission hired Peter C. Cheeks to study and to recommend changes in the administrative relationship between the solicitor and the division.[41]

Cheeks came to the probably predetermined conclusion that the Service should relocate to the Department of Justice. He also sought to induce the Service to cooperate in the transfer by recommending that it become the central policing agency for the entire federal government. He praised the division, proclaiming it a "large and efficient body of men" whose work "should not be limited," but should "take in every conceivable crime or offense committed against the laws of the U.S." Under Cheeks's plan, the chief of the Service would even get a promotion to the rank of commissioner.[42]

Considering that the Service had been on the verge of disappearing three years before this report, Cheeks's recommendations represented tremendous bureaucratic possibilities. Viewed through the prism of modern bureaucratic behavior, the solicitor's proposal appears to have been a heaven-sent opportunity to fulfill an agency head's dream. Brooks would simultaneously be able to rid himself of a superior who disliked his agency and to expand the Service's mission and power.

Brooks's thoughts and actions at this juncture have not survived.[43] Brooks, however, did manage to undermine the solicitor. The first indication that the solicitor's campaign had failed appeared in a news account of the commission's work, which said that it had made no recommendations for radical changes in the Service.[44] This inaccurately characterized the commission's report, which urged the creation of a highly centralized federal policing capacity—an idea not likely to find favor in the press at the time. After the commission released its report there were no new developments for a year, which indicated that the solicitor was having problems with his proposal. Finally, in November 1878 Secretary Sherman issued a muddled order that essentially maintained the status quo. Offering the remarkable explanation that he was disinclined to change the arrangements that Salmon Chase had created in 1863, Sherman actually increased Brooks's power by giving him greater authority to appoint all Service employees (subject to an assistant secretary's approval). Sherman gave Talbot the authority over the Service's pay scales and control of monies paid to informers. Talbot, however, lost his battle to divest himself of responsibility for the division, because the Service stayed in the Treasury Department.[45]

Brooks, whose bureaucratic style conformed to prevailing attitudes, had also declined the solicitor's broad invitation to expand his power. Empire building was not the norm within the federal establishment, and there was nothing in Brooks' record that intimated that he had any ambitions to violate tradition. In general, Brooks adopted a defensive posture in his bureaucratic behavior. His assistance to other agencies seems less a ploy to expand the Service's mandate than an effort to cultivate useful contacts that would enhance his ability to deflect threats to his agency.

Brooks continued to benefit from his defensive demeanor during the remainder of his tenure. Shortly after his victory over the solicitor, he again faced and resolved another threat—this time from Congress. For the first three years of Brooks's tenure as chief, Congress had budgeted $100,000 to deal with counterfeiting. Then, inexplicably, the appropriation plummeted to $60,000 for fiscal year 1879. In addition, Congress, concerned about the Service's habit of using its funds to assist other federal agencies with noncounterfeiting problems, altered the language of the appropriation significantly. The new appropriation stipulated that the money could only be spent for detecting and punishing counterfeiting, "and for no other purpose whatever."[46]

Congress's actions inadvertently threatened to alienate the division from its sources of support within the federal bureaucracy. If the Service could not use its operatives to assist other departments and bureaus, those organizations would turn to other means for dealing with their policing problems, thereby diminishing their interest in preserving the division. In the next appropriation act, however, the Service not only received authority to suppress counterfeiting, but also to investigate violations of veterans' pay and bounties and the revenue laws. The new clause did not expand the Service's power but merely ratified what had become customary within the Treasury Department. Congress, however, made no specific references to the Service's assisting other departments. Brooks apparently had resolved that issue by striking a bargain: If Congress would refrain from actually prohibiting the practice, the Service would not use any of its appropriation to pay for that assistance. In the future, the departments and bureaus requesting aid would use their own appropriations to pay the Service's operatives for their time.[47]

Although this solution conformed with Brooks's defensive approach to bureaucratic issues, it also represented a small step in achieving greater autonomy for the Service. By codifying custom, Congress also legitimized it. Furthermore, the bargain that permitted continued assistance to other agencies had great potential for widening the Service's contacts and, therefore, its authority within the federal establishment. Brooks's tactical solution to an immediate threat had created new possibilities for enlarging the Service's independence.

Brooks made two more inadvertent contributions to the evolution of the Service's independence. First, he managed to obtain congressional recognition of the Service's existence. Having left the means for suppressing counterfeiting to the discretion of executive officers in 1863, Congress had continued to appropriate a lump sum of money without acknowledging formally the Secret Service's existence. That changed, however, in 1882, when Congress divided its expenditures to deal with counterfeiters into two categories. For the first time, Congress authorized a separate appropriation for the administration of the Service and identified it by name. A second appropriation provided for all other expenses.[48]

This change may have occurred for budgetary reasons. When Congress drastically cut the Service's budget in 1879, Brooks had managed to restore half the loss in the next fiscal year. The division's general budget, however, began a long-term slide in fiscal year 1882, and Brooks may have negotiated a partial solution to this problem by obtaining an agreement to fund its administrative costs as a separate item. That would at least preserve the general appropriation for fulfilling the Service's mission, since those costs would no longer have to be paid out of the regular budget. Whatever the motive, the Service had obtained congressional recognition of its existence, which was an important victory in its long battle for autonomy.

Brooks's other contribution involved yet another battle with a solicitor. Early in Cleveland's administration, a new solicitor assumed office and almost immediately forbade the use of division funds to buy counterfeit money, on the grounds that to "buy cft. [sic] money from a cftr. [sic] incites the counterfeiter to commit a crime."[49] This order struck at the heart of the Service's mission. Operatives routinely purchased counterfeit notes as a means to gain the confidence of criminals and to infiltrate counterfeiting organizations. Although this practice had been standard since Wood's regime, Washburn had codified it for administrative purposes in one of his first general directives.[50] The new solicitor's order thus threatened to deprive the operatives of an essential technique for conducting their investigations. Indeed, this order crippled investigations throughout 1885, seriously jeopardizing the Service's effectiveness and mission.[51]

Brooks initially tried two tactics to eliminate this threat. First, he asked U.S. district attorneys their opinion of the legality of buying counterfeit money. He probably expected considerable support from these officials, since his operatives had developed close relations with many of them. The results, however, were mixed. Most of the attorneys agreed with the Service's position, but others refused to take a position.[52] With this ploy faltering, Brooks coaxed the solicitor into visiting the New York office to talk with Andrew Drummond about the necessity of making buys. Drummond thought he had convinced the solicitor, but the ban continued.[53]

Brooks's subsequent tactics are unrecorded. While his operatives struggled with the consequences of the solicitor's ban, Brooks apparently turned to his allies in Washington. The number of his supporters probably had increased, since the division had continued to expand its activities with other agencies and bureaus under his direction. By the mid-1880s his operatives had helped to investigate Garfield's assassination, fraud in naval contracts, and land frauds. During Cleveland's inaugural, the Service had patrolled the parade route and had provided protection for the president until he entered the White House.[54] These activities, and perhaps his credibility with Congress and the Democratic White House, had given Brooks the support he needed to deal with the solicitor's interference, although the campaign to do so lasted seven months. In mid-December 1885 Brooks notified his operatives that the ban on buys had been repealed.[55]

Brooks now wanted more than a simple repeal; he wanted to end the Service's relationship with the solicitor. In August 1886 Brooks wrote to Drummond that the secretary of the Treasury had approved a reorganization of the Service "according to the views of the chief," and that the solicitor would henceforth have nothing to do with the division, except to give legal advice "when asked."[56] Since neither the details of Brooks's bureaucratic maneuvers nor the precise nature of the resulting reorganization have survived, it is difficult to reconstruct how Brooks achieved his victory. Nevertheless, his defensive tactics had once again won an increased measure of autonomy for the division.

Brooks had had a remarkable twelve years as Chief. By the time he voluntarily retired in 1888, he had defeated his titular superior twice on matters affecting the division's bureaucratic position in the Treasury Department, and once on a matter crucial to the Service's ability to perform its mission. Furthermore, he had devised effective solutions to congressional threats to the Service's authority and budget, and he had won formal recognition of its existence.

Further progress toward autonomy had to await Andrew Drummond. Although Drummond served as chief for only four years (1891–94), he drew upon his seventeen years of field experience to alter fundamentally the structure of cooperative federalism that governed the Service's relations with other policing agencies.

Cooperative federalism seemed a practical necessity for the Service. Although its mandate gave it the authority to police the entire country, it never had an adequate staff to achieve that responsibility. In addition, its lack of arrest and search powers required the Service

ILLUSTRATIONS

Counterfeit state bank notes seized in October 1830 from Peter LaRue in New York City. (Courtesy of the New York City Municipal Archives)

It is ordered that all measures of this Department for the suppression of offences respecting the coin and securities of the Government, and for the punishment of those committing them, shall be under the supervision and direction of the solicitor of the Treasury, and that all detectives and other persons in the employ of the Department and engaged in the prosecution of these measures shall report to him, and receive their instructions from him

S. P. Chase, Secretary of the Treasury.

Treasury Secretary Salmon P. Chase's December 1863 order consolidating all detection efforts against counterfeiting in the Solicitor's Office. (Courtesy of the National Archives)

The obverse of a counterfeit greenback printed in 1864 or 1865. (Courtesy of the American Numismatic Society)

Signature of Henry O. Wright, the first operative hired by William P. Wood, on the reverse of a counterfeit greenback, probably from 1865. (Courtesy of the American Numismatic Society)

William P. Wood, chief of the Secret Service from 1865 to 1869. (Courtesy of the U.S. Secret Service)

Hiram C. Whitley, chief of the Secret Service from 1869 to 1874. (Courtesy of the U.S. Secret Service)

Elmer Washburn, chief of the Secret Service from 1874 to 1876. (Courtesy of the U.S. Secret Service)

James Brooks, chief of the Secret Service from 1876 to 1888. (Courtesy of the U.S. Secret Service)

Andrew Drummond, chief of the Secret Service from 1891 to 1894. (Courtesy of the U.S. Secret Service)

Opposite: During his long career, Bill Brockway (a) had many partners in counterfeiting before the Service sent him to prison for the last time in 1895. John Nixon (b) and Orlando Bradford (c) were the principal partners with Brockway in his last syndicate. (Courtesy of the National Archives)

107

DESCRIPTION AND INFORMATION.

Taken *March 5th*, 189*6*, of *William E Brockway* ; Aliases, *E. W. Spencer*

; Home, *64 Ave D N Y City*

Album Vol. *#10*   Legitimate occupation, _____ Nationality, *American.*

Photograph No. *1184*   Criminal occupation, *Counterfeiter*

Age, *74* years; Height in stocking feet, *6* feet *9½* inches.

Weight, *170* pounds; Color of hair, *Gray curly.*

Color of eyes, *Gray blue* : Complexion, *Medium*

Style of beard, *Moustache'd* ; Color of beard, *Gray*

Peculiarities, scars, marks, etc.. *Slim build. Features
long and spare; very long neck; faint anchor
on back of left wrist 3 inches long and ½ inch
wide; long sharp nose.* *(2 Vol o P 1068)*

SOCIAL RELATIONS AND PAST HISTORY.

*For previous record See Vol. 8 P 46.
Was arrested in New York June 3 1882, for
violating Sec #5463 U S Rev. Statutes, indicted May
10th 1882, and nolle prosequied March 23. 1896*

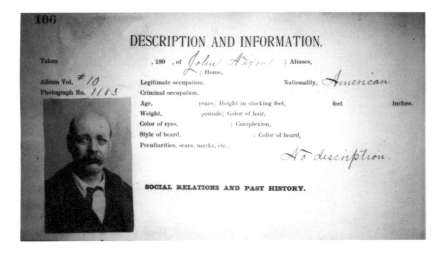

106

DESCRIPTION AND INFORMATION.

Taken _____, 189_, of *John Nixon* ; Aliases,

; Home,

Album Vol. *#10*   Legitimate occupation. _____ Nationality, *American*

Photograph No. *1183*   Criminal occupation, _____

Age, _____ years; Height in stocking feet, _____ feet _____ inches.

Weight, _____ pounds; Color of hair, _____

Color of eyes, _____ ; Complexion, _____

Style of beard, _____ : Color of beard, _____

Peculiarities, scars, marks, etc.. *No description*

SOCIAL RELATIONS AND PAST HISTORY.

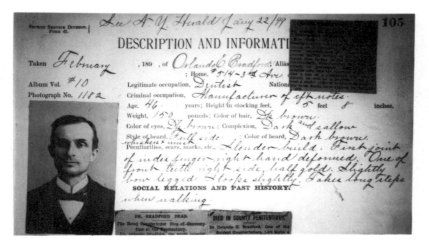

See N. Y. Herald Jany 22/99

105

DESCRIPTION AND INFORMATI...

Taken *February* , 189_, of *Orlando E Bradford* ; Alias...

; Home, *#514-3rd Ave*

Album Vol. *#10*   Legitimate occupation, *Dentist*   Nationa...

Photograph No. *1182*   Criminal occupation, *Manufacturer of #ft notes.*

Age, *46* years; Height in stocking feet, *5* feet *8* inches.

Weight, *150* pounds; Color of hair, *Dk brown.*

Color of eyes, *Dk brown* : Complexion, *Dark and sallow*

Style of beard, *Full side* : Color of beard, *Dark brown.*

whisker & mous

Peculiarities, scars, marks, etc.. *Slender build. First joint
of index finger right hand deformed. One of
front teeth right side, half gold. Slightly
bow legged. Stoops slightly. Takes long steps*

SOCIAL RELATIONS AND PAST HISTORY.

when walking

DR. BRADFORD DEAD. | DIED IN COUNTY PENITENTIARY.

DESCRIPTION AND INFORMATION.

Candelero Bettini, an Italian counterfeiter, ran an international syndicate with his wife in the early 1890s. Their notes were printed in Italy and distributed in New Orleans, New York, Boston, and San Francisco. Finally arrested in 1896, Bettini received an eight-year sentence; the jury refused to convict his wife. (Courtesy of the National Archives)

During a career that spanned more than forty years, Gaetano Russo proved to be an exception to the general rule that violent behavior was atypical among counterfeiters. At various times he committed arson, assault, and murder in addition to engaging in several counterfeiting schemes. (Courtesy of the National Archives) to rely on local police and U.S. marshals for those vital needs. Under-staffed and disadvantaged, the Service apparently had no recourse other than to seek help from larger and more powerful policing organizations.

Two basic problems at the outset of its operations (beyond those Wood created by his personnel and tactical policies) complicated the division's ability to utilize cooperative federalism effectively. First, the Service's mandate made it a rival to those upon whom it had to rely. This rivalry was sustained by the fact that federal officers col-lected fees for making arrests and serving warrants, while opera-tives did not. As a matter of organizational pride and as a means for demonstrating their own effectiveness, operatives naturally wanted to make their own searches and arrests. To do so, at least officially, they had to request that the resident marshal deputize them. By ac-ceding to such requests, however, the resident marshal would de-prive his own deputies of income, which he was usually loath to do.

Existing relations between federal marshals and local police fur-ther complicated the rivalry issue. Patrol officers and detectives fre-quently uncovered information about counterfeiting. Since the mar-shals paid rewards for such information, the local police developed a mutually beneficial relationship with them rather than Service oper-atives. The local police and the federal marshals thus perceived the Service as threatening long-standing, lucrative arrangements. Solic-itor Jordan had sought to allay their fears by giving police access to rewards and by assuring the marshals of monetary assistance to in-vestigate counterfeiting cases on their own.[57] Some operatives tried, with mixed results, to make the federal system work by cultivating relations with the local police.[58] Those efforts and Jordan's assur-ances, however, did not necessarily resolve the rivalry problem, as the marshals' hostility to the Service during the 1874 scandal had demonstrated.

Corruption within the local and the federal police created a second, even greater complication for a genuinely cooperative feder-al policing system. While deputy marshals and local officers could make money through the fees and reward system, they could make a great deal more by private deals with criminals. Enticed by such prospects, local detectives and deputy marshals had little incentive to work with the Service and powerful motives for thwarting its efforts.[59]

Problems with interagency rivalry and corruption may have con-

tributed to Whitley's efforts at empire building. His attempt at independence for the Service had foundered on the shoals of the 1874
scandal, however, and Solicitor Wilson's reforms forced the Service
to confront the problems of rivalry and corruption once again. With
no real alternatives available, the Service's operatives made a serious
effort to work within the framework of cooperative federalism and
around its problems, becoming adept at creating workable solutions.
Operatives partially solved the rivalry issue, for example, by actively
seeking the cooperation of the local police. They used two tools, money and information, to attain the assistance of local police. Although
both inducements had been available before, the operatives used
them much more systematically and selectively after 1876.[60] They
usually paid patrol officers for their assistance; they also provided police commanders with information about noncounterfeiting crimes
they had gleaned from their own contacts. In return, the police became fairly steady sources of information and assistance to the Service's activities.[61] Although corruption continued to be a problem,
operatives could withhold both money and information, the inducements to cooperation, as a way to control it. They also developed a
personal network of relations with police whom they learned to
trust.[62] In effect, operatives practiced selective association with the
police to avoid the more noisome aspects of their behavior, while simultaneously enlisting their assistance.

Cultivating cooperation with the local police permitted the operatives to sidestep their rivalry with the marshals and their deputies,
who continued to insist on their own prerogatives.[63] With the local
police becoming more cooperative, Service operatives turned more
frequently to them for help in making searches and arrests. Police
commanders, for instance, would willingly obtain a search warrant
and arrange a raid by their officers on a pretext provided by an operative. The operative would accompany the raid, conducting his own
search, while the suspects would be kept occupied by the patrol officers' pretended search. If the real search produced any evidence of
counterfeiting, the patrol officers would be conveniently on hand to
make the arrest.[64]

Such ploys depended for their success upon an operative's access
to reliable information. Cooperative federalism, however, did not
guarantee such access. Given the nature of nineteenth-century detective work, it could not have been otherwise. A detective's relation-

ship with his informers was highly personal. Operatives could not rely on informers borrowed from either local detectives or deputy marshals, because they would have had no personal knowledge of the trustworthiness or reliability of those informers.[65] Such knowledge was essential, because it affected an operative's judgment, tactics, and success in investigating a case. In these circumstances, operatives could not reasonably expect, or indeed desire, to share informers with their rivals.[66]

By recruiting its own informers, the Service was able to balance the need to cooperate with other police agencies with its organizational mandate. The Service had adopted a long-term strategy for suppressing counterfeiting that concentrated its operatives in the largest urban centers, where they sought to penetrate criminals' networks by starting at the lowest level and gradually working upward to identify and to arrest the manufacturers.[67] Informers were absolutely crucial to this strategy, because they provided the information and introductions that made possible the buys of counterfeit notes— which explains the depth of Brooks's reaction to the solicitor's order banning such deals. When Cleveland's new solicitor issued his blanket ban on buys, he threatened the Service's basic strategy and its independence as an organization. Deprived of the ability to build its own cases, the Service would have been reduced to a subordinate partner in its relationship with the local police and the marshals. The delicate balance between the dictates of federalism and the Service's separate bureaucratic identity would have collapsed.

Drummond perceived this danger more clearly than Brooks had. Adopting his usual tactics, Brooks had merely worked to overturn the solicitor's order. Although he had succeeded, Brooks had seen no need for anything more radical than a typically quiet bureaucratic end run. Drummond, in contrast, had regarded the solicitor's order as a threat requiring more drastic action. He began a crusade to expand the Service's powers, in order to deter future threats to its independence.

In November 1885 Drummond suggested that Brooks ask Congress to grant the Service the authority to obtain search warrants. Believing that informers would continue to provide the names of suspected counterfeiters, Drummond argued that ready access to search warrants would compensate for the inability to make buys.[68] Information from informers, however, did not provide a reliable basis for making searches or arrests since an operative could not confirm it by making purchases from suspects. With their own search authority, operatives could at least act on their informants' information by, for example, raiding a manufacturer's house in order to obtain the evidence against him. If the raid failed to produce the evidence, the operatives would at least be protected from civil suits.[69]

Drummond's proposal ignored the remedy to the Service's problem that was already in place. If an operative had information about counterfeiting, he could give it to a marshal and request that the marshal issue a search warrant. That, however, would leave the disposition of the case to the mercies of a rival agency, thus reducing the operative to little more than a glorified informer. In theory, that was the procedure the Service was supposed to use; in practice, however, it had devised an entente cordiale with the local police. Drummond, in effect, designed his proposal to ensure the continued independence of the Service. Although Brooks's victory over the solicitor had undermined the necessity of pursuing Drummond's idea, Brooks had not forbidden Drummond from pursuing it on his own.[70]

Drummond's efforts to implement his plan reveal a sophisticated understanding of the political process, as well as a practical use of his limited resources. Since Drummond's position as chief operative for New York did not give him the benefits of the Washington environment, he turned to his own contacts in the urban federal establishment to generate support for his idea at the local level. Working through the U.S. district attorneys in the New York area, Drummond testified before grand juries in Brooklyn and Manhattan. In his testimony, he argued that the power to obtain search warrants would protect the Service's officers by making searches more orderly and safe.[71]

His argument produced results. The Brooklyn jury petitioned Congress to give the Service this authority. Operative John Bell copied that resolution to present it to a New Jersey grand jury, which also endorsed the idea. That prompted Drummond to send copies of these endorsements to the chief operatives in St. Louis, Boston, Philadelphia, San Francisco, and Pittsburgh.[72]

Although Drummond's surviving records fail to mention whether those operatives obtained similar support, he had begun a process that developed its own momentum. When Bell succeeded Brooks as chief in 1888 and forced Drummond out of the Service, that did not end the campaign for expanding the power of the Service.[73] Instead, its scope broadened. Brooks's brother, John Brooks, Drummond's successor as chief operative in New York, suggested to Bell that operatives should seek appointments as deputy marshals so that they could make their own arrests.[74] Brooks did not fully explain the origins of this idea nor why he chose to advocate it at that time. Whatever its origins, Brooks's call for arrest powers, combined with Drummond's demand for search authority, created the potential for fundamental change in the Service's relationship with its rivals. Bell, however, rejected Brooks's suggestion.

Although a Democrat in a Democratic administration, Bell was not a long-term member of either the Service or the federal establishment. Prior to joining the division in 1885, he had been police chief of Newark, New Jersey. He apparently owed his career in local and federal law enforcement primarily to political contacts; he had even admitted that he was "not an expert officer."[75] Neither his record nor his affection for western dress had inspired confidence in his abilities. The new Republican administration asked him to resign in 1889; he refused and remained for another year.[76]

Despite his lack of credentials and short tenure, Bell may have aided the campaign to expand the division's powers. In early 1890 the House Committee on the Judiciary held hearings on the search-warrant proposal. The committee included a section of the New York grand jury's resolution, which provided strong support of search-warrant power for the Service. Drummond's campaign had thus percolated into the congressional process, despite his absence from the Service.[77]

When the solicitor finally fired Bell in June 1890, he appointed James Brooks as temporary chief. Seven months later, and reportedly at Brooks' insistence, Drummond became Chief.[78] Though brief, Drummond's tenure as chief marked a major turning point in the Service's development. Under his guidance the division redefined its position in federal policing. He had assumed office less than a month before Congress authorized his pet project: In February 1891 Congress acted on the Judiciary Committee's recommendation and authorized judges or U.S. commissioners to issue search warrants to marshals "or any other person specially mentioned in such warrant."[79] This was clearly a personal victory for Drummond. His conception and early direction of the campaign had been so astute that it had wended its way toward fruition, despite his three-year forced absence from the division.

It is less clear how much credit Drummond could claim for the second major change during his tenure. His own long federal service, his authorship of the search-warrant power, and his friendship with James Brooks probably gave Drummond the credibility to move aggressively to secure even more power for the division. The details of his activities as chief have not survived, but the results have. Drummond probably recognized the potential inherent in John Brooks's long dormant suggestion that operatives should have appointments as deputy marshals. Perhaps mindful of the controversy that the idea might generate, Drummond again showed his political agility by altering Brooks's idea to achieve a more emphatic result. By August 1892 he had convinced the Appropriations Committee to make an important single-word addition to the division's general budget authorization. Instead of the standard phrase that the appropriation was "for the expenses of detecting and delivering" counterfeiters into the custody of the United States marshals, the new appropriation stipulated that the money was "for the expenses of detecting, *arresting*, and delivering" counterfeiters to the marshals.[80]

Drummond had created a quiet revolution in the structure of federal policing. Having acquired the power to make its own searches and arrests, the Service greatly strengthened its independent organizational status within the federal policing system. These new powers enhanced both its prestige and power. No longer a supplicant in need of subterfuges to perform its mission, the division had obtained equality with its rivals.

Congress soon afterward made the division the dominant partner in suppressing counterfeiting by abolishing the fee system for the marshals in 1896. This change had no effect on the way operatives performed their work but dramatically altered the deputy marshals' behavior. Deprived of their fees, they lost interest in cooperating with the Service. Operatives then had the unusual luxury of complaining that their erstwhile partners "do not, and will not give the same attention to counterfeiting cases, as when fees were given by the Government, and consequently most of the Deputies want the Secret Service Agents to do all the work."[81] With the abdication of the marshals, the Service had no serious challengers to its basic institutional mandate.

The Service's new powers and independence greatly enhanced its usefulness and prestige within the federal environment. Between 1894 and 1908 (when another crisis beyond the purview of this study further altered the Service's relations with other federal agencies), it became the general detective agency for the federal government, performing investigations for the Departments of State, War, Interior, and Justice. Its special operations included engaging in espionage and counterespionage activities during the Spanish-American War, infiltrating anarchist groups, and investigating cases of involuntary servitude, lynchings, western land frauds, and the beef trust.[82]

Solicitor Wilson's efforts to make the Service a subordinate agency within federal policing had failed. The Service, however, had not deliberately engineered this defeat. The Service's road from disgrace to autonomy had run through largely uncharted territory. Simply by surviving the 1874 scandal, the Service had retained the opportunity to react to and to benefit from changing circumstances. The chiefs had been able to anticipate neither the threats nor the opportunities. Responding defensively, they had sought to preserve rather than to expand the division's mandate. Over time, however, a successful defense had encouraged more aggressiveness, particularly by James Brooks and Drummond. Their long tenures in federal service had given them a familiarity with both the players and the rules of the game, which they used to enhance the division's independence.

Gradually the cumulative effect of defensive measures subtly translated into institutional power for the Service. By the 1890s it had become a successful bureaucracy, whose deceptively narrow mandate to pursue counterfeiters justified a broad range of additional policing activities within the federal government. More important, the Service's ability to prosper provided the bureaucratic basis for its projection of federal power beyond Washington into local communities.

DISMANTLING
THE MONEY
MARKET

DEFT MANEUVERS within Washington's bureaucratic thicket en-sured the Service's survival but contributed little to its day-to-day ac-tivities to suppress counterfeiting. It was thus necessary that opera-tives learn to manipulate their environment as effectively as the chiefs were managing the hazards of Washington. Federal detectives had to develop skills that would complement those of their leaders in order to ensure that the Service's continued survival rested on genu-ine accomplishments in the field as much as on adroit political tactics in Washington.

The scope and complexity of the counterfeiters' illegal market required that the Service devise and apply an effective intervention strategy nationwide. There were few if any precedents to guide the Service in the fulfillment of this enormous operational task. Further-more, budgetary problems constrained its ability to implement mea-sures to dismantle the counterfeit market. Finally, the Service had to transform criminals' traditional expectations of and relations with law enforcement. Suppressing counterfeiting by efficiently, economi-cally, and honestly achieving the maximum penetration of federal power into the urban underworld therefore became the Service's cen-tral challenge.

Ironically, the era's distrust of detectives and its devotion to limited federal power and fiscal restraint forced the Service to adopt increasingly centralized controls over its agents and their activities. After a chaotic beginning the chiefs gradually increased their control over money and information in order to regulate their operatives' activities. Their efforts created a powerful federal policing capacity, which their putative bosses—solicitors like Edward Jordan and Bluford Wilson—had struggled to prevent.

Because of congressional penury, the Service's budget steadily, and occasionally dramatically, declined from an initial high appropriation of $200,000 in William P. Wood's first year as chief. By the end of Elmer Washburn's brief reign in 1876 Congress had reduced the Service's budget by half. James Brooks's triumphs in bureaucratic survival had not saved the Service from further budget cuts. The appropriation had decreased a further 40 percent during his tenure, although his success in obtaining supplementary funding for the Washington headquarters beginning in 1882 had helped to protect the Service's operating budget. Nevertheless, Congress had kept the Service on limited funds for the remainder of the period, increasing its appropriation only at the end of the 1890s (see Figure 5.1).

Limited and declining budgets posed a significant problem for the Service's field operations. Detective work was labor-intensive, time-consuming, and unpredictably expensive. Good cases could take weeks or even months to develop. Extended investigations entailed expenses that the operatives could not necessarily control. For example, a detective might need money to pay informers, to make buys, to travel, and to cover miscellaneous expenses such as renting a room from which to watch suspects' homes. Furthermore, since several investigations might have been under way simultaneously, the operative needed reliable help for varying periods of time and for a range of tasks. The unavoidable expenses pursuant to investigations thus had the potential to create budgetary chaos.

Restricted budgets also complicated the management of personnel and geographical space. Since their policing effort had to match the far-flung activities of counterfeiters, the chiefs had to balance the need to maintain a truly national law enforcement system with the reality that their budgets severely limited the number of operatives they could hire.[1] Wood began with fifteen operatives in 1865 and increased his force to thirty-four before his forced retirement. No subsequent chief had the money to retain that many operatives, whose

FIGURE 5.1

Secret Service's Annual Appropriation, 1866–1899

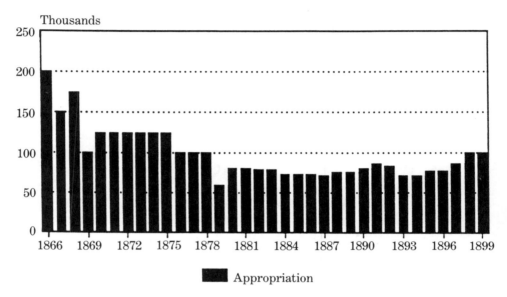

Source: Congressional Record

numbers hovered around thirty until early in Brooks's reign, when the force abruptly declined by nearly half within two years. After dropping to a low of fourteen operatives in 1880, the force slowly increased to a high of thirty-five in 1898.

In these circumstances the chiefs had to devote much of their time to fiscal matters. Wood, who probably did not possess the temperament for such administrative duties, belatedly addressed this issue only when he could no longer ignore the financial consequences of his operatives' flagrant behavior. The operatives had hired assistants and had set their compensation without consulting Wood, had charged expenses to their accounts without adequate explanation, and had made deals with counterfeiters on their own initiative. In general, they had wreaked havoc with the Service's budget.[2] Inadequate controls over finances had thus threatened to eviscerate the Service's activities by depriving the chief of the ability to dispense monies in the most effective manner. Toward the end of his tenure Wood sought to impose order on this fiscal chaos by undermining his operatives' entrepreneurial behavior. He prohibited operatives from hiring assistants or making deals without his prior approval, and established limits on the daily subsistence allowance and the pay of assistants.[3]

Despite these late efforts Wood failed to exercise sufficient administrative control of his force in order to achieve maximum results within the constraints of the budget. Hiram C. Whitley, who remained indifferent to financial issues, provided no remedies. He justified his budget by arguing that his small force could not adequately cover the entire nation without frequent travel, which entailed expenses. Whitley also had a rather cavalier attitude toward controlling the cost of buying counterfeit money. At one point he obtained permission to spend $5,000 for a buy, which was an astronomical sum for the era. Not until late in his tenure did he attempt to restrain the operatives' habit of hiring assistants without prior approval.[4] Finally, and perhaps most importantly, the 1874 scandal revealed that Whitley's indifference gave his assistant chief, Ichabod C. Nettleship, the opportunity to embezzle funds through spurious charges for incidental expenses.[5] Elmer Washburn's brief tenure, however, marked a turning point in the management of the Service. Compared with his predecessors, Washburn produced a blizzard of regulations that provided the basis for strict accountability in financial matters and obedience to centralized direction.

Since the operatives' inattention to financial issues had consistently been a major problem, Washburn introduced several new measures to enforce economy. He ordered that every charge for buys, information, assistance, or incidentals "must be dated and otherwise itemized to the fullest extent, and fully explained by notes . . . and vouchers must be obtained for money expended in every practicable case."[6] Furthermore, while he recognized the tension between the practical realities of the operatives' work and the restrictive controls over costs, Washburn firmly advocated thrift. He announced that he would evaluate the operatives' performance on the basis of whether or not they "took the cheapest practicable method to accomplish" their mission.[7]

The demand for itemized accounts permitted centralized scrutiny over literally every penny an operative spent, but only if the chiefs reviewed these accounts. Beginning with Washburn, every chief scrutinized the operatives' financial reports with a dedication that at times approached ferocity, and operatives became acutely conscious of the need for accurate reports.

Washburn also centralized control over buys. He discontinued the practice of permitting operatives to maintain a ready-cash fund at their offices, which they could use to make deals, and ordered that future buys be for "the smallest practicable amount"—a change which marked a significant departure from the Service's previous operational habits.[8] These new arrangements dramatically increased the chief's control over an essential part of the operatives' work. Previously, operatives had largely ignored the regulation that they ask headquarters for permission to make buys. They now had to seek approval, because they had no independent ability to finance these transactions. By exercising this control the chiefs could not only regulate the monies available for this purpose, but also make more careful decisions about which investigations represented a sound investment of the division's scarce resources.

Although these new arrangements achieved their bureaucratic intent, they also tended to make the operatives' work more difficult, because they restricted their capacity to conduct investigations. The chiefs, for example, frequently harassed the operatives about the size of their staffs. Each chief operative maintained a retinue of assistants and informers, whose number varied from one district to another. Each chief operative also believed that he lacked sufficient staffing for the work of his district. Since they frequently had several cases under investigation at once, chief operatives occasionally fought testy battles with headquarters over conflicting demands for economy and results.[9] When protests and careful expositions about promising cases did not convince the chief to relent, operatives occasionally proved ingenious in evading restrictions. During a particularly difficult period in the late 1870s, when budget cuts interfered with the Service's work, Andrew Drummond replaced paid assistants with volunteers and family members—including his brother, brother-in-law, and sons—in order to continue his investigations. This expedient worked so well that he relied on it several times thereafter, as did other agents.[10]

Nevertheless, centralized direction of the operatives' expenditures became the norm after 1874, because the chiefs had begun to maintain careful and effective supervision over every aspect of the operatives' work.[11] Congressional penury, while certainly affecting the Service's size, did not ultimately cripple its effectiveness, because the system Washburn had introduced created a workable balance between budget constraints and operational needs.

While struggling with their budgets, the chiefs also sought to direct detective work effectively on a national scale. Existing detection methods, which were rooted in the practices and the traditions of crime-ridden urban neighborhoods, did not offer inspiring models. City police departments did not exercise substantial control over their detectives' behavior. As a result, police detectives essentially acted as entrepreneurs, exploiting the fertile opportunities that the underworld offered to advance their own personal interests, while relying on their political connections to protect them from the public's wrath over invasions of privacy, abuses of authority, corrupt bargains, and false accusations.[12]

Unfortunately the task of successfully suppressing counterfeiting would not permit the facile use of uncontroversial detection techniques. Only one aspect of counterfeiting, shoving, lent itself to simple investigative methods. Having received a complaint, a detective could interview the victim to obtain a description of the shover and begin searching for the alleged criminal. After locating the suspect, the detective could conduct another interview to discover whether or not the shover had knowingly committed the crime. Since many people inadvertently passed counterfeit notes, the detective could conceivably trace a particular note through the hands of several people before finding the guilty party. Conducting a series of interviews, mostly with innocent people in order to gather evidence of criminal wrongdoing, demanded primarily investigative skills. In such situations the detective had to appear honest and sincere, in order to gain the trust of those he interviewed. He also had to have keen observational skills and an ability to recognize the truth (or a lie) when he heard it.

However useful these investigative skills might have been in dealing with shovers, they were practically useless for coping with the sophisticated criminals who financed, manufactured, and distributed counterfeit notes. Shovers experienced considerable risks, because they had to deal with honest citizens in order to earn an income from counterfeiting. Other individuals involved in counterfeiting dealt with their fellow criminals, and they all knew that they were committing a crime. Counterfeiting at this level was essentially consensual.

Suppressing a consensual crime required different detective techniques than those employed in tracking down a shover. Essentially, an officer had to obtain the cooperation of the criminals he intended to arrest, so that he could destroy the entire network. That goal required instigative techniques. First, the detective had to conceal his identity—either by playing a role so that he could participate in discussions about criminal activities, or by using an intermediary. Then he had to induce suspects to commit a crime when and where he could observe them. Observing a single transaction (between, for example, a shover and a retailer of counterfeits) was only part of a long-term strategy for discovering all the individuals involved with a particular note. By spurning an immediate arrest, the detective hoped to infiltrate each counterfeiting network, developing evidence against each individual. Ideally, arrests would occur only after all the guilty parties had been identified.

A successful attack on an entire network of criminals therefore required several controversial skills. The detective had to cultivate knowledge of and contacts within the underworld, manipulate informers, rely on the information of known criminals, ignore minor crimes to build cases against major criminals, and offer the "small fry" some inducements (for example, reduced charges) to betray the "big fish."[13] An effective campaign against counterfeiters thus involved both investigative and instigative techniques. The public, not understanding the nature of the task, had little patience with most of these methods and was deeply suspicious of the instigative approach, because it so easily lent itself to abuses. Federal detectives, however, could not operate effectively without this approach, and sought to avoid controversy in its applications. The chiefs reconciled the dilemmas of creating an effective national detective force in an era of public hostility toward federal power by increasing their control over two of the Service's most sensitive and problematic characteristics: their operatives' relations with informers and the information that relationship produced.

Corrupt relations between urban criminals and detectives had become routine by the mid-nineteenth century. Based on their prior experience, criminals probably regarded the Service as just another detective force whose activities created both problems and opportunities for them. They also may have expected that their access to information would decisively shape their relations with this new agency.

The Service dealt with two types of criminal informers, voluntary and coerced. Voluntary informers generally had a variety of motives for offering information. Some treated the division as an employer of last resort. Counterfeiters who were temporarily down on their luck offered agents information and cooperation in exchange for a steady wage (usually $3 a day). Once they had accumulated sufficient funds to resume their careers, they usually discontinued their employment until the next time they needed financial assistance. Others used the Service to exact revenge on their peers for real or imagined grievances, or to drive competitors out of business. Coerced informers had less complex motives, because they had an immediate problem to solve. They were under arrest, possibly facing a trial and prison. Criminals, however, had learned that they could routinely win their freedom by providing information about other counterfeiters.[14]

Altering the traditional rules of negotiations between detectives and informers would require a coherent policy that controlled the excesses while effectively exploiting the benefits. Accountability was the key to such a policy. Since nineteenth-century detectives had never been held accountable for their behavior, the effort to monitor the activities of the operatives placed the chiefs in the position of having to create a new system for supervising detective work.

The parameters of operatives' accountability were defined when the inadequacies of Wood's original system were corrected by Whitley and Washburn. Jordan, probably advised by Wood, issued a reward circular in July 1865 in which he enticed informers to submit information on counterfeiting schemes to the Treasury in order to gain such benefits as the prospect of employment. Jordan thus authorized Wood to put criminals on the federal payroll without providing any guidelines for regulating their behavior.[15] Wood expected to regulate informers by asserting his right to approve their employment and the terms of all bargains. No operative was supposed to make his own deals with informers.[16] Wood did not, however, institute a consistent policy for approaching these negotiations. Instead he personalized each bargain, offering such comfortably traditional terms as freedom in exchange for information, and salaries for full-time employment in the division. Such attractive terms frequently made criminals officers without changing their deviant behavior. Promises of legal assistance led to such embarrassing incidents as Wood's helping the defense in the trial of Bill Brockway.

Wood required weekly summaries from the operatives at the end of each month, which gave them considerable freedom in deciding what to report. What they failed to report, however, frequently had operational consequences. For example, their backgrounds (many of them were criminals and former city detectives) and their right to collect rewards in addition to their regular salaries prompted them to continue their entrepreneurial approach to detection. These early operatives developed their own sources of information and refused to share them with others, including Wood. Wood not only made no effort to change this behavior but also assiduously pursued his own deals and arranged handsome rewards for himself.[17] This situation jeopardized the flow of information that Wood needed in order to coordinate the Service's activities. It also threatened to make the Service nothing more than an elaborate federal subsidy for the operatives' convenience, as they pursued personal aggrandizement.

Whitley sought a more systematic approach. First, responding to a query from Solicitor Edward C. Banfield in 1870 about the wisdom of using informers, Whitley launched a campaign to educate both his superiors and the public about the need for instigative techniques in detective work. He wrote Banfield a spirited defense of such techniques and a brief lesson on detection, which stressed the need for criminal sources to provide "the best and most reliable information" about counterfeiters.[18] Banfield never raised the issue again.

Having won this argument, Whitley found other opportunities to disseminate his gospel on informers. He defended their use in letters to editors and wrote a short pamphlet on the topic for the public. The appearance of the Service's first authorized institutional biography in 1872 gave him yet another forum for his views. Finally, he summarized his thoughts on the legitimacy of instigative methods in his *Circular of Instructions* that was distributed to operatives. The circular assured them of the underlying morality of this approach to detection.[19]

However useful this campaign may have been, Whitley had to transform his noble rhetoric into concrete controls and results. He eliminated the most egregious aspects of Wood's system by recruiting individuals more amenable to bureaucratic routines and by prohibiting operatives from receiving rewards. Whitley shrewdly compensated for the lost income with promises of prestige and salary increases, which were implicit in the new ranking system that he had instituted within the Service. Each district would now be commanded by a chief operative, who had earned promotion by his performance as an assistant operative.[20]

Whitley also refined Wood's concept of districts. Wood's system, which had defined a district by a state or federal judicial district boundaries, was unworkable because the Service did not have enough individuals to staff so many areas. Whitley redefined districts so that each contained a number of states. He then ordered a single operative to maintain a headquarters in a major city. George Egbert, for example, was chief operative of the Atlanta District, which encompassed the states of Virginia, Tennessee, Georgia, North Carolina, South Carolina, Florida, Alabama, and part of Mississippi.[21] The number of districts varied thereafter but always remained quite large.[22]

By creating large districts Whitley ultimately permitted greater centralized control of the Service's operations. Having fewer districts than operatives provided a reserve of agents. With all communications and weekly reports sent directly to him, Whitley could use his control of information and agents to concentrate the Service's attention where he judged it was most needed.[23]

Whitley also devised much more stringent criteria to justify hiring informers. He insisted that he would employ only those who had proven their worth. To earn a place on the division's roster, an informer initially had to build a case on his or her own, to present his or her results to an operative, and to permit Whitley to determine a single payment reward for his or her services. This arrangement initially distanced the Service from a new informer, permitted an independent review of the evidence by the chief, and avoided the Service's paying of expenses and salary before the informer had demonstrated any value.[24]

Those informers who did manage to get on the payroll did not always find the experience profitable, because Whitley expected them to produce quick results in order to justify their employment; when they failed to deliver, he was ruthless. For example, losing his patience with Perry Randolph, Whitley ordered Operative Thomas E. Lonergan to arrange a fake deal for counterfeit money in Missouri, where there was an outstanding arrest warrant for Randolph. Whitley notified the Missouri authorities of Randolph's whereabouts and told Lonergan to destroy all evidence of Randolph's connection to the Service. Peter McCartney, a prominent counterfeiter turned informer, received similar treatment. McCartney had exchanged information for his freedom during Wood's tenure and probably expected the same deal from Whitley. Whitley, however, framed McCartney when he stopped being useful. Unlike Wood, Whitley believed that unproductive informers belonged in jail, not on the streets, and he had no qualms about the methods used to achieve that goal.[25] Such ruthless behavior transformed the character of the relationship between informers and operatives. Under Wood they had been valued colleagues; now they became tools serving the division's mission. However unsavory Whitley's technique, it probably created a more formal and therefore more distant tone in the negotiations between the Service and its informers.

There were, however, several problems with Whitley's methods. He sought to solve specific difficulties in the Service's relations with informers while continuing many of Wood's habits regarding negotiations. Like Wood's, his solutions to the problems of handling informers rested on personal whim. He thus failed to eliminate all the difficulties in the relationship between the Service as a federal policing organization and informers as a valuable but problematic resource.

Washburn finally established a coherent framework for dealing with informers. He issued a circular in September 1875 that created standards for dealing with voluntary informers. It announced that the Service would reward any person who gave information "not already in the possession of the Chief" that led to the "detection, arrest, and conviction" of counterfeiters or to the "capture of their . . . implements and materials." Washburn stipulated, however, that an operative—not the informer—would investigate the information and "work the case to a conclusion."[26] These were the most stringent criteria for evaluating the worth of information that the Service had ever used. Informers' liberty in dealing with operatives thus became severely restricted. They were now subordinate to an operative during an investigation and had to wait until the conclusion of a case for any compensation.

However satisfying these new rules might have been to Washburn, they needed to be adjusted to reality. Some informers refused to work under such conditions. Others had an immediate need for cash, prompting operatives to advance them small sums against their eventual reward money. Occasionally, if the information proved particularly significant, the operative requested a per diem for the informer, even though the chiefs acquiesced only reluctantly and strictly limited the time for such employment.[27]

Nevertheless, there was now a framework for systematic relations with voluntary informers. Operatives adapted their behavior to both the letter and the spirit of Washburn's circular. They either read or handed a copy of the reward circular to informers who came to their offices, asked them to provide verbal or written summaries of their information, and instructed them to return in a few days for the chief's response. Operatives sought adjustments to this system only as the need arose and on a case-by-case basis.[28]

Washburn created a similarly coherent policy to deal with coerced informers. Perhaps simultaneously with issuing his reward circular, he announced a no-compromise approach to negotiations with arrested counterfeiters.[29] In its final form the new regulations reflected Washburn's typically rigid strategy for managing operational tasks:

> Operatives will neither promise, either by word or implication, immunity from punishment, nor anything in mitigation of sentence, to any person for any offence he many have committed. They will accept from those arrested any information about criminals which they may choose to impart, and promise to make known to the District Attorney who prosecutes the cases, and the Judge before whom the accused are tried, all they have done to aid this service in the detection of crime.[30]

This policy struck at the heart of one of the most hallowed traditions in criminals' relations with detectives. Exchanging information for freedom had become so common that it was assumed to be a standard operational practice. Drummond encountered this expectation in an interview with the wife of a counterfeiter who had obtained her husband's freedom by informing on a compatriot several years earlier. She asked no compensation for her information, because she was "of the opinion that any one she may give away will be allowed to give away somebody else & get off himself."[31] Since neither Wood nor

Whitley (despite his handling of some informers) had done anything to subvert this tradition, Washburn's new policy probably shocked counterfeiters who had entered interrogations expecting the Service to honor it.

Philadelphian Frank Vintree was one of the first to encounter the new policy. Whitley had arrested him in 1870 and had freed him after Vintree had supplied information and introductions for operatives to various of his counterfeiting associates.[32] Having obtained personal confirmation that the Service played by traditional rules, Vintree had promptly returned to his criminal work, building an extensive network of customers that encompassed large sections of western Pennsylvania. When Drummond arrested him again in late 1875, Vintree entered negotiations with his prior experience clearly in mind. He offered to supply the names of the manufacturers of his notes if Drummond would let him go. To his utter astonishment, Drummond refused. Stubbornly continuing to insist on immunity, Vintree was unable to believe Drummond's statement that "anything he did must be did [sic] voluntarily and without any promises whatever."[33] Vintree's confusion was understandable, because nothing in his experience had prepared him for the extraordinary shift that Washburn had imposed on negotiations with arrested counterfeiters. For the remainder of the century, the Service sought to inculcate the lesson that arrest meant trial and probably conviction. Counterfeiters could expect leniency only after conviction, and then usually in the form of a reduced sentence rather than outright freedom.[34]

Washburn's approach to relations with informers and his operatives' implementation of the new policies represented a dramatic departure from the norms. The Service had now structured operative-informer relations to serve its bureaucratic mission rather than the personal interests of criminals and detectives. As if to emphasize the distinction between the Service and other detective agencies, James Brooks refined the policy to include a warning to suspects about their rights. Beginning in 1879 operatives admonished suspects that everything they said would be documented and used against them in court, and that they need not answer any questions until they had consulted a lawyer.[35] At a time when the New York City police had introduced the sweatbox as an aid to interrogations, such attention to legal formalities served to emphasize that the Secret Service was a separate organization committed to different goals.

Devising more centralized control over the behavior of operatives and informers would have been insignificant if the Service had
been unable to utilize that control in an effective campaign to dismantle the market for counterfeits. Fortunately for the division, the
structure of the counterfeit market contributed to its own destruction. Since the market was concentrated in certain cities and regions,
the chiefs could deploy operatives more effectively if they were able
to decipher the clandestine patterns of counterfeiting activity.

Wood had used his participation in the Treasury's initial study of
counterfeiting in 1864 to analyze the national counterfeit market. The
results, which he included in his first official report as chief in July
1865, demonstrated that the mid-Atlantic and Midwestern regions
contained the highest concentrations of counterfeiters. Four cities
were prominent centers of activity: New York, Philadelphia, Cincinnati, and St. Louis.[36] Wood thus deployed most of his operatives to
the mid-Atlantic and Midwestern areas, devoting special attention
to their key urban centers. By adopting a principle of economy of
force, he established the basic pattern for managing the Service's
seemingly impossible task of projecting its authority over the entire
nation, and determined the areas in which it would subsequently concentrate its force. Two-thirds of all arrests between 1864 and 1899
occurred in the mid-Atlantic and Midwest areas. Within those regions, the Service made the bulk of its arrests in the major cities. In
the mid-Atlantic area, for example, two-thirds of all arrests took
place in cities, with more than twice as many occurring in New York
City as in any other urban center (see Table 5.1).

More important, the Service attacked the structure of the market from the outset. Local law officers' and federal marshals' poor record against counterfeiters was not always attributable to corruption
or indifference. In a parochial era, which tied law enforcement authority to specific localities, police officers and marshals had neither
the incentive nor the right to pursue criminals participating in a national market system. They were thus incapable of mounting a coordinated large-scale effort to deal with counterfeiters.

Such limitations do not, however, explain why police in cities
that served as manufacturing and distribution centers, and whose effective intervention would have created serious problems for counterfeiters, failed to act more decisively. It was corrupt relations between local detectives and criminals that eviscerated effective action

TABLE 5.1

Distribution of Counterfeiting Arrests by Chief's Tenure (10 Percent Sample)

Chief	New England[a]	Mid-Atlantic[b]	Midwest[c]	South[d]	West[e]	Total
William P. Wood (January 1863–May 1869)	12	65	32	9	5	123
Hiram C. Whitley (May 1869–September 1874)	7	100	59	32	24	222
Elmer Washburn (October 1874–September 1876)	12	25	17	17	8	79
James Brooks (October 1876–January 1888)	10	137	126	55	31	359
John Bell (Febrary 1888–May 1890)	4	38	32	21	9	104
James Brooks (June 1890–January 1891)	0	9	12	4	5	30

Andrew Drummond (February 1891–January 1894)	3	36	60	29	29	157
William Hazen (February 1894–March 1898)	11	74	136	82	45	348
John Wilkie (April 1898–December 1899)	6	31	34	23	19	113
Total:	65	515	508	272	175	1,535

Source: U.S. Secret Service, *Description and Information of Criminals, 1863–1906*, Record Group 87, 40 vols., National Archives, Washington, D.C.

[a] Connecticut, Maine, Massachusetts, New Hampshire, Rhode Island, and Vermont.

[b] Delaware, Maryland, New Jersey, New York, Pennsylvania, and West Virginia.

[c] Illinois, Indiana, Iowa, Michigan, Minnesota, Missouri, Ohio, and Wisconsin.

[d] Arkansas, Florida, Georgia, Kentucky, Louisiana, Mississippi, North Carolina, South Carolina, Tennessee, Texas, and Virginia.

[e] California, Colorado, Kansas, Montana, Nebraska, North Dakota, Oregon, South Dakota, Washington, and Wyoming.

in these crucial areas. Ordinary patrol officers might arrest shovers, but detectives had no interest in destroying lucrative personal arrangements with counterfeiters.

Neither Wood nor his successors limited themselves to arresting shovers. From the outset the Service sought to undermine the market by attacking its manufacturing and distribution systems. This strategy was particularly evident in New York. While the local police persisted in arresting shovers, Service operatives besieged manufacturers and dealers (see Table 5.2).[37] New York's counterfeiters had never experienced such a concerted assault on the infrastructure of their market system. The Service sustained its attack on the makers and dealers for the remainder of the century.

Wood also attacked distribution networks outside New York. Aiming at the heart of that system, he turned major dealers, such as John Disbrow, into informers who provided extensive descriptions of the market's main distribution artery into the Old Northwest. Armed with this information, several operatives infiltrated the dealers' network, which stretched from the western area of Troy, New York, to Buffalo. Wood also recruited a few operatives from this area to assist if problems arose with local law officials. These efforts culminated in a large-scale raid in that region in 1867. The Service arrested thirty-eight dealers, whose network of customers extended from New England to Illinois.[38]

Whitley continued this initiative with the Service's first major effort to deal with counterfeiting in the upper South. Operatives gained access to the network serving this area through a dramatic ploy. Assistant Operative Drummond concocted a scheme to gain the dealers' confidence by arranging to have the police in a small town arrest him and an informer he had recruited. Drummond and the informer then escaped from jail and headed for Cincinnati, where the dealers who supplied the upper South were headquartered. En route, the Louisville police, alerted of the jailbreak but not of Drummond's true identity, captured the escapees. Drummond reported that he had secured his release from his captors "through strategy," a phrase which in this context suggests bribery. Finally arriving in Cincinnati, Drummond discovered that news of his exploits had preceded him, ensuring a warm reception among the local counterfeiters. With Drummond providing inside information, four other operatives built cases against a large network that served customers in

TABLE 5.2

Counterfeiting Arrests by Region, Type of Counterfeit, and Chief's Tenure (10 Percent Sample)

Chief	New England[a]		Mid-Atlantic[b]		Midwest[c]		South[d]		North[e]	
	N	C[f]	N	C	N	C	N	C	N	C
William P. Wood (January 1863–May 1869)	7	0	31	2	18	0	6	1	3	0
Hiram C. Whitley (May 1869–September 1874)	0	1	15	3	11	0	1	4	0	2
Elmer Washburn (October 1874–September 1876)	4	4	6	6	9	2	5	4	0	1
James Brooks (October 1876–January 1888)	1	4	9	70	12	78	2	31	4	18
John Bell (February 1888–May 1890)	1	3	11	24	2	25	5	12	0	8
James Brooks (June 1890–January 1891)	0	0	6	3	2	9	1	3	2	2
Andrew Drummond (February 1891–January 1894)	1	2	10	26	7	49	2	25	3	25

Continued on next page

TABLE 5.2
(*Continued*)

Chief	New England[a]		Mid-Atlantic[b]		Midwest[c]		South[d]		North[e]	
	N	C[f]	N	C	N	C	N	C	N	C
William Hazen (February 1894–March 1898)	2	9	18	53	23	98	11	59	4	36
John Wilkie (April 1898–December 1899)	3	3	5	23	5	29	4	15	2	15
Total:	19	26	111	210	89	290	37	154	18	107

Source: U.S. Secret Service, *Description and Information of Criminals, 1863–1906*, Record Group 87, 40 vols. National Archives, Washington, D.C.

[a] Connecticut, Maine, Massachusetts, New Hampshire, Rhode Island, and Vermont.

[b] Delaware, Maryland, New Jersey, New York, Pennsylvania, and West Virginia.

[c] Illinois, Indiana, Iowa, Michigan, Minnesota, Missouri, Ohio, and Wisconsin.

[d] Arkansas, Florida, Georgia, Kentucky, Louisiana, Mississippi, North Carolina, South Carolina, Tennessee, Texas, and Virginia.

[e] California, Colorado, Kansas, Montana, Nebraska, North Dakota, Oregon, South Dakota, Washington, and Wyoming.

[f] N = arrests for counterfeit notes; and C = arrests for counterfeit coins.

Kentucky, Tennessee, and the Carolinas. Their investigation occupied the summer and fall of 1873, culminating in a sweep that snared seventy-two dealers and shovers in October and another twenty in December.[39]

Counterfeiters tried various stratagems to deflect the impact of this assault on their marketing system. Unaccustomed to the idea of a nationally coordinated attack on their businesses, and thoroughly immersed in the corrupt culture of police-criminal relations, they expected the situation to improve once the Service's detectives had established the right to share in their profits. In the meantime they sought short-term solutions to their immediate problems.

Some counterfeiters who had lost their note suppliers tried to find new sources in the manufacturing centers. However, some producers and distributors, trying to cope with the Service's disruptions, temporarily suspended operations until they could determine whom they could trust. Others, assuming that they were experiencing localized difficulties, contacted their distant associates about the prospects of working elsewhere. A few retired, such as an anonymous counterfeiter who sent Whitley his plates with a note saying that "the sender, seeing that his confederates were little by little all arrested by officers of the Division, gives up the plate—having resolved to quit the business forever."[40]

Criminals were not alone in noticing the disruptions caused by the Service. In June 1867 a merchant who had been in business along the Erie Canal for twenty years told Operative John Beverly that he had never known a period until recently when "it [counterfeit notes] was not offered [to] him every day."[41] Other operatives reported similar shortages of counterfeits throughout the marketing system.[42]

These successes demonstrated that, despite its managerial problems prior to Washburn's tenure, the Service was capable of seriously damaging the market structure for counterfeits. The damage, however, had not necessarily been fatal, because Wood and Whitley had used faulty tactics to execute their strategies. Although they had seized a great deal of equipment and numerous plates, they had also partially fulfilled counterfeiters' expectations that once the Service had established its bargaining powers business would return to normal. By hiring so many counterfeiters, for example, Wood had made it difficult to prosecute them for their crimes. He had also relied on traditional assumptions about exchanging information for freedom, which had created a strong impression that Service operatives were indistinguishable from other detectives. Despite some changes, Whitley essentially had perpetuated Wood's approach to negotiations, allowing too many cooperative counterfeiters to go free to continue their businesses. Harry Cole, for example, had informed on Joshua Minor to gain his freedom; and Cole had obtained a pardon for his past crimes in order to become a credible witness against Minor. Cole subsequently moved to Philadelphia and promptly returned to counterfeiting.[43]

Cole's behavior illustrated the fundamental flaw in the Service's strategy prior to 1875. If there had been a finite number of permanent manufacturers and dealers, the policy of allowing the lesser participants in a counterfeiting ring to exchange information for freedom would probably have been fairly successful. Counterfeiters, however, were not organized into a permanent hierarchy. With few exceptions, individuals typically played different roles in different schemes; as circumstances changed, a retailer might become a wholesaler or even a manufacturer. By allowing so many counterfeiters to go free, Wood and Whitley had failed to cope with this flexibility and diluted the effects of the Service's assault on the manufacturing and distribution system.

Once Washburn corrected its managerial and operational deficiencies, the Service was capable for the first time of making a concerted attack on counterfeiters. Centralized controls and the no-compromise doctrine were crucial to the new approach. Using coordinated measures that undermined counterfeiting's profitability and doomed its participants to conviction, the Service systematically dismantled the national counterfeit market.

Andrew Drummond's relations with and investigations of Harry Cole illustrate the difficulties that the operatives confronted in apprehending counterfeiters. After moving to Philadelphia in 1871, Cole came to the Service's attention four years later, when he ordered $50,000 in counterfeit fives from Tom Congdon, a New York City manufacturer. This deal collapsed when the division seized Congdon's mill. Cole suffered a dual disaster from this seizure. First, he lost the profits that his consignment of notes would have earned. Equally important, Cole no longer had direct access to a manufacturer, which threatened his ability to continue doing business. Then, as if to underscore his plight, the New York police arrested Cole early in 1876 and lodged him in the Tombs.[44]

Apparently deciding that he could solve all his problems by turning to the Service, Cole initiated a complex game in which he and his wife Effie sought to trade information for his freedom, so that he could launch his own manufacturing venture. Cole was actually innocent of the charges against him, a fact to which Drummond could testify, because he had had him in custody at the time of the alleged offense. Cole therefore needed to inveigle Drummond into helping him—which Drummond was reluctant to do, because the Service, having had so many public scandals, was wary of appearing to defend any more criminals. Cole sought to at least arouse the Service's interests by appearing to assist in its task. In February 1876 Effie Cole contacted Drummond with an offer to inform on Nathaniel Kinsey, Jr., who was making a new plate in Cincinnati. Drummond promptly contacted Chief Washburn for instructions and received permission to cultivate this new informer.[45]

Effie Cole's cooperation proved interesting and useful. She not only provided details on Kinsey but also volunteered information about Joe Gordon's plans to steal some of the government's specially made fiber paper for bank notes from the manufacturer. She also gave Drummond the news that Tom Congdon, awaiting trial and trying to recover from the seizure of his mill, wanted to buy some of Gordon's supply. Washburn, impressed by her assistance, agreed to her request that Drummond testify in Cole's defense.[46]

With Drummond's help, Cole won an acquittal and returned to Philadelphia, where he joined his wife in cooperating with Drummond. At this point the Service seemed to have simultaneously gained two valuable informers and ended their active counterfeiting careers.[47] The Coles' cooperation, however, took an abrupt turn in the late summer of 1876. In July Effie Cole told Drummond that Charles Ulrich, one of the era's premier counterfeit engravers, had just been released from an Ohio prison and planned to work on a plate for Joe Gordon. This possible lead intrigued Washburn sufficiently that when Harry Cole offered to travel to Cincinnati to talk to Ulrich, he authorized the trip.[48] Cole returned with little useful information and, more important, stopped cooperating.

Later events revealed that Cole had in fact convinced Ulrich to come to Philadelphia to work on several plates for a manufacturing scheme that he had concocted with printer Jacob Ott. Ulrich evaded the Service's surveillance and arrived in Philadelphia in November 1876. He engraved two plates, one for a fifty-dollar note and the other for a five-dollar note. Cole in the meantime managed to buy a press and supplies without attracting Drummond's attention. The conspirators established their mill in the house of a relative of Effie Cole. During the spring and summer of 1877 they printed two versions of fifties, altering the bank name on the original plate to double its usefulness. They also printed a large issue from Ulrich's other note plate, which became known as the Tamaqua Five—one of the most notoriously successful counterfeit notes of the late nineteenth century.[49]

Suspicious of Cole's behavior after the abortive Cincinnati trip, Drummond sought information on this new venture. He tried without success to uncover Cole's plans until the spring of 1877, when an informer finally gave him reason to place Cole's house under continuous surveillance. Cole, however, proved extremely adept at evading Drummond's assistants. In June Drummond thought he had located Cole's mill but lacked sufficient proof. Before Drummond could gather further evidence, Cole had finished printing and had moved the mill. While Drummond struggled to find the new location, Ulrich reworked his five-dollar note plate and finished another plate for a new fifty. Ott printed these issues during the winter, and the trio dismantled their plant in March 1878.[50] Cole had succeeded in producing five large counterfeit issues, despite Drummond's best efforts to discover his operations. This was a major embarrassment to the Service at a time when it was still struggling to correct its various problems.

Although badly outmaneuvered, Drummond had accumulated substantial knowledge about Cole's counterfeiting group. He decided to maintain his surveillance and await developments. Late in the summer of 1878 his persistence began to produce results. His assistants, who had grown more skilled through practice, tracked Cole and Ulrich's movements closely. When Ulrich left Philadelphia in August, they secured the cooperation of Operative Henry Curtis in New York to track him to Scotch Plains, New York.[51] Deducing from his behavior that Ulrich was once again at work on plates and perhaps counting on his isolation from Cole to shield the Service's countermeasures, Chief Brooks ordered his arrest. Ulrich, who had a reputation for betraying his friends, promptly agreed to turn informer. Under close observation from Operative Curtis, he resumed work on the plates and waited for Cole to visit. When Cole finally arrived up in late December, Curtis had two assistants hiding in a closet and listening to the counterfeiters' conversation about the progress on the plates and Cole's plans for a new mill.[52] Armed with this information, Drummond concentrated on locating the stationers and print-supply dealers who had sold materials to Cole in Philadelphia. He also managed to identify all of Cole's suppliers for his first mill, putting together an enormous amount of evidence to prove Cole's continuous involvement in counterfeiting. Such evidence would be used in Cole's trial in order to influence the judge to impose a severe sentence.[53]

With all the evidence in hand, Chief Brooks ordered the arrest of Ulrich, Cole, and Ott in January 1879. This time there were no mistakes. Ulrich made a deal that typified the Service's new policy regarding informers who were participants in counterfeiting organizations. He agreed to be a witness against Cole and Ott, and to plead guilty to his own role in their scheme. In exchange he received a suspended sentence, which did not amount to a license to continue criminal activities. If in the future the Service arrested Ulrich for counterfeiting, his suspended sentence would be added to whatever new sentence he might receive. Ulrich understood his situation quite well; he never again engaged in counterfeiting except to act as an informer for the Service.[54]

Cole also pleaded guilty, but with different results. He received a twelve-year sentence. Ott attempted to defend himself in a trial, but the evidence was too overwhelming. He was convicted and sentenced to ten years. Neither Cole nor Ott ever again participated in counterfeiting. Cole died in prison in 1885; Ott served his time and disappeared from the Service's records.[55]

This successful campaign to end Cole's counterfeiting career was not atypical. Indeed, during the late 1870s the Service reaped the benefits of its new policy of centralized control of operatives' activities. Under Washburn's stern guidance, the Service launched its first effective and systematic plan to suppress counterfeiting throughout the national market. Between 1875 and 1879, operatives arrested such major counterfeiters as Peter McCartney, Miles Ogle, Benjamin Boyd, Nelson Driggs, Frederick Biebusch, Irvine White, and Tom Congdon.[56]

Previously, arrests of important criminals such as McCartney, Ogle, and Driggs had hurt the national market only temporarily. Although counterfeiters had lost equipment and, frequently, valuable plates, the traditional practice of exchanging freedom for information permitted them to return quickly to their careers and rapidly revive the manufacturing and marketing system. The new arrests, however, permanently damaged that system from New York City to St. Louis, causing it to lose its resilience.

Damage to the counterfeit manufacturing and marketing system derived first from the long prison sentences (typically eight to fifteen years) that the major counterfeiters received. Such lengthy enforced absences created major disruptions in their careers. Counterfeiters' inability to earn an income from crime while in prison made it unlikely that they would have the resources to start over. More important, the incarceration of major counterfeiters deprived the criminal subculture of individuals whose experience and resources would have transmitted the knowledge of counterfeiting to the next generation of criminals.

Arrest and incarceration were not the only tools the Service used to dismantle the counterfeiters' market. The logistics of the market's distribution system and its pricing mechanisms created other opportunities as well. Before manufacturers finished an issue, they arranged for its sale by contacting wholesalers who would assume control of its distribution. The wholesalers then began recruiting potential customers, using personal contacts and the mail to create their sales network. Information about a new issue began circulating in the counterfeiters' networks before its actual appearance.

Secrecy was vital to price while a new issue was being readied for the market. In order to maximize their profits, everyone involved in its manufacture and distribution had to avoid allowing any information about the new issue to reach the public. New notes sold for higher prices, because the lack of public awareness made them much easier to pass; as soon as a new counterfeit's existence became widely known, dealers had to lower their prices to compensate their customers for the increased risk. If the risk was too great, customers might refuse to purchase the new notes, thereby bankrupting the dealers.

Inefficiencies in the distribution system also created a potential threat to profits. A new note did not appear simultaneously throughout the market. Instead, it usually "broke," or debuted, first where it had been produced and then gradually spread to other areas as the dealers either traveled to different regions or used mailed orders.

Using its ability to coordinate information, the Service took advantage of the counterfeiters' distribution routines and need for secrecy to undermine their businesses. Operatives relied on voluntary informers, who regularly reported rumors about new issues, in order to initiate the procedures for a counterattack. When a rumor was substantiated, the local operative kept the chief informed of developments while simultaneously working with his source to infiltrate the new network. Ideally, the operative sought to identify all the participants and arrest them before they could complete their scheme. If, however, a note had entered the distribution network, the chief acted to limit the damage by disrupting the smooth functioning of the market. He achieved that by sending a description of the new note to all his operatives throughout the country, ordering them to spread news of its existence. To publicize a new note, each operative asked local police commanders to give their patrol officers a description of it with instructions to show it to all the business owners on their beats. Then the operative requested that the newspapers publish descriptions as a warning to the general public. In effect, the Service used community resources to enhance the capacity and effectiveness of federal intervention in the underworld.[57]

Where a new note first appeared was unimportant, because the Service made its existence known throughout the nation. This centrally coordinated publicity campaign dramatically enhanced the counterfeiters' risks and threatened their profits. Harry Cole's network suffered considerably from these tactics. Several dealers who had made large profits from the Tamaqua Five (which had managed to break before the Service had sufficient information to use this strategy) invested heavily in Cole's Hanover Five. Prompt publicity about the Hanovers bankrupted many of those dealers, because their customers refused to buy them.[58]

In the meantime, the operatives' superior access to information gave them opportunities to seize large quantities of new notes when they first appeared in their districts. Knowing that a note consignment was on its way, operatives usually had several days to prepare for its arrival. They alerted their informers, some of whom had managed to become members of the network that was expecting to distribute the note locally.

Phil Hargraves, for example, bought a large amount of counterfeits from a Philadelphia manufacturer in 1879. Operative Andrew Drummond knew that the boodle was on its way, and had identified Billy Cluff as Hargraves's boodle carrier before the shipment had arrived in New York. Drummond kept Cluff under close surveillance and arrested him with most of the notes in his possession.[59]

Although Drummond was unable to prove Hargraves's connection to the captured notes, he had in effect seized his assets, depriving him of any profits. That was almost as effective as having arrested Hargraves, whose losses in this disaster were so great that he never again had the resources to buy notes. Like so many other counterfeiters, Hargraves apparently had retained too little investment capital to deal with such a contingency. Trying to recoup, Hargraves switched to dealing in counterfeit coin. One of Drummond's informers, however, became Hargraves's new boodle carrier in his coining network, and within a year Drummond had Hargraves under arrest.[60]

The Service's efforts to develop a centrally coordinated attack became fruitful by the 1880s, when the counterfeiters' national market began to unravel. Hargraves's switch to coins was symptomatic of its disintegration. Counterfeiters had always engaged in coining, but only as a secondary activity. Technical problems made fake coins unsuitable to the market's demands. Faulty dies, usually made from plaster of paris, frequently broke, and coiners could not escape the laborious process of hand-finishing each coin. These production problems severely limited both the quantity and the profitability of coins available for distribution. Despite these problems, counterfeiters decided that they had no alternative other than coining, if they intended to continue earning income from counterfeiting.

Following the Service's successes in the late 1870s, note production and distribution dramatically declined. In New York, the national market's most important center for manufacturing and wholesaling, counterfeit notes practically disappeared until the end of the 1880s. National arrest data revealing the same pattern prompted cautiously optimistic assessments within the Service that counterfeiting had entered a long-term decline (see Table 5.3).[61]

The Service's optimism was not ill-founded. Switching to coin production represented a general admission among counterfeiters that participating in the national market now involved too much risk. By forcing this shift, the Service affected the evolution of this crime, because coining's low cost encouraged decentralization and fragmentation of the market. Intercity networks, which had existed for decades, would atrophy from disuse. With their networks degenerat-

TABLE 5.3

Arrests by Secret Service and Local Police in New York City, 1865–1899

	1865–71	1876–79	1880–84	1885–89	1890–94	1894–99
Shoving						
Secret Service	55	16	43	49	40	69
New York City Police	26	58	36	84	99	129
Dealing						
Secret Service	50	12	5	14	8	51
New York City Police	3	1	0	2	0	0
Manufacturing						
Secret Service	55	10	15	32	23	53
New York City Police	3	4	5	7	4	21

Sources: Register of Monthly Reports, 1864–1871, and Daily Reports of Agents, 1875–1899, in U.S. Secret Service, Record Group 87, National Archives, Washington, D.C.

ing, counterfeiters would lose the knowledge and the skills that they needed to maintain them. The next generation of counterfeiters would then find their opportunities circumscribed through the loss of the means to conduct business outside their immediate neighborhoods. Even New York's Bowery, once the center of national counterfeiting, fell into desuetude. Two of Operative William Hazen's assistants toured the Bowery in early 1898 without finding a single suspect, which was an astonishing result given the previous importance of the area.[62]

If the counterfeiters hoped that their switch to coining would ease the problems they had with the Service, they were sadly mistaken. Seeking to profit from sales to the now more localized and smaller distribution networks for counterfeit coins that still functioned on the same principles as those for note distribution, coin counterfeiters remained vulnerable to the same surveillance and infiltration tactics that had plagued note counterfeiters. For example, Hargraves's efforts to become a wholesale coin dealer were deterred when he sold his product to one of Drummond's informers and then welcomed the informer into his organization as a boodle carrier.

When Hargraves obligingly introduced this individual to his customers, Drummond had no trouble in rounding up all the principals.

Note production did revive in the 1890s, but in ways which indicated that the national market had shriveled to a pale shadow of its former self. Italian counterfeiters posed an important problem to the Service because their overseas production firms were secure from interference, and because their ethnicity gave them access to a burgeoning intercity immigrant community. But their near monopoly on the note business—at least in New York—simplified the Service's task, by permitting operatives to concentrate their efforts. During the 1890s the Service had little difficulty in infiltrating Italian counterfeiting rings with informers and making a significant number of arrests. Italian criminals, therefore, proved no more effective in maintaining the national market than other counterfeiters had been.[63]

There were other, non-Italian counterfeiters, however, attempting to work with notes. Secret Service circulars announcing newly discovered issues, as well as an increase in arrests for note-related cases during the late 1890s, demonstrate that some criminals continued to seek profits from counterfeiting.[64] Technology had democratized production to the detriment of the national market. Photographic equipment became widely available in the late nineteenth century, encouraging several criminals to attempt counterfeiting independent of a national network. Note production and sales became a local affair, with firms appearing randomly in such cities as New York; Chicago; New Orleans; Dallas; Sandusky, Ohio; Evansville, Indiana; Neosho, Missouri; and Seattle.[65]

This new generation of manufacturers, however, did not pose as great a threat as their predecessors had. The quality of their products was abysmally low. Of 153 counterfeit issues produced between 1898 and 1910, the Service judged only 43 to be sufficiently crafted to create a problem for the public.[66] Furthermore, the number of different counterfeit notes they produced compared unfavorably to that of their predecessors. An 1865 survey of counterfeits had found nearly 4,000 different issues in circulation.[67] The new generation of counterfeiters failed to match that level of productivity, which raised questions about their ability to supply a national market. Finally, few of these firms' products managed to achieve wide distribution. According to one operative, more notes continued to be made in New York than anywhere else; however, so few of these notes were distributed west of the Alleghenies that rural counterfeiters had begun coining to compensate for the collapse of the national market.[68]

The Secret Service had thus succeeded in making counterfeiting a furtive and risky business. By the 1890s the Service had also developed a reputation within the underworld as an organization that was dangerous to provoke. A customer offered a counterfeit five by a New York saloon keeper in 1896 refused, on the grounds that "he would not have that on him for any money, as it was worth fifteen years in prison to be found with that in his possession." Other thieves expressed similar reservations about arousing the Service's interest.[69]

Changes in confidence games provide some collateral evidence that counterfeiting was in serious, perhaps even fatal, disarray toward the end of the nineteenth century. The green-goods game had been a staple for counterfeiters for decades, providing a rough indicator of a continuing demand for counterfeit money. By the 1890s, however, the offers to sell counterfeit notes now contained extremely contrived descriptions of the products' ability to elude detection.[70] Such elaborate statements were indicative of the underlying insecurities of customers, who perhaps needed a great deal of reassurance that there would be no risks in their contemplated crime. These reassurances were apparently insufficient. The green-goods game abruptly disappeared by the end of the century, indicating that criminals no longer regarded this ploy as worth their effort. It also may be that after nearly four decades of swindling their customers, the green-goods criminals had reached the limits of public credulity. A concerted campaign against green-goods operators by the Postal Inspectors may also have discouraged these criminals.

The Service had progressed substantially from its problematic origins. To achieve its mission, it had become a law enforcement agency in which both formal procedures and actual behavior successfully regulated the crucial interaction between criminal informers and detectives. By the 1890s counterfeiting had ceased to be a criminal enterprise organized to meet the demands of a national market. Although criminals did not entirely abandon it, the counterfeiting business had become a faint shadow of its former self.

The Service had accomplished its mission despite severe restrictions in financing and staffing. Congress's authority over its budget had not proven to be any more constraining than the efforts of the solicitors to preserve cooperative federalism in law enforcement. Tension between competing political commitments in Congress had provided yet another opportunity for the Service to tilt the balance of policing power in its favor. While it had undoubtedly shared the public's general reaction against the state-building trends of the Civil War, Congress had also assumed new commitments to the economy —especially to federal sovereignty over the currency—which it had no desire to rescind. Influenced by these competing commitments, Congress had sided with the prevailing sentiment in favor of localism while refusing to renounce its determination to protect the currency. As penurious as it had been, Congress had never failed to provide an appropriation for the Service.

Scarce monetary resources had affected management and operational tasks within the Service but had not undermined its mandate. The Service's strategists had devised solutions to the challenge of suppressing counterfeiting that had fundamentally increased federal authority across the nation, demonstrating that neither huge budgets nor large staffs were critical to the expansion of federal authority.

CRIMINALS AT BAY

Counterfeiters in the
Federal Courts

WHILE ARRESTING COUNTERFEITERS created many dilem-
mas for the Secret Service, convicting them in a federal court provided yet another set of challenges. The Service's operatives had to
overcome a number of obstacles before they could incarcerate their
adversaries. The structure of the federal court system, the attitudes
and behavior of its participants, and the nature of the trials all posed
serious problems that operatives had to solve in order to achieve their
objective.

National and local interests often conflicted in the original federal court system. This system included the Supreme Court, circuit
courts, and district courts and defined the national interest in specific
civil and criminal matters. Local residents, however, served as
judges, prosecutors, U.S. marshals, and—perhaps most critically—
as jurors in the district courts in which the Service would bring its
cases against counterfeiters. This situation initially proved to be a
major obstacle to the successful prosecution of those criminals, because local rather than national norms shaped the conduct of federal
trials for counterfeiting. Although this arrangement conformed to
the theory and the practice of federalism, the traditional antipathy
toward centralized government frequently thwarted the national interest in punishing counterfeiters. Unsympathetic to the concept of a

national law enforcement agency, local residents' natural insistence on applying local values to counterfeiting cases impeded the Service's efforts to create uniform national standards for prosecuting offenders.

Communities' experiences with paper money and counterfeiters prior to the 1860s complicated the Service's task. They became exposed to both the idea of a national currency and the need to protect its integrity only after the Civil War. Most Americans were familiar with the dubious history of state bank notes, and probably distrusted them. Too many unreliable banks had issued notes, and numerous counterfeiters had emitted their own copies without suffering unduly for their crimes. Local residents, particularly those sitting on juries, needed to be schooled to the notion that the vigilant prosecution of these criminals could preserve the integrity of a national currency. The Service's operatives were the only available teachers, and the courtroom was the only arena in which they had the opportunity to offer instruction to the general public.[1]

The actual conduct of trials posed the ultimate challenge to the Service's goal of suppressing counterfeiters. A trial was not merely a test of the evidence against an accused counterfeiter, nor was it simply a contest between a criminal and the state. It was instead more akin to a game in which contending interests engaged in complex interactions to achieve their own ends.

This game had four players and two umpires. The players included a Secret Service operative, an accused counterfeiter, an assistant federal district attorney, and a defense attorney. Judges and juries acted as umpires who decided different parts of the trial game. Each of the players naturally sought to influence the umpires with their repertoire of techniques. Few of those techniques relied on strictly legal formalities in the years immediately following the Civil War. Instead, the players employed informal conventions, which had governed the dynamics of trials for decades before the Service began operations.

In 1865 the Secret Service was the newest player in this game. Despite its neophyte status the Service eventually compiled an impressive record of successes, because its operatives learned how to manipulate the judicial system in order to convict counterfeiters. In effect, they altered the rules of the game. They did not, however, institute their own personal rules. Rather, they supplanted the traditional conventions of trials with a more legalistic standard of conduct. That standard, which intruded into local communities to impose greater uniformity on the criminal justice system, represented the Service's version of centralized state power.

The Service's operatives dealt with obstacles to convicting counterfeiters at each stage of the judicial process. The first important issue they encountered involved channeling all counterfeiting cases into the federal judicial system. Prior to 1865, when local police officers occasionally arrested counterfeiters, the state courts had usually handled these cases. The Service, however, wanted to avoid those courts without losing the assistance of the local police.

Money solved this problem. The solicitor of the Treasury worked hard to assure local police that they would be rewarded for arresting counterfeiters and turning the cases over to the Service.[2] After the Service's reorganization in 1874 it regularly paid police officers (and informers) for their help for the remainder of the century. Enticed by these promises, the police eagerly became auxiliaries to the Service.[3] In effect, the Service purchased the acquiescence of the police in order to expand federal authority into their domain, and thereby gained control over the prosecution of counterfeiting. This arrangement permitted the Service to direct nearly all counterfeiting cases into the federal judicial system.

Money, however, could not solve the next problem the Service encountered: How should the operatives guide their cases through the commissioners' courts? As the first stage in the federal judicial process, the commissioners' courts offered both the prosecution and the defense opportunities to achieve their separate agendas. Serving in lieu of federal justices of the peace, a commissioner held a hearing to determine whether the evidence justified presenting a case to a grand jury, and whether it required bail from the defendant to assure his or her future appearance in court.[4] At this stage the government sought to present sufficient evidence to convince the commissioner to rule in its favor on both issues, but not enough to forewarn the defense. The defense, on the other hand, could move for a dismissal on grounds of insufficient evidence or argue for a low bail if the commissioner ruled to hold the case for a grand jury.

An analysis of the Service's national arrest records reveals that defendants had approximately a one-in-three chance of their case being dismissed in commissioners' courts. Their chances, however, varied according to the nature of the charge and its source. In New York City defendants had nearly a one-in-two chance of a dismissal if the police had arrested them, but only a one-in-five chance if the Service had brought them before the court.[5] The dramatic differences in dismissal rates at the local level probably derives from the kinds of arrests involved. Local police officers typically arrested only shovers. The law stipulated that the prosecution had to demonstrate the defendants' guilty knowledge and intent to pass a counterfeit note, and the police frequently hindered the prosecution's case by failing to collect sufficient evidence to satisfy the law. Operative Frederick Tapley commented on this problem in 1867, remarking that cases he received from the Rochester, New York, police were "very incomplete and little is known of them."[6] Further complicating matters, innocent citizens who had acquired counterfeit notes or coins in change did not recognize them as such, and would, for example, offer them to a store clerk who did. Flimsy evidence usually made it impossible to distinguish between a professional shover and an innocent victim, and commissioners tended to resolve the doubt in favor of the defendant in such cases.[7]

Service operatives did arrest shovers, but they also built cases against the less visible members of the counterfeiting circle—the manufacturers and the wholesalers. Their evidence, which tended to be much more substantial and meticulously assembled than that of the police, created a prima facie case that neither defense lawyers nor commissioners could easily ignore. The strength of the evidence was not, however, a guarantee that a commissioner would rule in the Service's favor. In one New York case early in the Service's campaign against counterfeiters, the commissioner discharged the accused on the grounds that his confession had been "extorted from him under fear" and that the evidence, including a printing press and a number of engraved plates for making counterfeit notes, was insufficient.[8] Despite such occasional odd rulings, the Service's considerably lower dismissal rates at the local level indicate that its operatives were presenting their cases in a more convincing and professional manner than had been customary prior to 1865.

Winning on the evidence meant that an operative had achieved only half a victory at this point in the judicial process. The operative next had to convince the prosecutor and the commissioner to ignore local customs in setting bail. Low bail—typically $500 or $1,000—

had become a tradition in counterfeiting cases by the 1860s, and posed no problem to professional criminals. Since so many counterfeiters had legitimate careers as small business owners, they could easily raise the necessary amount from their legitimate business associates, who perhaps would express indignation at the government's accusations against their colleague. Sometimes a counterfeiter did not want to jeopardize his or her legitimate relationships. The counterfeiter then arranged "straw bail," a situation in which a false bondsman was contracted to swear to possessing sufficient property to pay the bond in case of forfeit, and the counterfeiter would subsequently fail to appear in court. This ploy was often successful, because the commissioners' courts did not have the resources (or perhaps the time or the inclination) to check the backgrounds of bondsmen. When the court ordered the bail bond executed for nonappearance, there would be no property to seize, because none had been listed, or the property listed did not belong to the bondsman.

The Service's campaign to undermine these customs developed in an ad hoc manner but gradually became a systematic effort to make high bail a norm in counterfeiting cases and to eliminate the straw bail problem. At first, individual agents fought the practice of straw bail. Operative Abner B. Newcomb, for example, insisted in an 1866 New York case that a defendant's bail should be backed by real estate deeds. Failing to meet that criterion, the defendant went to jail.[9] The patchwork nature of the locally run federal judiciary, however, made this approach difficult to enforce uniformly. In that same year Operative Charles Benedict could not convince the New Orleans commissioner to set high bails. Counterfeiters in New Orleans were able to "pay and get out of the way."[10]

A major raid that netted thirty-eight important counterfeiters in upstate New York early in 1867 prompted a new tactic—the direct intervention by William P. Wood, chief of the Secret Service. The importance of these cases, which represented months of work against a long-standing network of counterfeiters stretching from Troy, New York, to Buffalo, probably encouraged Wood to act. He pressured the commissioner to set high bails for all those arrested, arguing that the government should be "fully protected" against these defendants. That convinced the commissioner and created consternation among the defendants. Business associates who had intended to become their bondsmen balked at the high price of bail, leaving the counterfeiters stranded in jail, because they lacked sufficient resources to pay their own bail.[11]

Wood's personal intervention in such an important case significantly advanced the campaign against low bails, though the problem continued. Chief Hiram C. Whitley continued Wood's success by enlisting the solicitor's assistance in this campaign. At Whitley's insistence, Solicitor Edward C. Banfield wrote to the district attorney in Cleveland to demand high bails for counterfeiters. Whitley soon saw changes in bail arrangements there and urged the same treatment for Cincinnati.[12]

In the meantime, the Service also attacked straw bail. Whitley used intimidation to deal with this issue. He rounded up a number of "bogus bondsmen" and frightened them out of business.[13] Most operatives, however, took the more plodding but probably more effective approach to straw bail. They laboriously investigated the assertions of potential bondsmen in their affidavits. When they found discrepancies, the operatives took their information to the district attorneys for prosecution. Although the number of such incidents was small, the fact that the Service took such pains probably had the intended effect.[14]

By the 1870s, the Service's campaign began to change the customs of the bail system. After 1875 operatives rarely complained about the amount of bail required, and the typical sum was now between $3,000 and $5,000 (or higher in major cases).[15] Straw bail was no longer problem, although the occasional case demonstrated that operatives monitored this problem closely. In effect, the Service had managed to replace local customs pertaining to bail with behavior that reflected its own criteria. The Service had thus isolated counterfeiters from their sources of comfort and support in the initial phase of the federal judicial process.

Victory in the commissioners' courts did not ensure that the Service would triumph in a subsequent trial. The long road to conviction involved many byways, which proved to be even more complex and challenging to the Service than were the shorter pathways through the commissioners' courts. Contemplating their prospects in a trial, counterfeiters deployed an array of strategies and tactics that potentially transformed every trial into a maze of possibilities. They had, for example, to decide whether or not to bargain with the Service, and if so, how and when in the trial process. Judges and prosecutors also contributed to the difficulties. These titular allies often raised legal issues, voiced hostility to the Service, and displayed enough incompetence in their work to make the journey through a trial a harrowing experience.

The games each participant played varied according to the circumstances of each case. In general, however, a trial had three stages: pre-trial maneuvers, the trial itself, and the sentencing period. The Service's basic strategy was to evolve uniform standards defined by centralized authority to overcome these obstacles.

Pretrial maneuvers required the Service's operatives to deal with three different players: counterfeiters, defense attorneys, and prosecutors. Judging from the ease and the alacrity with which counterfeiters initially entered into negotiations with Service operatives, bargaining with law enforcement officials had been the norm for counterfeiters prior to 1865. The Service, however, introduced an unusual dimensions to these negotiations. First, individual operatives did not have the authority to make deals on their own. Instead, they submitted a proposed deal to the chief for approval.[16] (Solicitor Jordan probably initiated such a requirement, although the record does not clearly substantiate this.) The requirement permitted a central review of a case, which allowed uniform standards for negotiating with counterfeiters. It also avoided one of the most important sources of corruption in local law enforcement: unsupervised detectives making private arrangements with professional thieves. Given the character of many operatives during Wood's reign as chief, these arrangements did not eliminate all opportunities for corruption. As the quality of the Service's personnel improved under Wood's successors, however, corruption essentially disappeared from its ranks.[17] The Service's newly instituted commitment to regulate negotiations with criminals clearly distinguished its practices from those of local police agencies.

This insistence on achieving bureaucratic goals radically altered the context of bargaining sessions. Prior to 1865 the basic deal involved the counterfeiter exchanging equipment for freedom. Over the next ten years the Service only occasionally followed that custom, because the chiefs gradually insisted on many more concessions in these discussions.[18] By the beginning of Elmer Washburn's tenure in 1874, the Service demanded not just all the equipment but also all the notes, the names of associates within the network, and at least a guilty plea if not some sort of sentence. In effect, while insisting that the counterfeiter abandon his livelihood and accept some punishment for his criminal behavior, the Service offered only clemency in exchange.[19]

Finding these terms unattractive, some counterfeiters sought different outcomes to the bargaining process. During and after the 1870s they turned their negotiations with the Service operatives over to their defense attorneys, who became mediators between the two antagonists. This arrangement permitted the counterfeiter to consider his or her options more carefully, instead of trying to deal with an operative personally under stressful circumstances in which he or she might make mistakes. Negotiations became more measured. Counterfeiters offered little at the outset and more later, only if their situation warranted it.

The tactics of Bill Brockway, one of the premier counterfeiters of his era, illustrate the seesaw nature of these negotiations. Brockway had a typically weak position from which to bargain, because he had some outstanding charges against him when Drummond arrested him in November 1880. As his opening gambit, Brockway sent his lawyer, William Guild, to Drummond with an offer to surrender a number of plates and some of the bonds he had recently made—as well as all the $100 notes, whose manufacture had occasioned his most recent arrest. In exchange, Brockway wanted a promise that the Service would not insist on prosecuting him for past offenses.

Drummond countered by asserting that Chief James Brooks wanted Brockway in prison and demanded additional plates besides those Brockway was offering. The prosecuting attorney, who also participated in these talks, proposed to Guild that Brockway plead guilty to the current charges in exchange for a suspended sentence. This unusual move was probably dictated by Brockway's age; he was sixty-four, and none of the negotiators anticipated that he could continue his counterfeiting career. Drummond recommended that Brooks accept this arrangement, but three days later Brooks countered with a demand for more plates. Brockway considered this for a week. Then, with his lawyer present, he met Drummond for a final round of negotiations. After protesting that he did not have any more plates, Brockway finally admitted to possessing the plates for the $100 note, and he agreed to provide information against his associates in the manufacture of that note. Brockway appeared in court three days later to enter his plea and to receive a suspended sentence.[20]

Although suspended sentences were not the typical outcome of such negotiations, guilty pleas were common. They indicated that the Service was a tough and relatively successful opponent in these bargaining sessions—especially in cases that it had initiated, although guilty pleas were also common in cases that the Service inherited from the police. In both instances, the percentage of cases settled by negotiation greatly exceeded the norm in the late nineteenth century, and may have contributed to the more rapid diffusion of this tactic within the criminal justice system. (The Service's successes may have prompted local prosecutors to imitate their tactics, although there is no direct proof of this.)[21]

The high rate of guilty pleas may not have been due only to the Service's hard-nosed approach to these bargaining sessions. As professional criminals, counterfeiters regarded imprisonment as an occupational hazard; and if they did try to plea bargain, they probably entered negotiations with some expectation of serving time, once they learned that the Service did not adhere to the norms of local policing.

While relatively common, plea bargaining was not the typical outcome of the contest between counterfeiters and the Service. Such negotiations were voluntary and based on each side's estimate of its relative strengths and weaknesses. The operative in charge of a case often would refuse to plea bargain. The reasons for this refusal varied. Occasionally a defense attorney simply made a ridiculous offer. An attorney named Post, for example, approached Drummond with the proposition that he would not argue to quash an indictment against his two clients on a technicality, if Drummond would agree to hold them in jail until the end of the court's term and then discharge them on good behavior. Retorting that "it was no part of my duty to provide immunity to any criminals," Drummond rejected this proposal.[22] The attorney in another case suggested that his client would inform on his partner in crime, if Drummond would agree to draw up a deliberately flawed indictment. Since Drummond had a particularly strong case against this counterfeiter, he dismissed this ploy.[23] In yet another case the prosecutor asked Drummond's consent to a conventional offer to plead guilty in exchange for a suspended sentence. Drummond successfully objected to this offer on the grounds that the accused counterfeiter was a hardened criminal who did not deserve clemency.[24]

A common theme—the determination to punish where the evidence was strong—runs through all such cases in which operatives refused to deal. This appears to have been both a moral and a bureaucratic imperative for operatives. Beginning with Chief Whitley, they tended increasingly to reflect conventional middle-class attitudes toward criminals. The Service's organizational objectives, stressing severe sentences and resolutely opposing clemency, also demonstrated those attitudes.[25]

It is, therefore, not surprising that so many counterfeiters rejected plea bargaining to take their chances in trials. They did not necessarily make this decision out of fear of dealing with the Service. They believed that they had a number of important advantages in the trial game that offered them better prospects.

Initially, criminals' estimate that they would fare better with a trial was fairly accurate. In a trial the Service had to deal simultaneously with all the players and umpires, whose perspectives, objectives, and tactics differed from those of the Service. Accommodating some of those differences while opposing others, the trial game increased the possibilities for errors that might allow an accused counterfeiter to escape altogether.

Judges, for example, often discarded their official neutrality to interject their own opinions into trial proceedings. During Chief Wood's reign this problem was common. Part of the difficulty that the Service encountered in dealing with judges derived from Wood's occasionally outrageous behavior. In 1867, for example, Wood sat at the defense table during one of Bill Brockway's early trials and actively assisted Brockway's lawyers, which provoked Judge C. L. Benedict to denounce the Service in the courtroom. Benedict was not mollified by Brockway's testimony that Wood had put him on the government payroll, nor by Wood's confirmation that he had hired Brockway with full knowledge of his offenses. Instead, he was incensed by the spectacle of a government officer publicly lending aid and comfort to a criminal. He thus refused to honor the bargain that Wood had struck with Brockway and sentenced the counterfeiter to fifteen years.[26]

Such episodes did not improve the Service's public image during its formative stage, and badly damaged its relations with judges who were already suspicious of its detective methods. Wood's habit of hiring criminals to work cases and to testify against their former associates only generated more distrust. Further complicating matters, judges found the practice of buying counterfeit money in order to establish guilt and to assemble evidence extremely problematic.

Operative Frederick Tapley encountered both problems with his cases during 1866 in Rochester, New York, and in Philadelphia. In both cities the judges intervened because of their objections to buys and the hiring of criminals. In the Rochester case the judge told the prosecutor that the evidence made it appear that the government "was putting up jobs, to induce men into crime and then convict them." Although the judge was certain of the defendants' guilt, he advised the prosecutor not to call a key witness who had bought counterfeit notes from the defendants to testify against them. In the Philadelphia case the presiding judge charged the jury not to convict a defendant because the government's principal witness was not reliable. Although the jury disregarded the judge's directions and voted for a conviction, the Service abandoned several other cases in which the same witness would have had to testify.[27]

Judicial hostility could even force the Service to cease work in a particular locality. A New Orleans judge's attacks on government witnesses in 1871 so disrupted the Service's cases that Chief Whitley discontinued operations there.[28]

The time-consuming nature of counterfeiting investigations often provoked judicial displeasure. The Service did not like to make arrests as cases solidified against particular individuals in a counterfeiting network, since doing so would alert others to their danger. Instead, operatives waited until they had gathered all the evidence they needed against everyone involved and then conducted simultaneous arrests. Evidence, however, was marked and dated as it came in. During a trial, therefore, the Service had to submit evidence in these cases that was sometimes relatively old. Stale evidence could irritate a judge, prompting him to suggest to the jury that long intervals between obtaining evidence and prosecuting a defendant implied that the government's case was fundamentally unsound.[29] Neutralizing this source of trouble became a major objective for the Service, especially since these judges had lifetime appointments and would probably preside over the Service's cases for decades. New York Judge Benedict, for example, served as district judge from the 1860s until the mid-1890s.

Unfortunately, there is little information to trace the development of rapprochement between the Service and the judges. Operative Henry Curtis's experience, however, provides some insight into the process. Proudly reporting the first time that Judge Benedict consulted with him about the sentencing of convicted counterfeiters,

he recollected that when he had first taken charge of the New York
District in 1876 he had

> found the Court before whom all our cases must come for trial strong-
> ly prejudiced against the Service[.] so much so that the first charge I
> heard him make[,] he virtually instructed the Jury not to believe the
> Secret Service officers unless they were corroborated by undisputed
> facts.

Considerably disturbed by this situation, Curtis worked for two
years to

> remove this prejudice which had been formed only because of the con-
> duct of the officers themselves in bringing suspicious cases into court,
> and testifying in such a manner as to impress the Judge with the be-
> lief that their evidence was wholly or partially manufactured.[30]

Curtis's analysis indicates that the judges' jaundiced views of the Service stemmed from their perceptions of the reliability of both individual operatives and their evidence. For example, the same Judge
Benedict who had given Curtis two years of grief told Andrew Drummond in 1875 that "he would be pleased to have any and all members
of the Secret Service come to him at any time and give any information that would throw light on any case that was being tried or where
a plea of guilty had been made."[31] Apparently judges learned to trust
some operatives more than others. (Interestingly, Curtis resigned in
1878, and Drummond replaced him.)

The Service operatives' relations with judges and their ability to
influence them varied with the particular individuals involved. Such
disparities did not provide a sound basis for the Service to meet its
institutional goals. Seeking a more coherent approach to this problem, the various chiefs turned to bureaucratic regulations in order to
create uniform techniques, which would strengthen the reliability of
the operatives and their evidence. Wood began the process with his
1868 *Circular of Instructions*. His regulations prohibited a great deal
of sloppy and often egregious behavior, and required operatives to
maintain a log of all counterfeiting materials they seized. Whitley reiterated these general admonitions and requirements in his 1873 instruction booklet.[32] Perhaps because neither Wood nor Whitley had
devised an effective way to monitor their operatives' behavior in the

field, the operatives had only occasional success in dealing with judges.[33]

With the beginning of Elmer Washburn's tenure as chief in late 1874, the Service's bureaucratic controls over its operatives tightened considerably. Washburn introduced much stricter requirements for handling evidence and required daily reports of his operatives' activities.[34] Finding these stricter regulations still insufficient, Washburn in 1876 finally issued an order that required a legal standard of his operatives' reports. Washburn stated that

> After the receipt of the Order, Operatives will write their reports in such language and form of expression, that they can verify their truthfulness by affidavit at any time they may be called upon to do so.[35]

By insisting that his operatives' field notes conform to legal standards of evidence, Washburn apparently turned the tide of judicial opinion in the Service's favor. Shortly thereafter judges began praising the Service as "absolutely necessary to the community."[36] By the late 1880s John Brooks could remark that "the reports made by our Assistants and self are accepted without question by our District Attorneys and Judges."[37]

This shift in attitude helped to establish the Service's legitimacy as both a federal agency and protector of local interests in a sound currency. Judges at times made this connection quite directly. Describing the Service as an "important and necessary institution,"[38] they instructed juries that "no matter how zealously and thoroughly the Government officers performed their duties, if they are not upheld by juries the currency of the country can never be protected."[39] On such occasions, citizens in the courtroom were schooled in the value of federal authority in their daily lives.

Friendlier relations also provided more practical dividends. Judges welcomed information on the careers and personal character of counterfeiters, and used that data to gauge the severity of the sentences they imposed.[40] Providing this information to judges materially assisted the Service in securing severe sentences for major counterfeiters, which in turn enhanced its reputation for effectiveness amongst its adversaries.

Even as the Service gradually eliminated the judges' hostility, it still lost some good cases through the ineptitude of prosecutors. Their failings usually derived from two related problems. First, the Service had to rely on the least experienced and the worst paid in the prosecutor's office—assistant district attorneys. Regardless of their intelligence and good will, these individuals were political appointees who had little interest in making a career of prosecuting counterfeiters.[41] It was therefore difficult to create and to maintain the long-term relationships with these prosecutors that were possible with judges.

Assistant district attorneys' inexperience led to the second problem: they had to learn the process of successfully prosecuting criminals and, inevitably made mistakes. Faulty indictments were one source of irritation. At various times judges in Philadelphia, Pittsburgh, and New York City, for example, issued directed verdicts of acquittal because of this problem, or refused to allow prosecutors to introduce evidence for charges not specified.[42] Other more common problems ranged from the failure to present all the evidence in a case, to inept handling of witnesses (especially those for the defense), and to inadequate closing statements to juries.[43]

Operatives employed a variety of solutions to these problems. First, they sought to forestall problems by frequent consultations with prosecutors prior to a trial. Operatives explained the background of a case, reviewed the evidence, asked for opinions on points of law (which may have been a subtle way of educating new prosecutors about the criminal justice process), and worked to secure more evidence where needed. They also monitored every trial, listening to the defense's arguments, to the judge's rulings, and to the prosecutor's presentation. As the trial developed, they often volunteered to return to the witness stand to refute claims by the defense. In summary, operatives made every effort to participate actively in the presentation of their cases in the courtroom, hoping that their close cooperation would help to avoid losing cases.[44]

When this approach failed, the operatives sought other solutions. Anticipating a not-guilty verdict, they often secured new warrants against the defendants and rearrested them as they left the courtroom.[45] Operatives also complained frequently about the performance of prosecutors, both to the chief of the Service and to the district attorneys. In an extreme example of this tactic, Drummond first complained bitterly to his superior that a particular assistant district attorney had lost eleven of thirteen cases that he had given him over a period of fourteen months. He talked with the district attorney, who admitted that this individual was particularly careless but refused to transfer Drummond's cases to someone else, because that "would be an insult and an injury to him." Such tender concern for feelings astonished Drummond, who retorted that he would refuse to give this prosecutor anymore business. Within a day Drummond received word that a new prosecutor would be assigned to his cases.[46]

Although not typical, Drummond's behavior illustrates the seriousness with which the Service's operatives sought to achieve the conviction of counterfeiters. Rather than assume that their jobs ended with an arrest, operatives insisted on creating a role for themselves in an arena officially reserved to the officers of the federal courts. Seeking to influence both judges and prosecutors, they were determined to secure every possible advantage in court over counterfeiters. That earnestness may have derived from the operatives' concern about the wiles of their adversaries, who also sought to manipulate the court system, deploying a variety of stratagems to avoid conviction. Some of these relied on trial customs and public attitudes; others depended on counterfeiters' ability to draw on the special resources of the urban underworld.

Defense attorneys worked within a legal system that bore many similarities to modern court practices, but with one significant difference. Evidence that had been illegally seized was still admissible in court. The most authoritative contemporary work on the subject, Simon Greenleaf's *A Treatise on the Law of Evidence*, stated categorically that

> though papers and other subjects of evidence may have been *illegally taken* from the possession of the party against whom they are offered, or otherwise unlawfully obtained, there is no valid objection to their admissibility if they are pertinent to the issue. The court will not take notice of how they were obtained.[47]

In 1886 the U.S. Supreme Court modified this rule slightly, holding that the government could not seize a defendant's private papers to use against him in a trial. The Court, however, also held that this decision did not apply to evidence in which a defendant had no property right, and specifically mentioned counterfeit money as an example.[48]

In these circumstances the Service's operatives' inability to obtain search warrants on their own was more relevant as a matter of bureaucratic integrity than a serious impediment to their work. Secure in the knowledge that the courts would accept it, operatives often illegally seized evidence against counterfeiters. They usually obtained this evidence in three ways. Operatives or their assistants frequently purchased counterfeit money from underworld wholesalers or retailers, carefully marking the buys with the date of purchase and the initials of the purchaser.[49] Since making buys required that the operative or his agent represent himself as a criminal, it did not conform to the ordinary norms for collecting evidence through a legal process. Subterfuge also prevailed in the second technique: Having located a counterfeiter's plant, an operative could arrange to have the police raid the place on some pretext, such as a search for a burglary suspect. The operative would join the raid, and while the police kept the counterfeiter occupied, the operative would search for and confiscate all the evidence that could be found.[50] Finally, operatives often conducted searches with or without a suspect's permission, ransacking a house or apartment and seizing personal effects with impunity.[51]

Regardless of how operatives had obtained their evidence, it was all admissible in court. This made it difficult for defense attorneys to overcome often overwhelming evidence of guilt. Their solution was to ignore the evidence. Instead of arguing the facts of the case, they relied on oratory and character assassination, both of which were rooted in courtroom customs, to sway juries.

Prior to the Civil War, when the public valued trials for their entertainment value, skillful oratory had been one of a lawyer's most important techniques. Edwin Stanton, for example, had a formidable reputation for winning difficult cases in which his client's guilt was obvious.[52] John M. Broomall, a prominent member of the bar in Chester County, Pennsylvania, enjoyed a long and prosperous career as a defense lawyer in criminal cases. He based his courtroom strategy on "shrewd appeals to emotion and . . . ruthless assaults upon the credibility of prosecution witnesses."[53]

Since the lawyers who defended counterfeiters had been reared in this tradition, it inevitably shaped their tactics in the years after 1865. They sought to undermine the credibility of the prosecution by attacking the character of its witnesses and by impugning the integrity of the Service.

Attacking the Service was relatively easy in the first decade of its existence. Not only did Chief Wood hire unsavory characters with criminal records, but he also paid them rewards for securing convictions of counterfeiters. That practice lasted only one year but incurred great damage to the Service's reputation.[54] For years afterward, according to Chief Whitley, defense attorneys cross-examining Service operatives and assistants sought "to show if possible that their pay is contingent upon the conviction of the accused."[55] Gradually, as the Service repeatedly presented evidence refuting this belief in numerous trials, defense lawyers resorted to this tactic less often. They did not, however, abandon it entirely.[56]

As generalized attacks on the Service's integrity became less useful, defense attorneys refined their standard tactics by focusing on minutiae to undermine a witness's character and testimony. Robert N. Waite, for example, tried to discredit one witness by proposing to prove that a lamppost did not stand where the witness had said it did.[57] That ploy did not work; however, A. H. Purdy, a master of this approach, and whose tactics made him a nemesis to the Service, had better luck. During the trial of James Holden, who had been arrested for shoving, Purdy asked the witness, Thomas McGovern, if he had played 176 games of pool in a saloon and had then left without paying. McGovern denied the accusation. When Purdy began his arguments for the defense, he called a saloon keeper named Smith who testified that McGovern had indeed played without paying. The prosecutor rose to object, providing Purdy with an opportunity to deliver a "long and forcible argument" against the objection. In the course of this ramble Purdy cleverly trapped the prosecutor and scored with the jury by commenting that

> he never before saw a Dist. Attorney trying to conceal from himself
> and the Court the villainy of a trusted Government [*sic*] officer[;] that
> if the man was a bad man he supposed the Dist. Attorney would like
> to know it so as the man's employers could get rid of him.

The judge sustained the prosecutor's objection. The prosecutor, however, was new at this game, and he failed to cross-examine Smith on the weak point in his testimony. Smith had sworn that McGovern had managed to play 176 games in four hours, which was physically impossible. Purdy's ploy therefore succeeded. Left with the impression that McGovern was unreliable, the jury acquitted the defendant.[58]

Having discovered the strategy of using minutiae to attack the government's case, some lawyers began experimenting with more elaborate versions. Rensselear Abrams, for example, hired two defense attorneys who called only one witness. Upon the conclusion of that testimony, they asked the judge for a directed verdict, on that grounds that the government had presented no evidence that a trade dollar (which Abrams was accused of counterfeiting) was a U.S. coin. They further argued that there was no evidence that trade dollars had ever been struck in the U.S. Mint, or that Congress had authorized their coinage, or that the coins found in Abrams's house had been finished.

Obviously unprepared by prior experience for such technical challenges, the prosecution requested time to prepare a rebuttal. When the trial continued, the prosecution presented a witness who swore to having received a trade dollar from the Mint. The defense promptly objected that this witness had not actually seen the coin struck. Despite that interesting objection, the judge allowed the testimony, and the government eventually won the case.

Although the government prevailed, the defense's strategy clearly surprised the assistant district attorney and the Service. Drummond commented that "there were many curious law points raised and ruled upon in the case [and] many that were quite novel."[59] His surprise suggests that the mid-1880s may have marked a turning point in defense strategies. By 1883 Drummond had had a dozen years of experience with defense tactics, and had his own counterattacks ready; yet he had to scramble to beat the defense's unprecedented maneuvers in this trial.

Highly technical defenses did not become the norm after this case, if for no other reason than that it would take time to test their efficacy. Lawyers would also need to take advantage of the better legal training that was becoming available before they could employ this strategy effectively. Nevertheless, some lawyers clearly paid attention to this approach and began to employ it sporadically.[60] In doing so, they may have begun to abandon their traditional reliance on appeals to emotions and character assassinations for much more rigorously legalistic strategies.

The Service's increasingly effective relations with judges and prosecutors, as well as the care with which operatives prepared evidence, helped to nudge defense attorneys in this new direction. Defense attorneys had to find methods to counter the Service's efforts, and a shift to technical issues at least had the virtue of novelty, which has always been a useful weapon in the courtroom.

Underworld customs for coping with trials also underwent changes. These customs varied from one jurisdiction to another and were shaped by the opportunities unique to each locality. In the first decade of the Service's operations key personnel in Philadelphia and in upstate New York's federal courts, for example, were more hostile to the Service and more corrupt than were their counterparts in New York City. Securing convictions was more difficult in such jurisdictions, which also offered criminals more opportunities to supplement their lawyer's stratagems with their own tactics.

Corrupt relations with the police and the courts permitted counterfeiters to concoct innovative solutions to their problems with the Service. Relying on the assistance of their associates in law enforcement and the judiciary system, counterfeiters sometimes sought to discredit accusations against them by having operatives arrested on false charges. John Simms, a major counterfeiter in Syracuse, New York, employed this tactic against operative Edwin Bruce in 1867. Simms had two friends file affidavits charging Bruce with counterfeiting. U.S. Commissioner Ruger, who was serving as associate defense counsel for Simms, then issued an arrest warrant for Bruce. In Philadelphia accused counterfeiter Henry Stewart had a city detective frame the chief witness against him, who happened to be an assistant to operative Stephen Franklin.[61] These maneuvers, however, did not always succeed. In Simms's case, Operative Frederick Tapley learned of the plans against Bruce and hauled Simms's two friends before a U.S. commissioner who was friendly to the Service. When they failed to identify Bruce in court, the commissioner confiscated their "evidence." News of this turn of events prompted Commissioner Ruger to withdrew from the defense. Simms hastily offered to plea bargain, but Tapley refused, intending instead to make an example of Simms and to vindicate the Service. He succeeded. The jury convicted Simms, and the judge sentenced him to ten years in prison and fined him $4,000.[62]

Despite the possibility of defeat, counterfeiters believed that the trial game was still worth playing. For example, in 1867 several Service operatives assisted Chief Wood in an investigation of thefts at the Navy Yard, where their inquiries resulted in the arrest of Phil

Stanley and some of his friends. Stanley retaliated on 3 July 1867 by filing a complaint against all the Service operatives, including Wood, for kidnapping. Stanley's timing was exquisite. Judge Benedict had just denounced the Service from the bench for Wood's participation in the defense of Bill Brockway.[63] Local distrust of the Service arising from that gaffe made Stanley's complaint plausible. The state court on Long Island entangled Wood and his operatives in a long legal battle that lasted for two years. Although the court eventually dismissed Stanley's charges, this case probably adversely affected the Service's reputation in New York.[64] It may also have contributed to Wood's dismissal as chief in May 1869; he was still then under indictment, which may have been embarrassing to the new secretary of the Treasury in the first Grant administration.

The counterfeiters' ability to entangle Service operatives in legal battles by involving their corrupt friends within the criminal justice system disappeared by the mid-1870s. Improvements in the Service's personnel, better relations with the local police, and changes in the Service's procedures may have combined to eliminate this particular threat.

Counterfeiters, however, still had other options. They could, for example, purchase the cooperation of witnesses. Storekeepers who had received counterfeit notes would sometimes have more interest in recovering their monetary losses than in punishing the shover. After having been paid off, these witnesses refused to appear in court.[65] Other witnesses, such as informers, might accept bribes not to appear.[66] If they declined a bribe, the counterfeiter's friends might resort to threats of physical violence. Such threats were rare and were hardly ever carried out, but they nonetheless represented a potentially useful tactic.[67] Finally, counterfeiters could hire witnesses who would attest to their sterling characters, creating an instant reputation for the defendant.[68] Jurors, unfamiliar with the defendant, might vote for acquittal on the basis of such testimony.

The Service fought defendants' attempts to tamper with witnesses. Operatives checked the backgrounds of defense witnesses and gathered evidence to refute their testimony. Witnesses who appeared in court to swear to falsehoods usually provoked the Service into charging them with perjury.[69] Such a retaliation undermined an important underworld custom of assisting one's associates. When there had been little risk in this practice, criminals could use perjured testimony to create obligations that they could exploit in the future.

The Service's watchfulness, however, increased the risks of incurring financial burdens and prison time for performing this favor.

If witnesses could not be fixed, a jury might be. Joe Gordon, one of Philadelphia's wiliest and most successful counterfeiters, used this tactic to fight conviction through the whole of 1877. In his first trial Gordon and his friends managed to bribe nine jurors to vote for his acquittal; in his second trial, Gordon bribed three jurors. According to his own accounting, which he relayed to Operative Drummond, these bribes had cost Gordon $4,000. Tried yet a third time in the fall, Gordon suborned four more jurors, forcing the government to postpone the trial until the next year.[70]

Bribing federal jurors was not common. The possibility of doing so, however, created yet another problem for the Service. When a particular jury seemed unsympathetic to its interests, the Service sought to manipulate the selection of jurors and to reschedule cases. Operatives consulted with prosecutors about jury lists and investigated the backgrounds of individuals whom they deemed unsatisfactory. Generally, the Service sought to impanel juries dominated by a community's "best citizens"—particularly business owners—on the assumption that they understood the need to protect the currency and would have little sympathy for criminals.[71] When a jury became uncooperative, or when the Service was not ready with its case, operatives asked prosecutors to postpone trials or to dismiss a jury and impanel a new one.[72]

These measures were not foolproof. The Service sometimes lost trials in which everything seemed favorable for a conviction, because juries occasionally proved to be impervious to the evidence when the defendant—not necessarily by design—struck a sympathetic chord. The Service lost cases for such varied reasons as a defendant's youth, health problems, and ignorance.[73]

Despite such defeats, the Service generally won the trial game. Its record far exceeded those of the local police. In New York, from 1875 to 1899 21 percent of cases brought to trial based on the evidence of the police ended with convictions; the figure was 40 percent for the Service.[74] Thus, the Service not only undermined many of the counterfeiters' defensive tactics, but also influenced juries to become more willing to convict in cases brought by the Service. The Service's record indicates that jurors had accepted an expanded federal policing presence in their local communities.

The Service's success resulted primarily from its refusal to adhere to the traditions that had governed police relations with the courts for decades. The police took no active role in defending the integrity of the trial system; their job ended with the arrest of a suspect. Rejecting that limited role, the Service's operatives actively participated in the trial process. They carved out an informal but nonetheless vital and effective place for themselves in guarding the integrity of the courts against the equally informal, illegal ploys of the counterfeiters.

Having successfully shepherded so many of their cases through trials, the Service displayed an equal tenacity in protecting their victories in the final arena—sentencing. Following conviction the counterfeiters' last hopes lay in a light sentence or a pardon. The Service consistently sought to dash such prospects. The Service operatives' initial lack of sufficient access to judges had prevented them from influencing the sentencing procedure. Operatives had to build judicial confidence in their agency and in themselves, and their behavior during Wood's reign had often complicated that task. Nevertheless, some progress did occur.

Judges seemed particularly interested in learning whether a convicted counterfeiter had a prior record, and tended to give more severe sentences when they knew of a criminal's past transgressions. The Service desired severe sentences for counterfeiters, because light sentences would not impress professional criminals. Since there was no central national record system of criminals' arrests and convictions, judges often had to accept the defense attorneys' and defendants' word about previous behavior.

Seeking to fill the information void, Service operatives volunteered to provide judges with certified records of prior convictions. Collecting such data could be time-consuming, especially in the Service's early years when it had no records. The fact that many counterfeiters had convictions in several jurisdictions further complicated matters. Chief Wood had expressed little interest in the sort of bureaucratic minutiae required for creating a national data base, and had failed to establish any procedures for centralizing information on arrests and convictions. His operatives had to rely on their personal knowledge of the past records of counterfeiters, which meant they could only occasionally provide the information judges needed for sentencing.[75]

Whitley had improved record keeping considerably by requiring extensive descriptions and photographs of persons arrested, as well as a full account of the outcome of each stage in the judicial process.[76] When Washburn succeeded Whitley in 1874, he refined these procedures by introducing standardized forms for entering data into a single record series.[77] By the mid-1870s the Service had adopted administrative procedures for record keeping that created the rudiments of a national information system.

The development of this record system at a time of improving relations with judges proved a boon to the Service. Operatives after 1875 routinely consulted judges during the sentencing phase, and their information (and probably their advice) frequently influenced the judges to impose longer sentences.[78] The relationship between judges and operatives often threatened to become a bit too cozy. Brooklyn Judge Thomas in 1899 told operative William Hazen that he had been surprised to discover that a counterfeiter sentenced to five years did not actually serve the entire five years. Hazen explained that state laws governing commutation time applied to federal prisoners as well. Judge Thomas subsequently increased his sentences to compensate for commutation time.[79]

While working to increase the length of sentences judges imposed on counterfeiters, the Service also sought to close the last door to early freedom—pardons. At the outset of this period, pardons were relatively common.[80] Counterfeiters easily abused the system, forging signatures and calling on their political friends for help to secure pardons.[81] With some exceptions, primarily during Wood's reign as chief, the Service consistently opposed leniency in any pardon cases that it encountered.[82] By the mid-1880s, if not earlier, the Service had made its opposition to pardons a matter of "resolute persistency."[83] Unfortunately, there are no data available to measure how effective this opposition was. The Service, however, played a consultative role in the process for granting pardons, which gave it at least an opportunity to influence the decision.

That opportunity brought the Service into tangential contact with local politics, since applications for pardons originated in a counterfeiter's own community. Criminals seeking pardons collected (or forged) the signatures of community notables and forwarded their applications through appropriate channels to the president. By becoming part of the review process, the Service gradually affected the relationships between criminals and their communities. Criminals with connections to local politicians or legitimate business owners found that these connections carried no weight with the Service. In this situation, the requirements of the state took precedence over traditional local assumptions about the ability to manipulate federal clemency.

Although a new player in the trial game in 1865, the Service managed to create an impressive record of successes against its adversaries. Like the counterfeiters, the Service sought to influence trials by developing relationships with key players whose decisions could affect the outcome. Unlike the counterfeiters, however, the Service achieved that influence by changing the rules of the game, forcing all the players to confront the evidence of the case. Winning the trial game was an important part of the Service's mission to protect the nation's currency by extending federal power into local communities. Counterfeiters would not have been impressed by a national policing effort that merely replicated their experiences with local law enforcement. Their encounters with the Service in the trial game, however, differed qualitatively and quantitatively from those with their local police. Conviction was more probable, and punishment was more severe.

The results of the trial game indicate that the Service made an equally important impression on the umpires in the federal court system. Over time both judges and juries showed increasing respect for and trust in the Service's activities. By overcoming the initial hostility toward them, the Service's operatives not only justified the expansion of federal policing power but also made it seem reasonable and desirable.

CRIME
AND POWER

ARMED WITH THEIR republican sensitivity to the dangers of centralization, Americans had created a political system in the first half of the nineteenth century that severely circumscribed the uses of federal power. Eschewing coercion to enforce its prerogatives, the federal government eagerly used its limited authority to enhance the nation's commitment to personal opportunity. Individual citizens regarded the federal government as a benevolent uncle who promoted territorial acquisitions, rapid western settlement, internal improvements, and the relocation of Native Americans. As a minimalist power, it served individual, group, and regional interests but not its own.

The trauma of the Civil War ruptured the antebellum era's entrenched customs regarding the uses of centralized power. It did not, however, obliterate the memory of those customs or uproot the political system that had nurtured them. When the most public and controversial experiments in state building foundered in the morass of Reconstruction and economic mismanagement during the depression of the 1870s, most Americans readjusted to the comfortable system in which courts and political parties governed the nation through cooperative federalism.

This return to "normalcy," however, concealed a fundamental shift in the uses of federal power in the United States. No matter how quickly Americans sought to reestablish the federal government's antebellum role as the benevolent uncle, the government had irrevocably expanded its regulatory and coercive authority by asserting its power over the currency.

Prior to the Civil War, in one of the most extraordinary displays of indifference to the concept of a nation-state's sovereignty, the political culture of courts and parties had allowed the business community to usurp the federal government's constitutional monopoly over the nation's currency. With Jackson's veto of the charter of the Second Bank of the United States, state banks had assumed control over the money supply, with chaotic results. Notes circulated in a confusing system of discounts and premiums that created innumerable obstacles to rational economic growth. This situation severely restricted the ability of notes to serve as an acceptable medium of exchange, and thereby undermined an essential function of money.

Furthermore, the sheer number of banks and the diversity of their notes created extraordinary opportunities for counterfeiters. In the absence of effective law enforcement, counterfeiters developed highly successful production and distribution networks that enabled them to take advantage of the inadequacies of the nation's chaotic currency. The proliferation of counterfeits eviscerated public trust in paper money. People cynically adopted a "beggar thy neighbor" attitude, knowingly passing counterfeits as long as others would take them. Whoever failed to find another sucker in this game simply lost money from their own ineptitude.

The lack of a uniform currency, therefore, both victimized many ordinary citizens and impeded national economic development. Politicians who deplored these consequences had no opportunity to remedy the situation until the Civil War, which created a national emergency that justified extraordinary measures. It is clear that supporters of federal control of the currency intended far more than a temporary assertion of federal power. Indeed, they believed that a uniform currency would link individual self-interest to the central government, thereby strengthening a citizen's loyalty to the nation. Surveying currency problems since the nation's foundation, Sen. John Sherman argued during debate over the National Banking Act of 1863 that: "If we are dependent on the United States for a currency and a medium of exchange, we shall have a broader and more generous nationality."[1]

An enhanced sense of nationalism would not necessarily have translated into increased federal power. In some important ways, individuals such as Sherman were merely legislating their version of the federal government as benevolent uncle. Although their success in establishing a uniform currency did make a significant contribution to the rapid evolution of the nation's industrial economy in the late nineteenth century, Congress's assertion of federal sovereignty over the currency during the war created new possibilities for an expansion of centralized power that proponents of this idea had not foreseen.

A declaration of sovereignty is equivalent to an assertion of an absolute right to regulate and to coerce. Congress tended to emphasize the first power but to ignore the second. In doing so it created a major opportunity for incremental state building that contradicted the prevailing political culture's devotion to cooperative federalism.

The National Banking Act of 1863 established standards that banks were required to meet in order to participate in the new currency system. These regulations tended to favor the larger, better capitalized banks in the nation's major cities. From the outset, then, Congress linked its sovereign control of the currency to the fortunes of urban banking. This connection reinforced a steady trend toward closer federal ties to cities during the nineteenth century, and did not in itself represent a major shift in cooperative federalism.

When Congress assumed control of the currency, it also inherited the major crime problem of counterfeiting, a flourishing criminal enterprise that had not yielded to the feeble ministrations of either federal marshals or city police departments. Furthermore, the ineffectiveness of law enforcement efforts against counterfeiters was common knowledge. If allowed to continue their depredations, these criminals would seriously undermine public trust in the new currency system. They in effect presented a direct threat to federal sovereignty over the currency.

Having no expertise to deal with this problem, Congress entrusted the Treasury Department with the task of forcing counterfeiters to abandon their activities. In creating the Secret Service, the Treasury spawned a new law enforcement agency whose activities undermined assumptions about the distribution of power within the federal system. The Service greatly enhanced the policing capacity of the central government by projecting its power into the uncharted underworlds of America's cities. It projected that power in a fundamentally unprecedented manner, because it was the only policing agency operating in the cities that sought to apply uniform standards of detection and prosecution to a national crime problem. The Treasury did not follow the customary nineteenth-century approach to federalism, which merely sought to balance competing powers in order to ensure that centralized authority did not dominate the entire system. In attacking counterfeiting, the Service brooked no rivalry from neither the local police or the federal marshals. Local customs yielded to the demands for obedience to the sovereignty of the nation-state.

Urban criminals suffered the most from this undiluted application of state power. Their social networks and work habits had evolved over more than a century into a subculture that was safely ensconced in the supportive environment of the nation's largest cities. Mutually convenient arrangements with the local police simply reinforced their ability to enjoy long and profitable careers in which counterfeiting represented one of many important opportunities. Although the Service did not transform this underworld, it did make counterfeiting an unprofitable venture in that environment. For the first time in their history criminals encountered a police force that did not follow traditional rules. Misperceiving what they faced, counterfeiters failed to devise effective countermeasures.[2] By the 1890s criminals had learned that the risk of arrest and imprisonment for counterfeiting was too high to be worth their trouble. They did not necessarily cease their simultaneous pursuit of legal and illegal sources of income, but they diverted their attention to less risky ventures.

Counterfeiting did not, of course, disappear entirely. A few people continued to try their luck. Some small business owners with the proper equipment occasionally printed notes; coiners were relatively more numerous and more likely to live in the marginal subculture of working-class ethnic neighborhoods. Their collective efforts only served to accentuate the Service's accomplishments in dismantling the previous elaborate structure of counterfeiting. With the disappearance of the knowledge and the experience that had sustained its national marketing system, counterfeiting was reduced to operating on a purely local scale.

Furthermore, even the previously secure neighborhoods that had provided a base of operations for so many counterfeiters were no longer as safe as they had once been. Over time the citizens in these communities, in what amounted to a cultural adaptation to the exercise of national power,[3] displayed an increasing propensity to report counterfeiters to the Service. This trend appeared sporadically in the late 1870s, when an occasional individual who had received a counterfeit note or coin came to the Service's office to complain.[4] The number of these complaints increased steadily until the 1890s, when they became almost a weekly occurrence. Although shopkeepers made some of these complaints, most of them came from ordinary neighborhood residents.[5]

There were probably several reasons for this trend. With the disintegration of counterfeiting as a broadly organized activity, counterfeiters no longer had access to potential markets outside their own neighborhoods. They therefore increasingly victimized their neighbors. Considering the marginal nature of many working-class incomes, these residents could least afford to absorb the loss involved in receiving a counterfeit. Some of these victims might attempt to avoid such losses by passing the counterfeit to someone else. That was not a particularly attractive option, because it made the victim who tried to shove a counterfeit susceptible to arrest. Although possessing or shoving a single coin or note was usually insufficient evidence of criminal intent to secure a conviction, working-class people could rarely afford the loss of time and money involved in an arrest and trial.[6]

Citizen complaints to the Service indicated that residents of working-class neighborhoods gradually discovered that they had an alternative to absorbing their loss or risking arrest: They could get their money back. Those who complained found the Service willing to act as mediator in the recovery of their loss.[7] By the late 1880s operatives typically sent the complainants back to the person from whom they had received the counterfeit with instructions to ask for a good coin or note. If that person (who was often a shopkeeper) refused this request, he or she was asked to come to the Service's office for a talk, or he or she was visited by an operative. Operative John Brooks reported in a typical case that "I told him [a saloon keeper] the consequences of any more complaints coming to us from his saloon from parties getting cft. [sic] money."[8] Considering the bluntness of the message, it is not surprising that victims generally recovered their money.

The Service's mediation efforts linked individual self-interest in the recovery of a loss to the federal government's exercise of coercive state power. Senator Sherman's prediction that a uniform currency would make "every stockholder, every mechanic, every laborer who holds one of these [national bank] notes . . . interested in the Government" had become a reality—although perhaps not in the way he had intended.[9] To victims of counterfeiting, the Service's capacity to coerce had become the guarantor of the value of their money.

Coercion and adaptation also played a prominent role in expanding the federal government's ability to police the business community. Businesspeople had long been accustomed to using "flash notes," imitations of coins and notes, as a form of advertising. Flash notes came in many forms, including tokens, coupons, and private script. They were widely used and popular, because their pictorial representation of currency expressed an offer in easily understandable terms. Congress, however, banned this form of advertising in 1867, giving the Service yet another opportunity to coerce compliance to a national standard of behavior.

The Service did not seriously address this problem until James Brooks became chief in 1876; shortly thereafter, he initiated a coordinated campaign to suppress flash notes entirely. His operatives visited various businesses that used the notes to inform them that they were violating a federal law. Most businesspeople were astonished by the news and quickly acceded to the division's demand that they not only cease publishing flash notes, but that they also surrender all dies, molds, plates, and supplies immediately. Those few who had resisted later regretted doing so, because operatives issued warrants for their arrest.[10]

By 1884 Brooks reported that flash notes had become far less of a problem for the Service. His campaign had not simply reduced the use of these notes but had also established the Service as an arbiter of advertising for urban businesspeople. As news of the crackdown spread by word-of-mouth and through various business journals, anxious businesspeople sought approval of their advertising ideas from the operatives and the chief of the Service. The responses they received made it quite clear that the Service had a low tolerance for any proposal that even faintly resembled the national currency.[11]

In fact, this campaign uncovered the deadly serious, even humorless attitude the Service took toward protecting the currency. Andrew Drummond launched an investigation of toy money in August 1881, which occupied much of his time for several months. Having obtained the names of toy-money manufacturers from a Manhattan toy dealer, he personally visited each company and confiscated all their supplies and equipment. Drummond also had the district attorney write to other manufacturers, who promptly surrendered all their supplies. In November 1881 this campaign climaxed when R. H. Macy solemnly surrendered 160 boxes of toy money to Drummond for destruction.[12]

Drummond's campaign was not an aberration. Other operatives were constantly looking for violations, no matter how slight. John Brooks seized a painting of a U.S. note that he found hanging in a saloon in 1891; years later, William Hazen, on the advice of the chief, informed a confectionery store that its plan to make molds for chocolate candy in the shape of a dollar coin was illegal.[13] From the Service's perspective, these were not trivial cases; rather, they demonstrated how dedicated the operatives had become to the proposition that, in Drummond's words, "the Securities and Coins of all countries should be held sacred, that people, especially manufacturers, should not seek to transform them into curiosities."[14]

The Service's campaign against counterfeiting thus had important ramifications beyond the modification of criminal behavior. Crime in effect became a tool for broadening federal power in unexpected ways. Diverse groups—criminals, ordinary citizens, and businesspeople—experienced the Service's coercive power in different ways. Criminals learned to fear its punitive character; victims of counterfeiters benefited from its redemptive power; businesspeople adapted to its regulatory strictures.

Congress's assertion of sovereignty over the currency thus created a framework for expanding the coercive power of the federal government, which was employed by means that gained the eventual support of a public still suspicious of centralized power. The initially hostile reaction to the Service, which was well founded given the behavior of the first operatives under Wood and Whitley, dissipated as the division implemented measures to control both the personal conduct and the investigative procedures of its employees. While not necessarily perfect by modern standards, those measures were exemplary for their time and earned the respect of both judges and juries.

In the 1890s the Service used its respect to create a public image as a valuable, indeed essential, federal agency. It began to court publicity in a systematic way for the first time. The chiefs controlled the campaign, while individual operatives continued to maintain the vow of secrecy. William Hazen, whose background as a Cincinnati police detective may have made him an influential player in the decision to launch this campaign, initiated the practice of granting interviews to the press in 1894. He used the occasion of the Service's annual report, which had never been disseminated as a separate document to the public, as an excuse to offer a general discussion of the problem of counterfeiting and the Service's activities in suppressing it. [15]

The press's response to this innovation was apparently sufficiently satisfying to Hazen that he made himself available for other, more broad-ranging interviews. Perhaps capitalizing on the press's natural curiosity in a government agency that for decades had refused to cooperate with it, Hazen provided an official interpretation of the Service's activities. News agencies, such as the United Press International and the Associated Press offered standardized news items to their subscribers, ensuring that Hazen's perspective would become the national version. In 1897 his commentary appeared without any alterations in at least ten newspapers throughout the Northeast, the Midwest, and the South. [16]

As a former journalist himself, John Wilkie probably valued this practice even more than Hazen had, and continued it after his appointment as chief in March 1898. By controlling press access to the Service's activities, Wilkie managed to turn even potentially embarrassing issues into triumphs. In one of the last great counterfeiting schemes of the century, two Philadelphia printers manufactured such a high-quality $100 note that the Treasury had to recall the entire legitimate issue. When a team of operatives tracked down the culprits, their arrest and trial became a national advertisement for and celebration of the Service, instead of a commentary on the incompetence of detectives dealing with clever criminals. The *New York Evening Sun* editorialized that "The successful pursuit of the counterfeiters reflects more credibly upon the efficiency of the Federal detective system and its agents," and that the case "directs the attention of the country to the value of the service [*sic*] and the cleverness of its men." The *Philadelphia Telegram* opined that "the professional criminal never willingly falls in the way of the Secret Service. The chase is as relentless as death, and only death or capture ends it." Furthermore, in an invidious comparison of the Service with local detectives, the *Telegram* informed its readers that "the men of the Government police seek none of the public praise which is a weakness of the municipal detective. Their business is to catch offenders against the Federal laws, and not to get their names in the papers, and they generally run their quarry to earth, which is more than can be [said] for the city policeman." Similar comments appeared in editorials throughout the nation, confirming the strong and positive public image of the Service.[17]

Such praise also impressed ordinary citizens. Wilkie began receiving letters from individuals asking for his assistance in solving cases of bank robbery, murder, kidnapping, and labor unrest. (He had to decline these requests for help on the grounds that he lacked jurisdiction.) His receipt of such pleas testifies to the widespread perception of the Service's effectiveness and the implicit recognition of its legitimacy in expanding federal power into local communities.[18]

The Service's long campaign to suppress counterfeiting culminated with the virtual elimination of this threat to the national currency and the emergence of the Service as a respected law enforcement agency. The Service's bureaucratic autonomy and its administrative capacity to extend national power into local communities evolved simultaneously within the federal system. The chiefs freed the Service from the confines of subordination to the marshals and city police, and created administrative regulations that made operatives responsible for enforcing national standards of behavior in regard to the currency. While the chiefs struggled in the bureaucratic thicket of Washington, the operatives contended with the twin problems of public suspicion and criminal inventiveness. The separate but interrelated efforts of the chiefs and the operatives ultimately coalesced by the 1890s to produce a new policing ability with applications and implications well beyond the Service's official, narrow mandate.

An expanded policing capacity thus became a crucial element in U.S. state building prior to the twentieth century. Changing definitions of appropriate or necessary exercises of national authority, which were articulated primarily by different constituencies within the Republican Party, made that expansion possible. The party's support for new federal initiatives in economic and social affairs created unprecedented possibilities for the development of a more powerful central government. In currency matters, however, counterfeiting threatened to undermine Republican policy. The fate of that policy and its implications for state building, therefore, depended upon creating the ability to impose the federal government's will on a group of urban criminals. Developing that capacity and a corresponding policy took time, but when the Secret Service's efforts finally succeeded, it became a vital example of a federal agency with the means to coerce obedience among a far wider population than simply counterfeiters.

As the development of the Secret Service demonstrates, before the era in which tremendous national emergencies such as world wars became the principal agents of centralization, changes in party policy drove state building. But the leaders of the developing bureaucracies of the incipient nation-state provided the energy and the skills that transformed policy into power.

NOTES

In the following notes, RMR refers to the United States Secret Service, Register of Monthly Reports, 1864–1871; DRA refers to the Daily Reports of Agents, 1875–1910. Both record sets are located in the United States Secret Service, Record Group 87, National Archives, Washington, D.C. References to the U.S. Secret Service, *Description and Information of Criminals, 1863–1906,* Record Group 87, 40 vols., National Archives, Washington, D.C. are cited as *Description and Information of Criminals.*

INTRODUCTION

1. Robert H. Wiebe, *The Segmented Society: An Introduction to the Meaning of America* (New York: Oxford University Press, 1975), x, 36–37. For an excellent study of a local political system based on limiting government power, see Robin L. Einhorn, *Property Rules: Political Economy in Chicago, 1833–1872* (Chicago: University of Chicago Press, 1991).

2. This is an important theme in Morton Keller, *Affairs of State: Public Life in Late Nineteenth-Century America* (Cambridge, Mass.: Harvard University Press, 1977). For commentary on the origins and development of this centralizing process, see Jon C. Teaford, *The Municipal Revolution in America: Origins of Modern Urban Government, 1650–1825* (Chicago: University of Chicago Press, 1975); Jon C. Teaford, *The Unheralded Triumph: City Government in America, 1870–1900* (Baltimore: Johns Hopkins University Press, 1984); Hendrik Hartog, *Public Property and Private Power: The*

Corporation of the City of New York in American Law, 1730–1870 (Chapel Hill: University of North Carolina Press, 1983); Terrence J. McDonald, *The Parameters of Urban Fiscal Policy: Socioeconomic Change and Political Culture in San Francisco, 1860–1906* (Berkeley: University of California Press, 1986), 278–82; and Allen Steinberg, *The Transformation of Criminal Justice: Philadelphia, 1800–1880* (Chapel Hill: University of North Carolina Press, 1989).

3. For the best general review of these developments, see Bray Hammond, *Banks and Politics in America from the Revolution to the Civil War* (Princeton, N.J.: Princeton University Press, 1957).

4. Ibid., 92–94, 107, 568–69.

5. Bray Hammond, *Sovereignty and an Empty Purse: Banks and Politics in the Civil War* (Princeton, N.J.: Princeton University Press, 1970), 24–25, 87–88, 128; Richard Bensel, *Yankee Leviathan: The Origins of Central State Authority in America, 1859–1877* (Cambridge: Cambridge University Press, 1990), 11.

6. Hammond, *Sovereignty and an Empty Purse*, 226–27.

7. Ibid., 339–40.

8. Keller, *Affairs of State*, 78–80.

9. On the political controversies, see, for example, Keller, *Affairs of State*, 191–95, 380–84; Irwin Unger, *The Greenback Era: A Social and Political History of American Finance, 1865–1879* (Princeton, N.J.: Princeton University Press, 1964); and Walter T. K. Nugent, *Money and American Society, 1865–1880* (New York: Free Press, 1968). For an excellent analysis of the structure and operations of the financial system, see Bensel, *Yankee Leviathan*, 238–302. Bensel also argues that the Treasury's administrative incompetence in the performance of its new economic role vitiated the banking community's support for any further state expansion by the late 1870s.

10. On coercion, see Charles Tilly, *Coercion, Capital, and European States, AD 990–1990* (Cambridge, Mass.: Basil Blackwell, 1990), 1–5.

11. Charles Tilly, "Western State-making and Theories of Political Transformation," in *The Formation of National States in Western Europe*, ed. Charles Tilly (Princeton, N.J.: Princeton University Press, 1975), 608–9; Stephen Skowronek, *Building a New American State: The Expansion of National Administrative Capacities, 1877–1920* (Cambridge, England: Cambridge University Press, 1982), 42.

12. The current historiography on American state building does not deal with the contributions of federal law enforcement to that process. Decisively influenced by Morton Keller's masterful analysis of postwar political development, scholars interested in the history of state building generally agree that the expansion of federal power during the Civil War was an aberration, whose influence did not survive the debacle of Reconstruction. According to

this interpretation, Americans quickly reverted to their accustomed ways, because a temporarily inflated federal government lacked the means to perpetuate the gains made during the war. Local interests once again prevailed over national concerns. The antebellum system of courts and parties reasserted its control of federal largess, once again subjugating the national government to the needs of the localities that dominated the federal system. Even when the state-building process resumed late in the century, it was largely confined—in Stephen Skowronek's phrase—to "patchwork" efforts to improve the administrative capacity of the central government. For these arguments, see Keller, *Affairs of State* and Skowronek, *Building a New American State*. Richard Bensel offers the most comprehensive attempt to refute Keller's basic contentions, but even he admits that with the end of Reconstruction, "state expansion ground to a halt—not to resume until the turn of the century." See Bensel, *Yankee Leviathan*, 367. For a rare attempt to examine the expansion of federal policing in the post–Civil War years, see Wilbur Miller, *Revenuers and Moonshiners: Enforcing Federal Liquor Law in the Mountain South, 1865–1900* (Chapel Hill: University of North Carolina Press, 1991).

13. On the role of currency in the economy, see Lester V. Chandler, *The Economics of Money and Banking* (New York: Harper and Row, 1964), 16; and Hammond, *Banks and Politics in America*, 722–23. Bensel analyzes the reasons for the relative decline of the Republicans' hopes for the currency as a state-building mechanism after the Civil War, stressing the resumption of the gold standard as an antistatist measure. See Bensel, *Yankee Leviathan*, 281–302. Greenbacks, nevertheless, remained the single largest component of the nation's money supply until the end of the century. See W. Elliot Brownlee, *Dynamics of Ascent: A History of the American Economy* (New York: Alfred A. Knopf, 1974), 204. Their importance as currency, therefore, required measures to protect their integrity.

14. On the importance of trust, see Edwin J. Wilber and Edward P. Eastman, *A Treatise on Counterfeit, Altered, and Spurious Bank Notes, with Unerring Rules for the Detection of Frauds in the Same* (Poughkeepsie, N.Y.: Edwin J. Wilber and Edward P. Eastman, 1865), 4, 7, 18; and William Greider, *Secrets of the Temple: How the Federal Reserve Runs the Country* (New York: Simon and Schuster, 1987), 53, 226.

15. Arthur C. Millspaugh, *Crime Control by the National Government* (Washington, D.C.: Brookings Institution, 1937), 62–69; and Frederick S. Calhoun, *The Lawmen: United States Marshals and Their Deputies, 1789–1989* (Washington, D.C.: Smithsonian Institution Press, 1990), 49–63.

16. For discussions of the theoretical implications of policing and state building, see Charles Tilly, "Reflections on the History of European State-making," in *Formation of National States*, ed. Tilly, 59–60; and David

Bayley, "The Police and Political Development in Europe," in *Formation of National States*, ed. Tilly, 328–79. On the connections between crime and state power, see V. A. C. Gatrell, "The Decline of Theft and Violence in Victorian and Edwardian England," in *Crime and the Law: The Social History of Crime in Europe since 1500*, ed. V. A. C. Gatrell, Bruce Lenman, and Geoffrey Parker (London: Europa Publications Ltd., 1980), 335–36.

17. Leonard D. White, *The Republican Era: A Study in Administrative History, 1869–1901* (New York: Macmillan, 1958), 54.

18. Theda Skocpol, "Bringing the State Back In: Strategies of Analysis in Current Research," in *Bringing the State Back In*, ed. Peter B. Evans, Dietrich Rueschemeyer, and Theda Skocpol (Cambridge, England: Cambridge University Press, 1985), 9, 13–14; Rhodi Jeffrey-Jones and Bruce Collins, eds., *The Growth of Federal Power in American History* (De Kalb, Ill.: Northern Illinois University Press, 1984), xiv, xviii.

19. For a theoretical discussion of this point based on European models, see Bayley, "Police and Political Development," in *Formation of National States*, ed. Tilly.

CHAPTER 1
THE SOCIAL WORLD OF COUNTERFEITING

1. Langdon W. Moore, *Langdon W. Moore: His Own Story of His Eventful Life* (Boston: Langdon W. Moore, 1893), 15, 31–32, 46–48, 67, 71–86; Confession of Charles Young, in Frederick C. Tapley, RMR, March 1866; I. C. Nettleship, RMR, April 1866.

2. George P. Burnham, *American Counterfeits: How Detected, and How Avoided* (Springfield, Mass.: W. J. Holland, 1875), 165–73; Statement of Thomas Hale, in Abner B. Newcomb, RMR, March 1866.

3. Moore, *Langdon W. Moore*, 55–56, 59; Confession of Charles Young, in Tapley, RMR, March 1866.

4. Statement of Charles L. Treat, in Charles F. Newman, RMR, December 1865.

5. Kenneth Scott, *Counterfeiting in Colonial America* (New York: Oxford University Press, 1957), 23–25, 28.

6. John L. McMullan, *The Canting Crew: London's Criminal Underworld, 1550–1700* (New Brunswick, N.J.: Rutgers University Press, 1984), 58–60.

7. Richard Bowen, *Rhode Island Colonial Money and Its Counterfeiting, 1647–1726* (Concord, N.H.: Rumford Press, 1942), 7–9.

8. Scott, *Counterfeiting in Colonial America*, 61; Kenneth Scott, *Counterfeiting in Colonial New York* (New York: American Numismatic Society, 1953), 20; Bowen, *Rhode Island Colonial Money*, 50.

9. Bowen, *Rhode Island Colonial Money*, 12, 83.

10. Scott, *Counterfeiting in Colonial America*, 10.

11. Scott, *Counterfeiting in Colonial New York*, 153–55, 168–69; John S. Dye, *The Government Blue Book: A Complete History of the Lives of All the Great Counterfeiters, Criminal Engravers, and Plate Printers* (Philadelphia: Dye's Government Counterfeit Detector, 1880), 5; Seth Wyman, *The Life and Adventures of Seth Wyman, embodying the Principal Events of a Life Spent in Robbery, Theft, Gambling, Passing Counterfeit Money, & c.* (Manchester, N.H.: J. H. Cate, 1843), 257–58.

12. Stephen Burroughs, *Memoirs of Stephen Burroughs, to which are added notes, and an appendix* (Albany: B. D. Packard, 1811), 82–95; Wyman, *Life and Adventures*, 257–58; Sile Doty, *The Life of Sile Doty, 1800–1876* (Detroit: Alved of Detroit, 1948), 17, 33, 50; *Nile's Weekly Register* 2d ser., no. 26 (22 August 1818): 429.

13. Wyman, *Life and Adventures*, 257–58, 260–71.

14. See, for example, Kellow Chesney, *The Victorian Underworld* (New York: Schocken Books, 1972); Bronislaw Geremek, *The Margins of Society in Late Medieval Paris* (Cambridge, England: Cambridge University Press, 1987); Dick Hobbs, *Doing the Business: Entrepreneurship, the Working Class, and Detectives in the East End of London* (New York: Oxford University Press, 1989); McMullen, *Canting Crew;* Michael Weisser, "Crime and Punishment in Early Modern Spain," in *Crime and the Law: The Social History of Crime in Europe since 1500*, in ed. V. A. C. Gatrell, Bruce Lenman, and Geoffrey Parker (London: Europa Publications, 1980): 76–96; J. J. Tobias, *Crime and Industrial Society in the Nineteenth Century* (New York: Schocken Books, 1967).

15. Richard B. Stott, *Workers in the Metropolis: Class, Ethnicity, and Youth in Antebellum New York City* (Ithaca, N.Y.: Cornell University Press, 1990), 7; *Report of the Council of Hygiene and Public Health of the Citizens' Association of New York, upon the Sanitary Condition of the City*, 2d ed. (New York: D. Appleton and Co., 1866), 290–348.

16. Stott, *Workers in the Metropolis*, 194.

17. Ibid., 58–60.

18. Ibid., 22–23, 40, 95, 110.

19. Robert Ernst, *Immigrant Life in New York City, 1825–1863* (Port Washington, N.Y.: Ira J. Friedman, 1965), 48–83.

20. Ibid., 84–98. Carol G. Pernicone, "The 'Bloody Ould Sixth': A Social Analysis of a New York City Working-Class Community in the Mid-nineteenth Century" (Ph.D. diss., University of Rochester, 1973), 112. The number of saloons and groceries was calculated from the *Sanitary Condition of the City*, passim.

21. On the concept of illegitimate opportunity structures, see Hobbs, *Doing the Business*, 84–182.

22. Ibid., 102–3; *Sanitary Condition of the City*, 5, 37–38; Ernst, *Immigrant Life in New York City*, 57.

23. David R. Johnson, "A Sinful Business: The Origins of Gambling Syndicates in the United States, 1840–1887," in *Police and Society*, ed. David H. Bayley (Beverly Hills, Calif.: Sage Publications, 1977), 22–23, 30–32; *Sanitary Condition of the City*, 137; Ernst, *Immigrant Life in New York City*, 58; Timothy J. Gilfoyle, "The Urban Geography of Commercial Sex: Prostitution in New York City, 1790–1860," *Journal of Urban History* 13 (August 1987): 371–93.

24. On the essential characteristics necessary to the development of an underworld, see McMullen, *Canting Crew*, 7–25.

25. This composite portrait of criminals' employment patterns is drawn from Burroughs, *Memoirs of Stephen Burroughs;* Wyman, *Life and Adventures;* Doty, *Life of Sile Doty;* Moore, *Langdon W. Moore;* Edwin S. Bruce, RMR, October 1866; John T. Linscott, RMR, November 1866; Nettleship, RMR, April 1866; Charles Treat, RMR, April 1866; Hiram C. Whitley to Solicitor Banfield, 31 October 1869, in Hiram C. Whitley, RMR, October 1869; and affidavits in *United States v. Frederick Davis*, Criminal Case Files, U.S. Circuit Court for the Southern District of New York, New York.

26. Stott, *Workers in the Metropolis*, 22, 48–55.

27. Deposition of Frances Bundel, 30 September 1830, Indictment Papers of the District Attorney of New York City (hereafter cited as Indictment Papers), New York City Municipal Archives, New York.

28. Pernicone, "Bloody Ould Sixth," 40–41; Sean Wilentz, *Chants Democratic: New York City and the Rise of the American Working Class, 1788–1850* (New York: Oxford University Press, 1984), 404–5; Indictment of Edward Hulseman, 10 August 1840, Indictment Papers.

29. Deposition of Lewis King, 5 February 1830, Indictment Papers.

30. This profile in Tables 1.1 to 1.4 is based on an analysis of all counterfeiting arrests for every tenth year beginning with 1830. Aside from inadvertently revealing the low risk of police interference involved in counterfeiting, the sample's bias toward 1860 means that the generalizations drawn from the analysis are probably more accurate for 1860 than for 1830. That does not undermine the validity of the analysis, however, since my argument is that lower Manhattan developed its particular opportunity structure for crime during that thirty-year interval; thus, the effects of that development should be more apparent at the end of the period than at the outset.

31. Edward K. Spann, *The New Metropolis: New York City, 1840–1857* (New York: Columbia University Press, 1981), 432.

32. The distribution of occupations for 121 persons was: unskilled, 49 (40 percent); skilled, 45 (37 percent); business, 27 (22 percent). I have defined the business category to include anyone whose occupation gave him or her

the opportunity to deal with the public in a business context. This approach places some individuals who would ordinarily be reported as unskilled (such as waiters) or white-collar workers (such as clerks) in a higher status category, and therefore inflates that category to some extent. However, since criminals worked in an environment that stressed opportunities to hustle rather than upward mobility, I regard waiters or clerks who knowingly passed counterfeit notes on customers as members of a subculture with different values than those which would be reflected in a standard analysis of occupational data.

33. Stott, *Workers in the Metropolis*, 75.

34. Ibid., 73.

35. David Philips, *Crime and Authority in Victorian England: The Black Country, 1835–1860* (Totowa, N.J.: Rowman and Littlefield, 1977), 228–36.

36. Indictments of Margaret Moran, 8 October 1860, Sarah Chapman, 16 October 1860, and Margaret Donohoe, 16 October 1860, in Indictment Papers.

37. George P. Burnham, *Memoirs of the United States Secret Service* (Boston: Laban Heath, 1872), 422–28; Thomas Shortell, RMR, January 1867.

38. W. E. Brusle, RMR, August 1865; William Wood, RMR, September 1865; Nettleship, RMR, November 1865. For the locations of other "dens," see R. R. Lowell, RMR, September 1865; William Redfield, RMR, February 1867; C. V. Hogan, RMR, February 1867. On New York City as the principal center of counterfeiting in the United States, see chapter 2 of this book.

39. Andrew Drummond, DRA, 30 November 1880.

40. Geremek, *Margins of Society*, 123.

41. Newman, RMR, December 1865; John Murray, RMR, August 1866; John Byrne, RMR, May 1869; Dye, *Government Blue Book*, 6.

42. Treat, RMR, January 1866; Moore, *Langdon W. Moore*, 55.

43. For descriptions of lower Manhattan's underworld after the Civil War, see Edward Crapsey, *The Nether Side of New York; or, the Vice, Crime, and Poverty of the Great Metropolis* (1872; reprint, Montclair, N.J.: Patterson Smith, 1969), 154–63; James D. McCabe, Jr., *Lights and Shadows of New York Life; or, the Sights and Sensations of the Great City* (Philadelphia: National Publishing Company, 1872), 523; John H. Warren, *Thirty Years Battle with Crime, or the Crying Shame of New York, as seen under the Broad Glare of an Old Detective's Lantern* (Poughkeepsie, N.Y.: A. J. White, 1875), 286, 303, 312–13.

44. Drummond, DRA, 18 January 1881, 14 March 1881.

45. Henry Curtis, DRA, 2 and 3 May 1877, 22 January 1878; John P. Brooks, DRA, 24 September 1888, 19, 26, and 31 October 1888, 23 January 1889, 28 May 1890; *Description and Information of Criminals*, 31:188.

46. This description of working-class job opportunities and neighborhood development is based on *Sanitary Condition of the City*, 226–348; Thomas Kessner, *The Golden Door: Italian and Jewish Immigrant Mobility in New York City*, 1880–1915 (New York: Oxford University Press, 1977), 44–70, 127–60; and Emanuel Tobier, "Manhattan's Business District in the Industrial Age," in *Power, Culture, and Place: Essays on New York City*, ed. Joseph H. Mollenkopf (New York: Russell Sage Foundation, 1988), 89. On the spread of brothels, see Timothy J. Gilfoyle, "City of Eros: New York City, Prostitution, and the Commercialization of Sex, 1790–1920" (Ph.D. diss., Columbia University, 1987), 377–506.

47. Deposition of William Fairthorne, 7 October 1839, Indictment Papers. Only six individuals (of the sixty-nine who reported addresses in the sample; see above notes 30 and 31) gave addresses that were north of 14th Street.

48. See, for example, Drummond, DRA, 19 September 1882.

49. Drummond, DRA, 28 March 1876.

50. Curtis, DRA, 13 July 1876, 10 January 1879; Drummond, DRA, 13 January 1880, 2 April 1880.

51. Curtis, DRA, 6 May 1879.

52. Drummond, DRA, 28 May 1880, 5 and 19 February 1883, 28 April 1883.

53. Calculated from data reported in RMR, 1865–1871; and DRA, 1875–1899.

54. Drummond, DRA, 2 and 30 April 1880, 28 April 1883.

55. This same point may also explain the relative insignificance of the Germans and English in counterfeiting after 1865.

56. Johnson, "A Sinful Business," 23, and passim.

57. Kessner, *Golden Door*, 33–39; Moses Rischin, *The Promised City: New York's Jews, 1870–1914* (Cambridge, Mass.: Harvard University Press, 1962), 51–75.

58. Kessner, *The Golden Door*, 143, 149–50.

59. Ibid., 14–16; Rischin, *Promised City*, 76–94.

60. According to Kessner, there were 13,571 Jews and 12,000 Italians in lower Manhattan in 1880. See *Golden Door*, 15, 19.

61. Calculated from Table 1.8. The figures on German arrests in this table do not include Jews, as far as can be determined from the original arrest data reported in the DRA. It is not my contention that these figures represent the entire universe of Italian and Jewish counterfeiters. Instead, I attempt to explain the disproportionate presence of Italians in the arrest data.

62. With the obvious exception of Italians, where reference to the Mafia and the Camorra provide a convenient though usually misunderstood context for explaining criminal activities in urban America, there is little serious work on the patterns of ethnic participation in crime, particularly for the

nineteenth century. Studies of Jewish criminality tend to emphasize that such behavior was the exception, missing the point that crime is always the exception regardless of what group is being examined. See, for example, Rischin, *Promised City*, 89–91; and Jenna W. Joselit, *Our Gang: Jewish Crime and the New York Jewish Community, 1900–1940* (Bloomington: Indiana University Press, 1983). Joselit argues that crime was not the norm, while simultaneously documenting a considerable range of illegal behavior. For a more balanced account, which does not, however, deal in detail with specific aspects of Jewish criminality, see Arthur A. Goren, *New York Jews and the Quest for Community: The Kehillah Experiment, 1908–1922* (New York: Columbia University Press, 1970), 134–58. The best book on Italian crime is Humbert Nelli, *The Business of Crime: Italians and Syndicate Crime in the United States* (New York: Oxford University Press, 1976).

63. Ernst, *Immigrant Life in New York City*, 241n79. Although most if not all Jews belonged to the German community during the antebellum period, their criminal behavior can be isolated. Antebellum officials and newspapers were quick to identify Jewish malefactors. On this point, see ibid., 58. In the sample of counterfeiting cases for the antebellum period, none of those identified as Germans (a total of thirteen individuals) was further differentiated as Jewish.

64. Nettleship, RMR, December 1865; John Eagan, RMR, December 1869. Unfortunately, the lack of information on the backgrounds of these early Italian counterfeiters makes it impossible to trace the origins of their knowledge of counterfeiting. Coppini may have been a Sicilian, and that heritage may have provided him with prior knowledge of counterfeiting, but neither proposition can be proved.

65. On Coppini, see Drummond, DRA, 17 and 28 September 1876, 12 and 25 November 1876, and 28 December 1876. For the Gill-Lombardo group, see Drummond 20 March 1876, 6 and 7 June 1886. On other Italians, see Charles Anchisi, RMR, July 1869; Drummond, 22 March 1882, 4 February 1885, 10 June 1886; Brooks, DRA, 20 August 1888; George Hazen, DRA, 16 April 1897.

66. Brooks, DRA, 23 January 1889, 16 and 28 May 1890, 15 November 1890, 23 February 1892, 17 January 1893.

67. Kessner, *Golden Door*, 129, 158.

68. George Bagg, DRA, 18 and 20 January 1895.

69. Nettleship, RMR, December 1865. For the career history of Gaetano Russo, see *Description and Information of Criminals*, 15:n.p.

70. Drummond, DRA, 13 February 1881; Bagg, DRA, 22 January 1897.

71. Drummond, DRA, 11 October 1885, 19 November 1887; Brooks, DRA, 22 August 1888; *Description and Information of Criminals*, 15:n.p.; New Orleans *Daily Picayune*, 17 October 1913.

72. Brooks, DRA, 27 December 1892, 17 April 1893, 15 July 1893.

73. Drummond, DRA, 4 February 1885.

74. Ibid.

75. Drummond, DRA, 16 October 1885.

76. For discussions of the organization and the culture of the Mafia, see Anton Blok, *The Mafia of a Sicilian Village, 1860–1960: A Study of Violent Peasant Entrepreneurs* (New York: Harper and Row, 1974), and Nelli, *Business of Crime*, 3–23.

77. Informers' report, in Hazen, DRA, 4 November 1898.

78. Ibid., 7 November 1898.

79. Ibid., 11, 12, and 29 November 1898.

80. Ibid., 11 November 1898.

81. Ibid., 23 November 1898, 3 December 1898, 4 January 1899.

82. Drummond, DRA, 21 January 1886, 13 December 1886, 7 December 1887; Brooks, DRA, 13 March 1889; Bagg, DRA, 15 October 1894; Hazen, 12 May 1897, 27 December 1897; Hazen, 4 November 1898, 23 January 1899.

CHAPTER 2

THE MONEY MARKET

1. *New York Times*, 30 July 1862. Similar figures, possibly based on the same unidentified survey that the *Times* used for its story, can be found in the *Banker's Magazine and Statistical Register* 18 (December 1863): 497; and A. Barton Hepburn, *A History of Currency in the United States* (New York: Macmillan, 1915), 101, 165. An 1865 survey estimated that there were four thousand counterfeit or fraudulent bank notes circulating in 1862. See Edwin J. Wilber and Edward P. Eastman, *A Treatise on Counterfeit, Altered, and Spurious Bank Notes, with Unerring Rules for the Detection of Frauds in the Same* (Poughkeepsie, N.Y.: Edwin J. Wilber and Edward P. Eastman, 1865), 4. It should be noted, however, that there is an important distinction between the *number* of notes that had been counterfeited and the *amount* of all currency that was counterfeit. Contemporary accounts asserted that half of the currency in circulation was counterfeit, but that is impossible to verify.

2. Lynn Glaser, *Counterfeiting in America: The History of an American Way to Wealth* (Philadelphia: Clarkson N. Potter, 1968), 77–101. One important attempt to determine the state of the money supply, although not assessing its adequacy, is J. Van Fenstermaker, John E. Filer, and Robert S. Herren, "Money Statistics of New England, 1785–1837," *Journal of Economic History* 44 (June 1984): 441–53.

3. U.S. Congress, Senate, *Report of the Secretary of the Treasury, communicating the Results of the Investigation made pursuant to the joint resolution of the 26th of February, 1857, "to Prevent the Counterfeiting of Coins*

of the United States," 13 June 1860, 36th Cong., 1st sess., S. Exdoc. 53, serial 1033, 11.

4. Analysis of the deficiencies in antebellum detective abilities among local police forces is based on David R. Johnson, *Policing the Urban Underworld: The Impact of Crime and the Development of the American Police, 1800–1887* (Philadelphia: Temple University Press, 1979), 22–24, 41–43, 45–48, 64–67; Roger Lane, *Policing the City: Boston, 1822–1885* (Cambridge, Mass.: Harvard University Press, 1967), 9–10, 68–69, 147–48, 150–52; and James F. Richardson, *The New York Police: Colonial Times to 1901* (New York: Oxford University Press, 1970), 17–19.

5. *Banker's Magazine and Statistical Record* 19 (April 1865): 796–98; Glaser, *Counterfeiting in America*, 84–85.

6. See, for example, Howard Kennedy to the Secretary of the Treasury, 12 September 1843; secretary of the Treasury to Jacob Gould (U.S. marshal), 24 December 1846; Solicitor John C. Clark to the secretary of the Interior, 30 January 1850; and Petition of George M. Dole and others to the secretary of the Treasury, 18 May 1851 in Closed Cases (Misc.), Solicitor of the Treasury, Record Group 206, National Archives, Washington, D.C.

7. Frederick S. Calhoun, *The Lawmen: United States Marshals and Their Deputies, 1789–1989* (Washington, D.C.: Smithsonian Institution Press, 1989), 49–63.

8. Secretary of the Interior J. Thompson to James A. Bayard, chairman, Judiciary Committee of the U.S. Senate, 24 February, 1860 in House, *Miscellaneous Documents*, 36th Cong., 1st sess., Doc. 23, 1064; *U.S. Statutes at Large*, XII, 36th Cong., 1st sess., 102.

9. The customers whom counterfeiters served in the nineteenth century probably did not differ significantly from those they had served in the colonial era; however, insufficient evidence makes this impossible to prove.

10. James Downs, RMR, January 1866; Charles J. Deming, RMR, February 1866; Stephen D. Franklin, RMR, February 1866, July 1866; John T. Foure, RMR, November 1866; Andrew Drummond, DRA, 7 June 1876, 14 and 23 July 1877, 6 August 1879, 20 August 1880, 17 September 1880, 17 December 1883; Henry R. Curtis, DRA, 10 August 1877, 10 August 1878.

11. J. Holbrook, *Ten Years among the Mailbags; or, Notes from the Diary of a Special Agent of the Post-Office Department* (Philadelphia: H. Cowperthwait, 1855), 262–66; *Chicago Tribune*, 18 May 1858; *Philadelphia Public Ledger*, 21 November 1860. The inference that counterfeiters probably invented this con game is based on the Secret Service's discovery that counterfeiters frequently engaged in this game. See John Murray, RMR, November 1865, March 1866; and Abner B. Newcombe, RMR, December 1866.

12. Horace Kent, RMR, October 1866.

13. Secret Service, *Description and Information of Criminals*, 1:201.

14. See *Philadelphia Public Ledger*, 12 December 1870; and *New York Times*, 11 April 1874; 17 May 1893. See also Anthony Comstock to A. G. Sharp, 17 April 1885, in William Ferguson, U.S. Post Office Department, Bureau of the Chief Inspector, Correspondence and Reports Relating to Criminal Investigations, National Archives, Washington, D.C.

15. Calculated from the census of printing establishments in the U.S. Bureau of the Census, *Manufactures of the United States in 1860* (Washington, D.C.: Government Printing Office, 1865), passim.

16. William H. Griffiths, *The Story of the American Bank Note Company* (New York: American Bank Note Company, 1959), 34, 39, 43.

17. See Richard B. Stott, *Workers in the Metropolis: Class, Ethnicity, and Youth in Antebellum New York City* (Ithaca, N.Y.: Cornell University Press, 1990), 22–23, 48–55; Sean Wilentz, *Chants Democratic: New York City and the Rise of the American Working Class, 1788–1850* (New York: Oxford University Press, 1984), 30, 33, 52; and Bureau of the Census, *Manufactures of the United States in 1860*, passim. For Houston Street as the printing center, see *New York Times*, 26 August 1983, C17.

18. Murray, RMR, October 1866; Secret Service, *Description and Information of Criminals*, 1:437–39, 448, 464, 481, 8:47.

19. Allen R. Pred, *Urban Growth and the Circulation of Information: The United States System of Cities, 1790–1840* (Cambridge, Mass.: Harvard University Press, 1973), 86–87, 93–95, 173–77.

20. Richard C. Wade, *The Urban Frontier: The Rise of Western Cities, 1790–1830* (Cambridge, Mass.: Harvard University Press, 1959), 192, 218–19; Edward K. Muller, "Selective Urban Growth in the Middle Ohio Valley, 1800–1860," *The Geographical Review* 66 (April 1976): 178–99. For an excellent analysis of one Midwest city's vice district during this period, see John C. Schnieder, *Detroit and the Problem of Order, 1830–1880: A Geography of Crime, Riot, and Policing* (Lincoln: University of Nebraska Press, 1980).

21. Otto A. Rothert, *The Outlaws of Cave-in-Rock* (1920; reprint, Freeport, N.Y.: Books for Libraries Press, 1970), 18, 267–81. "In the Matter of Appointing the Marshal of Ohio a Special Agent to Arrest Counterfeiters," 1847, in Solicitor of the Treasury, Closed Cases (Misc.); Reuben G. Thwaites, ed., *Early Western Travels* (Cleveland: Arthur H. Clark Company, 1905), 13:295–96, 17:29, 22:202, 26:74; Wade, *Urban Frontier*, 123.

22. U.S. Attorney G. W. Clinton to Secretary of the Treasury R. J. Walker, 19 July 1848; and Agent Jonathan H. Green to Solicitor of the Treasury R. H. Gillett, 15 October 1848, in Solicitor of the Treasury, Closed Cases (Misc.).

23. Edwin S. Bruce, RMR, November 1866.

24. Calculated from U.S. Bureau of the Census, *Manufactures of the United States in 1860*.

25. Jeffrey Adler, "Internal Migration and Urban Growth: The Rise and

Fall of Ante-bellum St. Louis" (Ph.D. diss., Harvard University, 1986), 29–51.

26. Wade, *Urban Frontier*, 122–23; Jeffrey Adler, "Vagging the Demons and Scoundrels: Vagrancy and the Growth of St. Louis, 1830–1861," *Journal of Urban History* 13 (November 1986): 3–30. See also *New York Journal of Commerce*, 29 August 1857 (I am indebted to Jeffrey Adler for this reference to Biebusch's early career); Edward Quinton, RMR, November 1866; James Fitzpatrick, RMR, June 1869; and John Eagan, RMR, February and December 1870. For a summary of Biebusch's career, see *New York Times*, 25 October 1879.

27. Quinton, RMR, October 1866; James A. Pitts, RMR, November 1866.

28. Secret Service, *Description and Information of Criminals*, 1:26; John S. Dye, *The Government Blue Book: A Complete History of the Lives of All the Great Counterfeiters, Criminal Engravers and Plate Printers* (Philadelphia: Dye's Government Counterfeit Detector, 1880), 80–81.

29. Pred, *Urban Growth and the Circulation of Information*, 93, 149, 171, 185. The history of urban crime in the South has been greatly neglected, particularly from the perspective of white professional criminals. I do not intend to imply that such crime did not exist or that counterfeit money did not circulate in the South, but to offer an explanation for the lack of a production center in any southern city prior to the Civil War.

30. This analysis of the market areas is based on data reported in RMR, 1864–1871.

31. For the diffusion of a criminal subculture rooted in yet transcending local boundaries, see Henry Tufts, *The Autobiography of a Criminal*, ed. Edmund Pearson (1807; reprint, New York: Duffield and Company, 1930), 29–32, 179–80; Seth Wyman, *The Life and Adventures of Seth Wyman, embodying the Principal Events of a Life Spent in Robbery, Theft, Gambling, Passing Counterfeit Money, & c.* (Manchester, N.H.: J. H. Cate, printer, 1843), 68–78, 79–80; Sile Doty, *The Life of Sile Doty, 1800–1876* (Detroit: Alved of Detroit, 1948), 44, 96, 101, 139–40; Langdon W. Moore, *Langdon W. Moore: His Own Story of His Eventful Life* (Boston: Langdon W. Moore, 1893), 160–62, 195, 197; *Philadelphia Public Ledger*, 26 December 1836, 31 January 1867, 26 April 1871; William H. Bell (New York City detective), diary, 14 April 1851, New-York Historical Society, New York; John Landesco, "The Criminal Underworld of Chicago in the 1880s and 1890s," *Journal of Criminal Law and Criminology* 25 (May–June 1934): 346–47; David W. Maurer, *The Big Con: The Story of the Confidence Man and the Confidence Game* (Indianapolis: Bobbs-Merrill, 1940), 166–67; and Daniel A. Cohen, "A Fellowship of Thieves: Property Criminals in Eighteenth-Century Massachusetts," *Journal of Social History* 22 (Fall 1988): 65–92.

32. Curtis, DRA, 19 and 21 July 1875, 3 and 17 October 1876, 16 Novem-

ber 1876; Drummond, DRA, 24 July 1878, 28 March 1883, 28 June 1883, 26 December 1883; *Chicago Tribune*, 20 March 1885.

33. Dye, *Government Blue Book*, 87–93.

34. George P. Burnham, *Memoirs of the United States Secret Service* (Boston: Gaban Heath, 1872), 422–28; I. C. Nettleship, 26 October 1871, Reports of I.C. Nettleship, New Jersey Historical Society Collections, Newark, N.J.; Chief Hiram C. Whitley to Solicitor Edward C. Banfield, 16 November 1871, in Letters Sent from Headquarters of the Chief in New York, 1870–1873, U.S. Secret Service, Record Group 87, National Archives, Washington, D.C.; *New York Times*, 27 October 1871; Glaser, *Counterfeiting in America*, 143–44.

35. Murray, RMR, January 1867, March 1867; Samuel M. Felker, RMR, March, 1867; Frederick C. Tapley, RMR, June 1867.

36. Dye, *Government Blue Book*, 5–8; Secret Service, *Description and Information of Criminals*, 1:531; Henry O. Wright, RMR, August 1865; Robert R. Lowell, RMR, November 1865, February 1866; Charles Anchisi, RMR, April 1870.

37. Burnham, *Memoirs of the United States Secret Service*, 199, 211; Dye, *Government Blue Book*, 5–8; John S. Hammond, RMR, May 1866.

38. *New York Times*, 21 June 1868; Secret Service, *Description and Information of Criminals*, 1:58, 66; Murray, RMR, July 1866.

39. Drummond, DRA, 22 October 1875, 25 June 1877, 1, 5, 16, and 21 December 1877, 28 January 1878, 18, 21, and 25 January 1879, 5 February 1879, 5 March 1879, 29 May 1879; Burnham, *Memoirs of the United States Secret Service*, 199, 211, 359–66.

40. Wright, RMR, 31 August 1865; John Donn, RMR, March 1867; *New York Times*, 29 April 1888; Dye, *Government Blue Book*, 34.

41. Wright, RMR, 1 and 31 August 1865; Joseph Gaillard, RMR, October 1865; Alexander H. Bicknell, RMR, January 1867; Charles F. Newman, RMR, July 1867; Drummond, DRA, 5 August 1877; Dye, *Government Blue Book*, 50.

42. Agent Jonathan H. Green to Solicitor H. H. Gillett, 9 November 1848, in Solicitor of the Treasury, Closed Cases (Misc.); J. H. Walker, RMR, January 1864; Edwin Bruce, RMR, June 1866; Murray, RMR, July 1866; John Herron, RMR, September 1866; Eagan, RMR, May 1870; Curtis, DRA, 22 May 1878, 30 November 1878; Drummond, DRA, 27 February 1879, 27 November 1879, 15 December 1885; John P. Brooks, DRA, 25 March 1890, 3 June 1892.

43. Wright, RMR, 31 August 1865; Joseph A. Jackson, RMR, April 1866; Drummond, DRA, 5, 7, and 8 August 1877, 8 September 1877, 13 December 1877, 4 February 4 1878, 1 May 1878, 18 January 1879, 9, 10, and 13 June 1879, 26 February 1881, 19 March 1884. On the bachelor subculture, see

John Schneider, *Detroit and the Problem of Order, 1830–1880: A Geography of Crime, Riot, and Policing* (Lincoln: University of Nebraska Press, 1980), 36–45; and Elliott J. Gorn, *The Manly Art: Bare Knuckle Prize Fighting in America* (Ithaca, N.Y.: Cornell University Press, 1986), 131–33, 141–42.

44. C. S. Treat, RMR, April 1866; Donn, RMR, September 1866; John Linscott, RMR, November 1866; William D. Redfield, RMR, November 1866; Drummond, DRA, 14 November 1876, 27 October 1881, 1 November 1881, 1 and 29 January 1883.

45. Felker, RMR, September 1866; Thomas Shortell, RMR, January 1867; Anchisi, RMR, April 1870; Secret Service, *Description and Information of Criminals*, 1:531. Burnham, *Memoirs of the United States Secret Service*, 241–43, 333.

46. Confession of Charles R. Young, in Tapley, RMR, March 1866.

47. Humbert Nelli, *The Business of Crime: Italians and Syndicate Crime in the United States* (New York: Oxford University, 1976; Chicago: University of Chicago Press, 1981), 24–25.

48. U.S. Attorney D. S. Dickinson to Solicitor of the Treasury Edward Jordan, 4 January 1866, Bulletins, Circulars, and Lists Issued by the Chief, 1874–1938; Charles Benedict, RMR, August 1866; Shortell, RMR, December 1866; Redfield, RMR, September 1866; Fitzpatrick, RMR, May 1869; George Egbert, RMR, October 1870; Louis Dell'Ormo, RMR, February 1870.

49. Newcombe, RMR, April 1866; Thomas Bradley, RMR, April 1866; Anchisi, RMR, June 1869; Dell'Ormo, RMR, February 1870, April 1870; Chief Hiram C. Whitley to Solicitor Edward C. Banfield, 23 November 1873; Whitley, Reports of Operations for the Months of October and November, 1873, Department of Justice Source Chronological Files: Treasury, National Archives, Washington, D.C.

50. Bruce, RMR, May 1866.

51. Ibid., RMR, May 1866, June 1866, September 1866, October 1866; H. A. Sessions, RMR, December 1866

52. Newman, RMR, February 1866; Curtis, DRA, 1 September 1876.

53. Newman, RMR, February 1866; Gaillard, RMR, February 1866; Bruce, RMR, September 1866; Curtis, DRA, 8 August 1877, 1 September 1877.

54. For examples of the wholesalers' travails, see Drummond, DRA, 8 and 13 October 1876, 24 September 1877, 19 April 1880, 20 and 22 July 1880. On the problems of markets in general and illegal markets in particular, see George J. Stigler, *The Organization of Industry* (Homewoood, Ill.: Richard D. Irwin, 1968), 171, 172, 176; and Peter Reuter, *Disorganized Crime: The Economics of the Visible Hand* (Cambridge: MIT Press, 1983), 109, 114–15, 121, and passim.

55. Drummond, DRA, 21 September 1877, 2, 5, and 7 October 1877, 6 May 1878, 20 January 1883, 2 and 20 February 1883, 2 March 1883, 19 March 1884, 27 April 1884.

56. Newman, RMR, December 1865; William Reville, RMR, September 1866; Eaton, RMR, May 1867; W. W. Hall, DRA, 18 May 1876; Curtis, DRA, 2 August 1877, 2 March 1878; Drummond, DRA, 19 and 20 May 1876, 14 October 1876, 31 December 1877, 22 July 1880; John P. Brooks, DRA, 14 January 1893. Stigler, *Organization of Industry*, 176; Reuter, *Disorganized Crime*, 109, 114–15.

57. Linscott, RMR, January 1867; John Maloy, RMR, August 1867; Drummond, DRA, 8 November 1876, 25 January 1877, 20 November 1884; Curtis, DRA, 30 January 1878; Chief James J. Brooks to Solicitor Alexander McCue, 30 November 1887, in Letters Received from the Secret Service, Solicitor of the Treasury Records, Record Group 206, National Archives, Washington, D.C.

58. Drummond, DRA, 21 December 1877, 27 October 1881, 1 November 1881, 12 December 1882.

59. Edgar Bishop, RMR, January 1866; Mary Casey, RMR, February 1867; Curtis, DRA, 3 October 1876, 27 July 1877, 28 August 1878.

60. Wright, RMR, 31 January 1865; 28 February 1865; Donn, RMR, January 1866; Drummond, DRA, 5 May 1875, 19 February 1881, 22 September 1887; John P. Brooks, DRA, 16 February 1889, 19 November 1892; William P. Hazen, DRA, 15 July 1898.

61. Franklin, RMR, February 1866; Bruce, RMR, October 1866; M. B. Card, RMR, October 1866; James Henry, RMR, October 1866; Drummond, DRA, 13, 22, and 23 November 1875, 21, 23, and 27 July 1877.

62. S. B. Benson, RMR, May 1867; Whitley, Reports of Monthly Operations for October and November, 1873; Letter from James Brown, 6 September 1865, in Secret Service, *Description and Information of Criminals*, 1:127–32.

63. For a description of this process, see Drummond, DRA, 2 June 1876.

64. Secret Service, *Description and Information of Criminals*, 1:403; Russell Applegate, RMR, June 1870; Curtis, DRA, 1 May 1878; Drummond, DRA, 30 August 1876, 25 August 1877, 21 January 1881, 27 January 1885, 11 March 1886.

65. Drummond, DRA, 13 and 29 September 1886; John P. Brooks, 22 August 1890, 22 June 1893.

66. Benedict, RMR, August 1866; Curtis, DRA, 1 May 1878.

67. On this behavioral pattern see, Tufts, *Autobiography of a Criminal*, ed. Pearson; Wyman, *Life and Adventures of Seth Wyman;* Doty, *Life of Sile Doty;* Moore, *Langdon W. Moore;* and Drummond, DRA, 21 November 1876, 2 May 1880, 4 July 1877, 4 and 18 October 1877, 23 November 1877, 19 De-

cember 1877, 23 July 1880, 12 December 1882, 10 January 1883, 5 and 19 February 1883.

CHAPTER 3
LOCALISM VERSUS SOVEREIGNTY

1. On this point, see, for example, Morton Keller, *Affairs of State: Public Life in Late Nineteenth Century America* (Cambridge, Mass.: Harvard University Press, 1977); Robin L. Einhorn, *Property Rules: Political Economy in Chicago, 1833–1872* (Chicago: University of Chicago Press, 1991), esp. 188–230; Jon Teaford, *The Unheralded Triumph: City Government in America, 1870–1900* (Baltimore: The Johns Hopkins University Press, 1984); Eric Foner, *Reconstruction: America's Unfinished Revolution, 1863–1877* (New York: Harper and Row, 1988), 460, 469.

2. Foner, *Reconstruction*, xxvi.

3. On the IRS, see Wilbur Miller, *Revenuers & Moonshiners: Enforcing Federal Liquor Law in the Mountain South, 1865–1900* (Chapel Hill: University of North Carolina Press, 1991); on the Postal Inspectors, see David R. Johnson, *American Law Enforcement: A History* (St. Louis, Mo.: Forum Press, 1981), 76–81; Wayne Fuller, *The American Mail: Enlarger of the Common Life* (Chicago: University of Chicago Press, 1972).

4. Quoted in Harold M. Hyman, *A More Perfect Union: The Impact of the Civil War and Reconstruction on the Constitution* (Boston: Houghton Mifflin, 1975), 66.

5. Stephen B. Oates, *With Malice toward None: The Life of Abraham Lincoln* (New York: Harper and Row, 1978), 254.

6. Benjamin P. Thomas and Harold M. Hyman, *Stanton: The Life and Times of Lincoln's Secretary of War* (New York: Alfred A. Knopf, 1962), 152–53, 400, 475. For an account of these activities by one participant, see L. C. Baker, *History of the United States Secret Service* (Philadelphia: L. C. Baker, 1867).

7. *U.S. Statutes at Large*, XIII, 37th Cong., 2d sess., 749.

8. Salmon P. Chase, Order dated 22 December 1863, in Letters Sent Relating to Treasury Department Administration, OR Series 1861–1873, Treasury Records, National Archives, Washington, D.C.

9. Ibid.

10. Nelson W. Evans, *A History of Scioto County, Ohio, together with a Pioneer Record of Southern Ohio*, 2 vols. (Portsmouth, Ohio: Nelson W. Evans, 1903), 1:287–88.

11. Chase's request is reproduced in Baker, *History of the United States Secret Service*, 262.

12. Ibid., 19, 45–92, 127, and passim.

13. *New York Times*, 11 August (story from the *St. Louis Democrat*, 6 August), 9 and 14 October 1864; *Banker's Magazine*, 19 (December 1864): 492–93.

14. Walter S. Bowen and Harry E. Neal, *The United States Secret Service* (Philadelphia: Chilton, 1960), 12–13; Thomas and Hyman, *Stanton*, 63–64.

15. Fletcher Pratt, *Stanton: Lincoln's Secretary of War* (Westport, Conn.: Greenwood Press, 1970), 457–58.

16. Wood's escapades during the war were traced in *The War of the Rebellion: A Compilation of the Official Records of the Union and Confederate Armies*, series II (Washington, D.C.: Government Printing Office, 1897), 4:656, 934, 943; 5:229, 400–1; 6:40, 348, 432. He referred to his association with Baker's raid in summer 1864 in William P. Wood to Solicitor Jordan, RMR, 20 July 1865.

17. Wood to Secretary of War Edwin M. Stanton, 17 April 1863, in *War of the Rebellion*, 5:490.

18. U.S. Congress, House of Representatives, House Executive Document 179, 40th Cong., 2d sess., 1339, pp. 37, 49; Wood to Jordan, RMR, 31 December 1864.

19. *U.S. Statutes at Large*, XIII, 38th Cong., 1st sess., 351; *Banker's Magazine* 19 (April 1865): 819.

20. Secretary of the Treasury Hugh McCulloch to Stanton, 5 July 1865, in Solicitor of the Treasury, Letters Received from the Secret Service, Record Group 206, National Archives, Washington, D.C.

21. Solicitor Bluford Wilson to Secretary of the Treasury Benjamin Bristow, 27 July 1874, in Letters Received from the Secret Service. Wilson wrote to Bristow that "I have not been able to find any written order from any of your predecessors creating the Division . . ." and concluded that Jordan had established the Service after oral consultation with McCulloch. See also William P. Wood, Letter to the Editor, *New York Times*, 2 July 1867.

22. Cf. Bowen and Neal, *United States Secret Service*, 15; Hugh McCulloch, *Men and Measures of Half a Century: Sketches and Comments* (reprint, New York: Da Capo Press, 1970), 222.

23. Wood, RMR, December 1864 to June 1865.

24. Report of the Solicitor, 10 November 1866, in Department of the Treasury, *Annual Report, 1866* (Washington, D.C.: Government Printing Office, 1866), 183.

25. Bray Hammond, *Sovereignty and an Empty Purse: Banks and Politics in the Civil War* (Princeton, N.J.: Princeton University Press, 1970), 141, 248–49, 253.

26. Alan Trachtenberg, *The Incorporation of America: Culture and Society in the Gilded Age* (New York: Hill and Wang, 1982), 82.

27. On the importance of public trust in the currency, see William H. Griffiths, *The Story of the American Bank Note Company* (New York: The American Bank Note Company, 1959), 9. My conclusions about the interrelationships among federal power, urban development, and the national economy are drawn from my reading of Stein Rokkan, "Dimensions of State Formation and Nation-Building: A Possible Paradigm for Research on Variations," in *The Formation of National States in Western Europe*, ed. Charles Tilly (Princeton, N.J.: Princeton University Press, 1975), 562–600.

28. *Circular from the Solicitor of the Treasury to District Attorneys, Marshals, and Clerks of Courts of the United States* (Washington, D.C.: Treasury Department, 21 July 1865), in Letters Received from the Secret Service.

29. Ibid., 5.

30. Ibid.

31. Early examples of Solicitor Jordan's leadership of the division and his directives to Wood and others include Edward Jordan to D. C. Richmond, 7 July 1865, copy in C. F. Newman, RMR, 31 July 1865; Wood, RMR, 8 September 1865 (for August); Newman, RMR, December 1865.

32. This evolution can be traced through Wood's monthly reports in the RMR series. There seems to be no "official" date on which the New York office assumed its distinctive role; like Topsy, it just grew.

33. Frank T. Morn, *"The Eye That Never Sleeps": A History of the Pinkerton National Detective Agency* (Bloomington: Indiana University Press, 1982), 68–70.

34. For example, Solicitor John C. Clark to Hawkins Taylor, 21 February 1850; and B. C. Yates to Clark, 27 June 1851, in Solicitor of the Treasury, Closed Cases (Misc.), Record Group 206, National Archives, Washington, D.C.

35. The title appears without explanation beginning with the July 1865 monthly reports of the Service.

36. Pinkerton to Jordan [?], 28 December 1863, in Register of Letters Received, 1863–1903 (16 vols.), U.S. Secret Service, Record Group 87, National Archives, Washington, D.C., 1:383; Morn, *"Eye That Never Sleeps,"* 53.

37. These figures are based on my compilation of the employment records and backgrounds of *all* Wood's officers from the RMR, covering the period from December 1864 to September 1867, when the records of Wood's tenure end. A total of 206 men served as operatives or assistant operatives during that time, although not all at the same time. For example, Wood began with 15 men in July 1865; in April 1867 he had 84 employees. The total number of employees therefore varied considerably month by month.

38. Wood, RMR, July and August 1865.

39. George P. Burnham, *Memoirs of the United States Secret Service* (Boston: Laban Heath, 1872), 278–85.

40. Ibid., 160–63.

41. Wood, RMR, December 1864.

42. S. D. Franklin, RMR, December 1865; *New York Times*, 16 October 1866, 2 and 18 July 1867.

43. John Murray, RMR, July 1866; Virgil Barlow, RMR, December 1866.

44. Lynn Glaser, *Counterfeiting in America: The History of an American Way to Wealth* (Philadelphia: Clarkson N. Potter, 1968), 108.

45. See, for example, Wood, RMR, October 1865; Abner Newcomb, RMR, November 1866. During Wood's tenure as chief the degree of cooperation with the Service from other police agencies varied considerably. It is therefore possible that Wood's men developed this habit of making common-law arrests in part because of that pattern. See C. H. Rosch, RMR, August 1865; Franklin, RMR, September 1865; Newman, RMR, October 1865.

46. Franklin, RMR, August, 1865; Wood to Joseph Gaillard, 18 December 1865, copy in Gaillard, RMR, December 1865; E. L. Quinton, RMR, February 1866; Franklin, RMR, April 1866; Murray, RMR, April 1866; J. H. Downs, RMR, April 1866; Franklin, RMR, June 1866; Newman, RMR, May 1867; Barlow, RMR, June 1867; Newman, RMR, May 1869; I. C. Nettleship, RMR, June 1869; *New York Times*, 2 July 1867.

47. W. P. Wood, *Circular of Instructions to Operatives, Secret Service Division, Treasury Department* (Washington, D.C.: Government Printing Office, 1868), passim.

48. Wood and some of his operatives were charged in a civil suit with false imprisonment in 1867; the case came to trial in 1869. See Gaillard, RMR, October 1869.

49. William P. Wood, *Letter from Wm. P. Wood (Late Chief of the Secret Service Division, Treasury Department), to the Hon. George S. Boutwell, Secretary of the Treasury* (Washington, D.C.[?]: n.p. [1869]).

50. Burnham, *Memoirs of the United States Secret Service*, 15–34; Hiram C. Whitley, *In It* (Cambridge, Mass.: The Riverside Press, 1894), 41–42, 91, 99–100.

51. Whitley to Solicitor Edward C. Banfield, 16 June 1870, in Letters Sent from Headquarters of the Chief in New York, 1870–1873, U.S. Secret Service, Record Group 87, National Archives, Washington, D.C. That Whitley created a correspondence file with this title indicates the status that the New York office had acquired. Whitley began implementing his new system in the late fall of 1870. See Whitley to John Eagan, 17 November 1870, Ibid. Eagan was appointed chief operative for St. Louis.

52. Burnham, *Memoirs of the Secret Service*, 160–63.

53. Ibid., 213–16.

54. Ibid., 122–23; Thomas E. Lonergan to the President, 30 March 1881, in Department of the Treasury, Division of Appointments, Record Group 56, National Archives, Washington, D.C.

55. Based on an analysis of backgrounds contained in the RMR, the total group, for all categories in the analysis of Whitley's hiring practices, numbered 113.

56. H. C. Whitley, *Circular of Instructions to Operatives, Secret Service Division, Treasury Department* (Washington, D.C.: Government Printing Office, 1873), 3, 4, 5, 6.

57. Ibid., passim.

58. Whitley left no explanation of his motives for the changes he implemented. His motives can therefore be imperfectly inferred from his actions. But the federal bureaucracy was undergoing important changes at this time. See Cindy S. Aron, *Ladies and Gentlemen of the Civil Service: Middle Class Workers in Victorian America* (New York: Oxford University Press, 1987), 3, 5, 7, 8.

59. Whitley to Banfield, 8, 9, and 26 April 1870, Letters sent from Headquarters, U.S. Secret Service, Record Group 87, National Archives, Washington, D.C.; Whitley to Attorney General A. T. Akerman, 14 July 1871, 19 March 1872, Department of Justice, Source Chronological Files, Treasury, Record Group 60, National Archives, Washington, D.C., Whitley to Banfield, 14 May 1874, Reports of Operations of the Secret Service, U.S. Secret Service, Record Group 87, National Archives, Washington, D.C.; *New York Times*, 11 April 1874.

60. Whitley, *Circular of Instructions*, 9.

61. Whitley, *In It*, 46.

62. Constance M. Green, *Washington: Village and Capital, 1800–1878* (Princeton, N.J.: Princeton University Press, 1962), 358–61; Ross A. Webb, *Benjamin Helm Bristow: Border State Politician* (Lexington: The University Press of Kentucky, 1969), 139–41.

63. This account of the burglary, and the connections among the various principals, is reconstructed from U.S. Congress, House of Representatives, Joint Select Committee on Affairs in the District of Columbia, *Safe Burglary*, 43rd Cong., 1st sess., Report No. 785 (Washington, D.C.: Government Printing Office, 23 June 1874), 1–329; *Washington Star*, 1 and 11 June 1874; *New York Times*, 21 and 22 July, 25 August, 16 September, 4, 5 and 6 November 1874; Nettleship, RMR, July and October 1869; September 1870; Reports of I.C. Nettleship, Chief Assistant S.S. Division, vol. 10 (1871–1874), 280–81, I. C. Nettleship Collection, New Jersey Historical Society.

64. *Safe Burglary*, 1.

65. Webb, *Benjamin Helm Bristow*, 138–39; Leonard D. White, *The Re-*

publican Era: A Study in Administrative History, 1869–1901 (New York: Macmillan, 1958), 10, 372.

66. Wilson to U.S. Attorney George Bliss and others, 3 July 1874, in Letters Received from the Secret Service.

67. Wilson to Bristow, 27 July 1874, ibid.

68. It is unclear precisely when Whitley took this step, but he made his antipathy toward rewards clear in a letter to Wilson. See Whitley to Wilson, 24 July 1874, in Letters Received from the Secret Service.

69. For example, Joseph Burr to Wilson, 16 June 1874, in Letters Received from the Secret Service. This file contains several letters from U.S. marshals and attorneys responding to Wilson's inquiry about the Service's effectiveness.

70. Wilson to Bristow, 27 July 1874, ibid.

71. Whitley to Wilson, 24 July 1874, ibid.

72. Wilson to Bristow, 27 July 1874, ibid.

73. Wilson to Bristow, 5 September 1874, ibid. Bristow conveyed his orders in the form of endorsements on Wilson's letters. Webb, *Benjamin Helm Bristow,* 140, records Babcock's attempt to intervene for Whitley.

74. *Chicago Tribune,* 23 September 1874.

75. Ibid., 4 August 1872, 25 November 1918 (obituary). I am indebted to Professor Perry Duis for locating Washburn's obituary.

76. John J. Flinn, *History of the Chicago Police from the Settlement of the Community to the Present Time* (Chicago: Under the Auspices of the Police Book Fund, 1887), 138–39.

77. A. T. Andreas, *History of Chicago from the Earliest Period to the Present Time,* 3 vols. (Chicago: A. T. Andreas, 1884), 1:355, 855.

78. Washburn to Wilson, 28 January 1875, Extract, Exhibit A, in Reports of Operations of the Secret Service, 1874–1877.

79. Wilson to Bristow, 27 July 1874, in Letters Received from the Secret Service.

80. See chapter 4 for details concerning the backgrounds of operatives after 1874.

81. General Orders, No. 1, (31 October 1874), in *Criminals and Suspects, Record of Arrests and Convictions, 1869–1930,* U.S. Secret Service Records, Record Group 87, National Archives, Washington, D.C.

82. Washburn to Wilson, 28 January 1875, Extract, Exhibit A, in Reports of Operations of the Secret Service, 1874–1877.

83. For the development of bureaucratic routines, see chapter 5.

84. Bluford Wilson, Solicitor's Report, 18 November 1875, in Secretary of the Treasury, *Annual Report, 1875,* 602; Webb, *Benjamin Helm Bristow,* 187–212.

85. Washburn to Wilson, 28 January 1875, Extract, Exhibit A. Washburn mentioned that his men "sometimes" made arrests.

CHAPTER 4
FROM DISGRACE TO AUTONOMY

1. Wilbur Miller, *Revenuers and Moonshiners: Enforcing Federal Liquor Law in the Mountain South, 1865–1900* (Chapel Hill: University of North Carolina Press, 1991), 99–101, 143–44, 158.

2. James Q. Wilson, *The Investigators: Managing FBI and Narcotics Agents* (New York: Basic Books, 1978), 59.

3. Elmer Washburn, General Orders, No. 1 (31 October 1874), in *General Orders, Circular Letters, and Warning Circulars, 1874–1879*, U.S. Secret Service, Record Group 87, National Archives, Washington, D.C.

4. Washburn, General Orders, No. 2 (28 December 1874).

5. Ibid.

6. Ibid.

7. Washburn, General Orders, No. 4 (31 December 1874).

8. These figures include only operatives and chief operatives (who had charge of a district), not the numerous part-time employees.

9. Ironically, the Service's personnel records for the period after 1874 have largely disappeared. Since operatives had no need to record personal information in the Daily Reports of Agents, which at 715 linear feet is the single largest record series surviving for the years after 1874, there is very little information available about the backgrounds of operatives.

10. *New York Times*, 12 October 1895 (obituary); *Washington Post*, 13 October 1895 (obituary); James J. Brooks, *Whiskey Drips: A Series of Interesting Sketches, Illustrating the Operations of the Whiskey Thieves in Their Evasions of the Law and Its Penalties* (Philadelphia: William B. Evans, 1873), 87. The *Philadelphia Inquirer*, 25 November 1872, contains the confession of the man who shot Brooks. Brooks' application to the Service is in the Register of Letters Received, 1863–1903 (16 vols.), U.S. Secret Service, Record Group 87, National Archives, Washington, D.C., 4:17–18.

11. Brooks, *Whiskey Drips*, 130.

12. Ibid., 233–34.

13. James J. Brooks's religious and political affiliations were recounted in his obituaries in the *New York Times*, 12 October 1895; and *Washington Post*, 13 October 1895.

14. James J. Brooks was listed as Assistant Chief in an arrest record for 29 December 1874, in *Description and Information of Criminals*, 4:243.

15. James J. Brooks, DRA, 1 January 1875 to 20 October 1876.

16. *New York Times*, 13 February 1921 (obituary); Reports of I. C. Nettleship, Chief Assistant S. S. Division (1871–1874) 10:43, 53–54, 65, 91, 98, 102 in I. C. Nettleship Collection, New Jersey Historical Society; Register of Letters Received, 1863–1903, 5:72; Andrew Drummond, DRA, January 1875.

17. Drummond, DRA, 21 April 1885.

18. These and other examples of agents' backgrounds were gleaned from various newspaper clippings in Scrapbooks, 1894–1912, U.S. Secret Service, Record Group 87, National Archives, Washington, D.C.

19. On the importance of this issue for successfully managing organizations, see Wilson, *The Investigators*, 13–14.

20. Scanlon's response is recorded in Drummond, DRA, 12 June 1879.

21. Most of the Service's administrative records, and particularly its correspondence files, have not survived. It is therefore difficult to estimate just how systematically politicians attempted to influence appointments to the Service. Surviving evidence indicates that the politicians were more successful with William Wood than with his successors in finding places for their constituents. See, for example, Wood's monthly reports, RMR, July 1865 to June 1866, in which Wood listed the sponsors of several operatives. There are no comparable lists for subsequent administrations, although the issue of political influence appears sporadically in various places. See, for example, James Brooks to Andrew Drummond, in Drummond, DRA, 6 July 1878; Drummond to John P. Brooks, in Brooks, DRA, 13 February 1891; and John Wilkie to Senator John C. Spooner, 5 January 1907, in Letters Sent, 1899–1914, U.S. Secret Service, Record Group 87, National Archives, Washington, D.C.

22. Drummond, DRA, 9 July 1878, 21 September 1878; 5 April 1879; 22 April 1885; 2 March 1886.

23. Hiram C. Whitley to Solicitor E. C. Banfield, 8 April 1870, 25 October 1870; Whitley to James M. Moore, 4 March 1871; Whitley to Senator O. P. Morton, 12 June 1871; Whitley to M. T. Russell, 27 December 1872; Whitley to A. P. Callahan, 11 June 1873, in Letters Sent from Headquarters of the Chief in New York 1870–1873.

24. *New York Times*, 12 October 1895, 13 February 1921; Henry Curtis, DRA, 25 April 1877; John P. Brooks, DRA, 8 July 1889, 13 September 1889, 9 February 1892; Wilkie to L. W. Gammon, 3 October 1909, in Letters Sent, 1899–1918.

25. Drummond, DRA, 12 December 1875.

26. See, for example, John P. Brooks, DRA, 7 July 1893; William P. Hazen, DRA, 17 May 1899; Wilkie to E. A. Gorman, 4 January 1907, in Letters Sent, 1899–1914.

27. James P. Brooks, General Orders, No. 1 (23 August 1878).

28. Curtis, DRA, 18 January 1879; Drummond, DRA, 23 November 1881, 9 September 1885; J. P. Brooks, DRA, 21 July 1890; Ray Bagg, DRA, 15 April 1895; George Hazen, DRA, 14 November 1897; William Hazen, DRA, 22 November 1898.

29. Drummond, DRA, 16 July 1881, 29 August 1881, 2 October 1881.

30. Papers relating to the Dismissal of Special Operative M. M. Mulhall, Pittsburgh District, 1892–93; Bagg, DRA, October 1895.

31. Drummond, DRA, 2 June 1875, 18 November 1877, 3 June 1879, 16 to 18 August 1881, 30 March 1885; J. P. Brooks, DRA, 7 May 1889, 8 November 1890, 22 January 1891; Bagg, DRA, 6 August 1895; G. W. Hazen, DRA, 18 March 1898; Joseph A. Walker to Wilkie, 21 November 1902; G. W. Hazen to Wilkie, 24 May 1904, in General Correspondence, 1894–1918, U.S. Secret Service, Record Group 87, National Arhcives, Washington, D.C.; Wilkie to B. W. Bell, 13 October 1904, in Letters Sent, 1899–1914.

32. For its theoretical grounding this discussion relies on John Maniha and Charles Perrow, "The Reluctant Organization and the Aggressive Environment," *Administrative Science Quarterly* 10 (September 1965): 238–57.

33. Cindy S. Aron, *Ladies and Gentlemen of the Civil Service: Middle Class Workers in Victorian America* (New York: Oxford University Press, 1987), 166, 169–70.

34. J. Y. Donn, RMR, December 1865; Drummond, DRA, 15 to 17 August, 5 September 1877; G. W. Hazen, DRA, 7 October 1897, 15 November 1897.

35. Whitley, RMR, June, August, 1869; *Description and Information of Criminals*, 1863–1874, passim.

36. Newcomb, RMR, February 1870. The time required for these inquiries raised protests from the operatives; see, for example, Curtis, DRA, 4 December 1876.

37. Drummond, DRA, 1 to 8 January 1875, 20 and 25 February 1875, 3 July 1875, 16 February 16, 1888; J. P. Brooks, DRA, 27 June 1890; James Scanlon, DRA, 7 April 1894; *Seattle Daily Times*, 24 May 1904.

38. On the importance of the Treasury, see Leonard D. White, *The Republican Era: A Study in Administrative History, 1869–1901* (New York: Macmillan, 1958), 110.

39. On the issue of an executive's role in defending his agency's well-being, see Wilson, *The Investigators*, 163–64.

40. Department of the Treasury, *Annual Report, 1876* (Washington, D.C.: Government Printing Office, 1876), 628.

41. I have been unable to determine Cheeks's identity, although his familiarity with federal policing issues as well as the administrative structure of the Treasury and Department of Justice indicates that he was a federal employee.

42. Peter C. Cheeks, "A plan for the consolidation of the Special Agents of the various Depts. with the Secret Service division of the Treasury, who are to be known as 'Special Agents,' the Chief of whom shall be Commissioner. This Bureau to be henceforth under the control of the Department of Justice," n.d., submitted by Solicitor Rayner to the Honorable Richard McCormick, 22 November 1877, in Reports of Operations of the Secret Service Division, 1874–1877, U.S. Secret Service, Record Group 87, National Archives, Washington, D.C.

43. This discussion is based on the assumption that changes in the size and scope of a bureaucracy, as well as the location of its headquarters, are subject to negotiation among the principals involved. It is, of course, possible to conceive of a bureaucracy as a hierarchical flow chart in which subordinate agency heads simply do what they are told. That concept, however, does not account for the effects of interpersonal relations within hierarchical organizations nor does it explain the outcome of the Solicitor's proposal.

44. *New York Times*, 1 December 1877.

45. Order of Secretary Sherman, 23 November 1878, reprinted in *New York Times*, 1 January 1879.

46. *U.S. Statutes at Large* (Washington, D.C.: Government Printing Office, 1879) 20:384.

47. Ibid., 21:265; the bargain is not formally recorded but is mentioned in John Wilkie to Representative M. E. Driscoll, 1 February 1909, in Letters Sent, 1899–1914. For an example of the new arrangements, see Drummond, DRA, 22 January 1882.

48. *U.S. Statutes at Large*, 22:230, 313.

49. Drummond, DRA, 19 and 21 April 1885.

50. Washburn, General Orders, No. 2 (28 December 1874).

51. On the effects of this order, see, for example, Drummond, DRA, 9 and 12 June 1885, 31 July 1885, 27 November 1885, 3, 5, and 9 December 1885.

52. See Brooks's instructions to Drummond in Drummond, DRA, 3 May 1885, and the results in Drummond, DRA, 7, 8, 13, and 14 May 1885.

53. Drummond, DRA, 29 May 1885.

54. Curtis, DRA, 2 December 1876; Drummond, DRA, 4, 5, and 14 July 1881, 22 January 1882, 2 to 4 March 1885.

55. Drummond, DRA, 16 December 1885.

56. Drummond, DRA, 27 August 1886.

57. *Circular from the Solicitor of the Treasury to District Attorneys, Marshals, and Clerks of Courts of the United States* (Washington, D.C.: Treasury Department, 1865), 5.

58. R. R. Lowell, RMR, November 1865; Newcomb, RMR, December 1865; Stephen Franklin, RMR, September 1866; John Sharkey, RMR, January 1870.

59. On local police corruption, see Joseph Gaillard, RMR, March 1866; Newcomb, RMR, February 1866; John Murray, RMR, July 1866; William Redfield, RMR, October 1866; James Tullis, RMR, February 1867; Hiram C. Whitley, *In It* (Cambridge, Mass.: The Riverside Press, 1894), 104–5. On federal corruption, see Lowell, RMR, September 1865; Murray, RMR, October 1865; Frederick Tapley, RMR, January 1867.

60. This judgement is based on the scarcity of evidence that the Service used money or information to create relationships with the local police during Wood's regime. However, the lack of relevant records for a large part of Whitley's tenure makes the generalization tenuous. I am assuming from Whitley's efforts at empire building, and his remarks about paying rewards, that he did not seek such relationships.

61. Curtis, DRA, 26 and 27 December 1876; Drummond, DRA, 1 August 1875, 4 November 1875, 16 May 1876, 2 July 1876, 30 January 1877, 10 January 1880, 11 November 1883; James Brooks to Solicitor Henry Neal, 17 November 1884, in Solicitor of the Treasury, Letters Received from the Secret Service, Record Group 206, National Archives, Washington, D.C.; George Hazen, DRA, 15 September 1897.

62. Curtis, DRA, 25 January 1878, 23 December 1878; Drummond, DRA, 17 March 1875, 25 November 1875, 27 October 1877, 30 September 1879, 9 April 1880, 13 May 1880.

63. Curtis, DRA, 25 September 1876; Bagg, DRA, 21 May 1895.

64. Drummond, DRA, 14 August 1877, 8 October 1877, 15 February 1882.

65. I have found no evidence of such borrowing in the Daily Reports of Agents for the period 1875–1900.

66. A point that comfirms James Wilson's comment that "borrowing informants from another, and rival agency, is difficult and often impossible." Wilson, *The Investigators*, 58.

67. Although this strategy was implicit in Wood's activities, Whitley was the first to articulate it. See Whitley to Solicitor Banfield, 16 July 1873, in Letters Sent from Headquarters.

68. Drummond, DRA, 27 November 1885.

69. Ibid., 11 December 1885.

70. Ibid., 16 December 1885.

71. Drummond summarized his testimony in ibid., 1 February 1886.

72. Ibid., 5 and 29 January 1886.

73. Ibid., 2, 4 and 5 April 1888, 13 June 1888.

74. John Brooks, DRA, 1 and 19 May 1888.

75. *New York Times*, 24 April 1890; Walter S. Bowen and Harry E. Neal, *The United States Secret Service* (Philadelphia: Chilton, 1960), 154.

76. *New York Times*, 4 June 1890.

77. House Report 3042, 51st Cong., 1st sess., 2816, 2–3.

78. *New York Times*, 24 April, 10 June 1890, 12 October 1895; John Brooks, DRA, 5 January 1891.

79. *U.S. Statutes at Large*, 26:742–43.

80. *U.S. Statutes at Large*, 27:365.

81. William Hazen, DRA, 15 June 1898.

82. Bagg, DRA, 2 March 1896; William Hazen, DRA, 6 March 1898, 24 April 1898; Letters and Reports relating to Spy Suspects during the Spanish-American War, February to August 1898, U.S, Secret Service, Record Group 87, National Archives, Washington, D.C.; E. J. Parsons to U.S. Attorney Warren S. Reese, 26 January 1903, Commissioner of Immigration to Wilkie, 14 January 1905, Wilkie to the Commissioner of Immigration, 16 and 24 January 1905, in General Correspondence, 1894–1918; *Brooklyn Daily Eagle*, 12 March 1905; L. M. Shaw to the Attorney General, 30 March 1905; Wilkie to the Secretary of the Treasury, 22 December 1906; Wilkie to AG Charles J. Bonaparte, 15 January 1908; Acting Secretary of the Secret Service to Truman H. Newberry, 14 August 1908; Wilkie to Lawrence Richey, 24 September 1908; in Letters Sent, 1899–1914.

CHAPTER 5
DISMANTLING THE MONEY MARKET

1. This analysis is confined to the number of operatives (defined as full-time detectives) the Service employed; part-time assistants and informers, whose numbers varied widely from month to month and year to year, are not included here.

2. James Downs, RMR, November 1865; I. C. Nettleship, RMR, May 1866; John Murray, RMR, May 1866; Alexander Bicknell, RMR, May 1867. On illegal behavior, see chapter 3.

3. W. P. Wood, *Circular of Instructions to Operatives, Secret Service Division, Treasury Department* (Washington, D.C.: Government Printing Office, 1868), passim.

4. Simon Benson, RMR, February 1871; Hiram C. Whitley to Solicitor Edward C. Banfield, 14 May 1874, in Reports of Operations of the Secret Service, U.S. Secret Service, Record Group 87, National Archives, Washington, D.C.; Whitley, *In It* (Cambridge, Mass.: The Riverside Press, 1894), 108.

5. U.S. Congress, House of Representatives, Joint Select Committee on Affairs in the District of Columbia, *Safe Burglary*, 43rd Cong., 1st sess., Report No. 785 (Washington, D.C.: Government Printing Office, 1874), 197, 227–28, 282.

6. Elmer Washburn, General Orders, No. 2 (28 December 1874), in *General Orders, Circular Letters, and Warning Circulars, 1874–1879*, in U.S. Secret Service, Record Group 87, National Archives, Washington, D.C.

7. Ibid.

8. General Orders, No. 2; Henry R. Curtis, DRA, 27 September 1876.

9. For example, Andrew Drummond, DRA, 7 to 20 December 1875, 10 to 15 February 1878.

10. Drummond, DRA, 25 May 1877, 14 September 1877, 16 February 1878, 9 July 1882, 18 March 1884, 17 October 1884; Curtis, DRA, November 1878; John P. Brooks, DRA, 1 December 1888, 3 October 1890; Ray Bagg, DRA, 12 January 1895, 14 October 1896.

11. Drummond, DRA, 14 to 18 September 1875, 30 April 1876, 8 September 1877, 22 March 1878, 9 August 1884; John P. Brooks, DRA, 1 June 1889, 1 December 1891; William P. Hazen, DRA, 28 September 1899.

12. On the development of detectives and their reputations, see David R. Johnson, *Policing the Urban Underworld: The Impact of Crime and the Development of the American Police, 1800–1887* (Philadelphia: Temple University Press, 1979), 22–24, 41–43, 64–67, 170–72; Frank Morn, *"The Eye That Never Sleeps": A History of the Pinkerton National Detective Agency* (Bloomington: Indiana University Press, 1982), 58–59.

13. This discussion of detective work, and particularly the distinction between investigative and instigative activities, is based on James Q. Wilson, *The Investigators: Managing FBI and Narcotics Agents* (New York: Basic Books, 1978), 39–42, 57.

14. William P. Wood, RMR, March 1865; Wood to Operative Joseph Gaillard, 18 December 1865, in Gaillard, RMR, December 1865; Whitley, *In It*, 146–47; Andrew Drummond, *True Detective Stories* (New York: G. W. Dillingham Co., 1908–9), 47, 49, 51; Drummond, DRA, 6 February 1875, 14 August 1876, 31 August 1878, 22 September, 13 October 1879.

15. *Circular from the Solicitor of the Treasury to District Attorneys, Marshals, and Clerks of Courts of the United States* (Washington, D.C.: Treasury Department, 1865), 3–5, in Solicitor of the Treasury, Letters Received from the Secret Service, Record Group 206, National Archives, Washington, D.C.

16. Charles Newman, RMR, June 1865; Wood, RMR, August 1865; Robert R. Lowell, RMR, 28 September 1865.

17. Frederick C. Tapley, RMR, November 1865, May 1867; Samuel Picking, RMR, April 1866; James Tullis, RMR, January 1867; William Redfield, RMR, January 1867; William Hildreth, RMR, May 1867; Martin Igoe, RMR, June 1867; Benson, RMR, August 1867; Wood's penchant for rewards is mentioned in Joseph Burr to Solicitor Bluford Wilson, 16 June 1874, in Letters Received from the Secret Service.

18. Whitley to Banfield, 16 June 1870, in Letters Sent from Headquarters of the Chief in New York 1870–1873, in U.S. Secret Service, Record Group 87, National Archives, Washington, D.C.

19. *New York Times*, 11 January 1872; George P. Burnham, *Memoirs of the United States Secret Service* (Boston: Laban Heath, 1872), 84, 219, 228; Hiram C. Whitley, *Circular of Instructions to Operatives, Secret Service Division, Treasury Department* (Washington, D.C.: Government Printing Office, 1873), 4–7. Copies of Whitley's pamphlet have apparently not survived, but its contents can be surmised from these other sources.

20. Whitley, *Circular of Instructions*, 8–11.

21. Whitley to Egbert, 11 July 1870, in Letters Sent from Headquarters.

22. The Service's records contain no continuous data on the number and size of districts. For indications of their fluctuating number and size, see Elmer Washburn, General Order No. 1 (31 October 1874), in Criminals and Suspects, Record of Arrests and Convictions, 1869–1930, in U.S. Secret Service, Record Group 87, National Arhcives, Washington, D.C.; William P. Hazen, DRA, 29 March, 11 September, 1898, 1 June 1899.

23. Nettleship to Downs, 26 May 1871; Nettleship to W. W. Applegate, 1 June 1871; Whitley to M. G. Bauer, W. W. Kennock, J. J. Hoffman, and A. L. Drummond, 1 July 1873, in Letters Sent from Headquarters of the Chief in New York, 1870–1873; Whitley to Solicitor Banfield, 14 May 1874, in Reports of Operations of the Secret Service Division, 1874–1877; Whitley, *Circular of Instructions*, 11, 13, 18; Drummond, *True Detective Stories*, 143.

24. Nettleship to Benson, 14 March 1871; Whitley to Charles E. Anchisi, 25 September 1871, in Letters Sent from Headquarters of the Chief in New York, 1870–1873.

25. Whitley to Lonergan, 6 June 1870; Whitley to Applegate, 9 February 1871; in Letters Sent from Headquarters of the Chief in New York, 1870–1873.

26. Washburn, Circular No. 2 (1 September 1875), in Criminals and Suspects.

27. Curtis, DRA, 18 and 21 November 1876; Drummond, DRA, 15 November 1876, 4 September 1877, 24 March 1880; John P. Brooks, DRA, 12 July 1888.

28. Drummond, DRA, 14 August 1876, 27 June 1879; John Scanlon, DRA, 30 March 1894; Bagg, DRA, 13 March 1896.

29. Unfortunately, Washburn's original orders regarding the no-compromise policy have not survived. The only contemporaneous reference to this new approach appeared in the *New York Times*, 4 December 1875, in a story on Washburn's first annual report (which has not survived either).

30. Whitley, General Orders, No. 1 (27 June 1876).

31. Drummond, DRA, 26 February 1876.

32. Frank Vintree, RMR, May 1870.

33. Drummond, DRA, 12 October 1875, 12 and 13 November 1875; Bagg, DRA, 20 December 1896.

34. Operatives did occasionally recommend suspended sentences. See Drummond, DRA, 22 March 1880, 21 and 29 March 1882.

35. Drummond, DRA, 25 June 1879, 28 June 1883.

36. Wood, RMR, 20 July 1865. Wood's survey was hardly scientific since it was limited by the extent of his personal investigations from the summer of 1864 to the spring of 1865. It therefore contained some significant errors, including an underestimation of New York City's importance.

37. Local records represent the most valuable source for determining the patterns of the Service's activities, because national arrest data, particularly for the early years of the Service's operations, are very incomplete, making generalizations hazardous.

38. Tapley, RMR, April to June 1867.

39. Hiram C. Whitley, Report of Operations for the Month of July, December 1873; Whitley to the Solicitor of the Treasury, 23 November 1873, in Department of Justice Source Chronological Files: Treasury, Record Group 60, National Archives, Washington, D.C.

40. Stephen D. Franklin, RMR, December 1865; Ashbel Culver, RMR, February 1866; Edwin Bruce, RMR, June 1866; John Linscott, RMR, November 1866; M. B. Card, RMR, December 1866; John Gunsales, RMR, April 1867; Stephen Felker, RMR, May 1867; Charles Anchisi, RMR, December 1869.

41. John Beverly, RMR, June 1867.

42. Franklin, RMR, December 1865; Fitzroy Sessions, RMR, July 1867.

43. Nettleship, Reports, 9, 10, 12 and 25 October 1871; Whitley to [New York] Governor John T. Hoffman, 28 October 1871, in Letters Sent from Headquarters of the Chief in New York, 1870–1873.

44. John S. Dye, *The Government Blue Book: A Complete HIstory of the Lives of All the Great Counterfeiters, Criminal Engravers and Plate Printers* (Philadelphia: Dye's Government Counterfeit Detector, 1880), 5–8; Drummond, DRA, 26 February 1876, 15 April 1876.

45. Drummond, DRA, 26 and 29 February 1876.

46. Ibid., 15 and 19 April 1876.

47. Ibid., 21 and 26 April 1876, 17 June 1876.

48. Ibid., 27 July 1876, 14 August 1876.

49. Confession of Charles Ulrich, recorded in Curtis, DRA, 1 December 1878.

50. Drummond, DRA, 25 June 1876; Ulrich confession in Curtis, DRA, 1 December 1878.

51. Drummond, DRA, June to August 1878.

52. Curtis, DRA, 1 and 27 December 1878.

53. Drummond, DRA, 21 January 1879.

54. Ibid., 5 February 1879, 17 August 1880, 22 April 1882; Bagg, DRA, 19 and 21 November 1896.

55. Drummond, DRA, 5 February 1879, 5 March 1879, 21 April 1885.

56. Dye, *Government Blue Book*, passim.

57. Curtis, DRA, 18 September 1876, 15 September 1877; Drummond, DRA, 17 August 1876, 21 September 1877, 26 February 1880, 16 and 21 March 1884, 20 and 28 August 1884; John Brooks, DRA, 29 August 1890, 14 September 1893; Bagg, DRA, 24 November 1894, 21 July 1896; George W. Hazen, DRA, 30 June 1897, 3 January 1898.

58. Curtis, DRA, 30 January 1878.

59. Drummond, DRA, 20, 26 and 27 September 1879.

60. Ibid., 2 January 1880, 13 March 1880, 2 April 1880.

61. Ibid., 30 July 1881; James Brooks to Solicitor Alexander McCue, 18 November 1886, in Letters Received from the Secret Service; John Brooks, DRA, 7 March 1891, 7 and 8 September 1893; Bagg, DRA, 18 December 1894, 12 November 1896.

62. William P. Hazen, DRA, 19 March 1898.

63. For example, see John Brooks, DRA, 17 January 1893 to 20 February 1894; John Scanlon, DRA, 2 March to 30 April 1894; Bagg, DRA, 12 September 1894 to 3 January 1897. All these reports detail a continuous surveillance and disruption of major groups of Italian counterfeiters.

64. See, for example, *Minneapolis Tribune*, 6 July 1895; George Hazen, DRA, 19 August 1897.

65. Secret Service, Circulars on Counterfeit Notes, 1898–1910, U.S. Secret Service, Record Group 87, National Archives, Washington, D.C.

66. Calculated from the Service's evaluations in Circulars on Counterfeit Notes 1898–1910.

67. Edwin J. Wilber and Edward P. Eastman, *A Treatise on Counterfeit, Altered, and Spurious Bank Notes, with Unerring Rules for the Detection of Frauds in the Same* (Poughkeepsie, N.Y.: Published for the Authors, 1865), 4.

68. *Denver Times*, 12 January 1895.

69. Bagg, DRA, 3 June 1896, 1 March 1897; Josiah Flynt, *World of Graft* (New York: McClure, Phillips & Co., 1901), 198–201.

70. Cf. U.S. vs. W. H. Martin, September 1884, and U.S. vs. John Wise and Frank White, January 1895, both in Post Office Bureau, Chief Inspector's Correspondence and Reports, National Archives, Washington, D.C.

CHAPTER 6

CRIMINALS AT BAY

1. The Secret Service did not launch any "Know Your Money" campaigns designed to educate the general public about the problem of counterfeiting until the twentieth century.

2. See Solicitor Edward Jordan, *Circular from the Solicitor of the Treasury to District Attorneys, Marshals, and Clerks of Courts of the United States* (Washington, D.C.: Treasury Department, 1865), in Solicitor of the Treasury, Letters Received from the Secret Service, Record Group 206, National Archives, Washington, D.C.; and U.S. District Attorney D. S. Dickinson to Jordan, 4 January 1866, in Orders, Circulars, and Bulletins Issued by the Chief, 1874–1938, U.S. Secret Service, Record Group 87, National Archives, Washington, D.C. Dickinson wrote to Jordan on behalf of three New York City policemen claiming a reward for the arrest of a counterfeiter.

3. Elmer Washburn, Circular No. 2, 1 September 1875, in *General Orders, Circular Letters, and Warning Circulars, 1874–1879*, U.S. Secret Service, Record Group 87, National Archives, Washington, D.C.; John P. Brooks, DRA, 5 May 1893.

4. John C. Rose, *Jurisdiction and Procedure of the Federal Courts*, 4th ed., rev. (Albany, N.Y.: Matthew Bender & Co., 1931), 121–22, 126.

5. The calculations for the national figure are based on a 10 percent random sample drawn from *Description and Information of Criminals*. The New York figures are from an analysis of the Daily Reports of Agents, January 1875 to October 1936, and are based on *all* arrests reported. The national sample included 1,133 cases for which complete records were available covering the years from 1865 to 1899. Of that number, 379 (33 percent) were dismissed. In New York, complete records were found for 342 arrests by the local police, 434 by the Service. Dismissals were as follows: Local Police, 155 (45 percent); Service, 109 (18 percent).

6. Frederick C. Tapley, RMR, July 1867; Andrew L. Drummond, DRA, 22 March 1884.

7. Drummond, DRA, 29 March 1880.

8. Abner B. Newcomb, RMR, September 1866.

9. Newcomb, RMR, July 1866. See also A. D. Hatch, RMR, October 1866; and John Maloy, RMR, January 1867.

10. Charles Benedict, RMR, December 1866.

11. Tapley, RMR, April and May 1867.

12. Hiram C. Whitley to Banfield, 13 and 24 June 1871, in Letters Sent from Headquarters of the Chief in New York 1870–1873.

13. Whitley, *In It* (Cambridge, Mass.: The Riverside Press, 1894), 116. Whitley, who served as Chief from 1869 to 1874, gave no date for this campaign of intimidation.

14. Henry Curtis, DRA, 14 August 1878; Drummond, DRA, 11 March 1880; and George W. Hazen, DRA, 29 October 1897 provide examples of tracking down and prosecuting straw bail cases.

15. A break in the reports of Service operatives covering the years from 1869 to 1874 makes it impossible to know more precisely when high bail be-

came routine. However, the Daily Reports of Agents for New York, which began in 1875, revealed practically no complaints from operatives on this issue.

16. Newcomb, RMR, December 1865; Charles F. Newman, RMR, July 1867; I. C. Nettleship, RMR, April 1870.

17. I have been able to glean from the Service's records only two cases of corrupt dealings with counterfeiters between 1869 and 1899. Both cases were turned over to the courts; one resulted in a long prison sentence.

18. William Wood, RMR, 20 July 1865, details the cases of 198 counterfeiters arrested roughly between the fall 1864 and July 1865. These cases reveal a wide range of bargaining outcomes, but outright freedom for equipment was rare. For other details on bargaining prior to 1875, see Newcomb, RMR, December 1865; E. W. Pratt, RMR, October 1869; Wood, Letter to the Editor, *New York Times*, 2 July 1867; Reports of I. C. Nettleship, Chief Assistant S.S. Division, 25 to 27 July 1873, in I. C. Nettleship Collection, New Jersey Historical Society (hereafter cited as Reports.

19. See chapter 4 for further details on the evolution of bureaucratic controls over negotiations with counterfeiters.

20. Drummond, DRA, 11, 14, 20 and 24 November 1880.

21. The Service negotiated 114 guilty pleas out of the 434 cases for which there are complete records from the New York District between 1875 and 1899, for a rate of 26 percent. Of the 342 cases inherited from the local police in this district, 21 percent resulted in guilty pleas. According to Lawrence M. Friedman and Robert V. Percival, *The Roots of Justice: Crime and Punishment in Alameda County, California, 1870–1910* (Chapel Hill: University of North Carolina Press, 1981), 176, between 8 percent and 14 percent of all offenders pled guilty in that jurisdiction. For the history of plea bargaining, see the articles by Albert Alschuler, Lawrence Friedman, John Langbein, and Mark Haller in *Law and Society* 13 (Winter 1979).

22. Drummond, DRA, 21 October 1875.

23. Ibid, 12 June 1880.

24. Ibid, 8 June 1881.

25. James J. Brooks, Annual Report to the Solicitor of the Treasury, 30 November 1887, in Letters Received from the Secret Service.

26. *New York Times*, 2 July 1867.

27. Tapley, RMR, May 1866.

28. Whitley to Operative James Fitzpatrick, 8 August 1871; Whitley to Solicitor Banfield, 19 October 1871, in Letters Sent from Headquarters.

29. Drummond, DRA, 8 February 1881.

30. Curtis, DRA, 23 December 1878.

31. Drummond, DRA, 19 October 1875.

32. Cf. William Wood, *Circular of Instructions to Operatives, Secret*

Service Division, Treasury Department (Washington, D.C.: Government Printing Office, 1868), 6–8, and Hiram C. Whitley, *Circular of Instructions to Operatives, Secret Service Division, Treasury Department* (Washington, D.C.: Government Printing Office, 1873), 12–15.

33. Newcomb, RMR, December 1866; James Downs, RMR, June 1867; John Eagan, RMR, October, 1869; Nettleship, Reports, 15 February 1871.

34. Washburn, General Orders, No. 3, 29 December 1874; General Orders, No. 4, 31 December 1874.

35. Washburn, General Orders, No. 1, 27 June 1876.

36. Drummond, quoting a Philadelphia judge's charge to a jury, DRA, 31 May 1877.

37. Brooks, DRA, 23 May 1889.

38. Curtis, DRA, 28 March 1877.

39. Ray Bagg, DRA, 20 December 1895.

40. Drummond, DRA, 16 April 1875, 29 May 1885; Brooks, DRA, 27 May 1891; William P. Hazen, DRA, 10 January 1899.

41. Drummond, DRA, 21 May 1883.

42. Ibid, 14 November 1875, 30 October 1878, 21 May 1883.

43. Ibid, 21 January 1876, 24 and 25 November 1876, 13 March 1877, 24 March 1880; John P. Brooks, DRA, 15 January 1889; Bagg, DRA, 16 January 1895.

44. Drummond, DRA, 24 and 25 November 1876, 27 March 1880; Brooks, DRA, 23 July 1888.

45. Drummond, DRA, 11 September 1876, 21 May 1883.

46. Ibid, 14 and 15 January 1881.

47. Quoted in Bradford P. Wilson, *Enforcing the Fourth Amendment: A Jurisprudential History* (New York: Garland Publishing, 1986), 46, emphasis in original.

48. Ibid., 5–6, 51–53, 54.

49. This was standard practice from the outset of the Service's operations. For example, Henry O. Wright, RMR, 31 July 1865; Drummond, DRA, 23 August 1877.

50. Drummond, DRA, 15 February 1877.

51. R. R. Lowell, RMR, October 1865; Nettleship, Reports, 6 October 1871; Curtis, DRA, 1 July 1876, 2 May 1877; Drummond, DRA, 25 April 1885; Bagg, DRA, 21 September 1894; William P. Hazen, DRA, 25 March 1898.

52. Fletcher Pratt, *Stanton: Lincoln's Secretary of War* (Westport, Conn.: Greenwood Press, 1970), 26.

53. Anthony F. C. Wallace, *Rockdale: The Growth of an American village in the early Industrial Revolution* (New York: W. W. Norton & Co., 1980), 428.

54. Wood to Solicitor Jordan, 8 June 1866, in Letters Received from the Secret Service; John Y. Donn, RMR, July 1867, mentions a circular from Wood revoking rewards for convictions.

55. Whitley to Solicitor Bluford Wilson, 24 July 1874, in Letters Received from the Secret Service.

56. Examples of this tactic continued to appear until at least the mid-1880s. See Curtis, DRA, 1 April 1878; Drummond, DRA, 9 July 1880, 18 May 1881, 15 December 1882, 15 May 1883.

57. Drummond, DRA, 28 May 1883.

58. Ibid., 31 May 1883. Drummond paraphrased Purdy's remarks to the judge.

59. Ibid., 31 October 1883.

60. Ibid, 23 October 1883, 5 June 1885, 25 January 1886, 23 May 1887; John Scanlon, DRA, 8 April 1894; Bagg, DRA, 20 June 1896.

61. Tapley, RMR, June 1867; Stephen Franklin, RMR, May 1867.

62. Tapley, RMR, June 1867.

63. Joseph Gaillard, RMR, July 1867.

64. Ibid., RMR, October 1869.

65. Curtis, DRA, 23 October 1876; Drummond, DRA, 3 October 1879.

66. Nettleship, RMR, October 1865; Drummond, DRA, 4 July, 18 October 1877, 20 May 1878; William P. Hazen, DRA, 24 January 1899.

67. William D. Redfield, RMR, September 1866; E. W. Pratt, RMR, November 1869; Brooks, DRA, 31 December 1890, 9 November 1892.

68. James Downs, RMR, January 1866; Edwin S. Bruce, RMR, June 1867; Drummond, DRA, 13 February 1878, 3 and 14 September 1880, 15 July 1885.

69. William Hildreth, DRA, February 1867; Downs, RMR, July 1867; Drummond, DRA, 8 May 1877, 18 October 1877, 5 January 1878, 4 and 5 June 1880, 18 May 1881.

70. Drummond, DRA, 27 May 1877, 9 June 1877, 3, 20, 22, 29, and 30 November 1877, 1 December 1877.

71. Ibid., 11 November 1876; Curtis, DRA, 15 December 1878; U.S. District Attorney James B. Holland to the Attorney General of the United States, 3 May 1902, in General Correspondence, 1894–1918, U.S. Secret Service, Record Group 87, National Archives, Washington, D.C.

72. Drummond, DRA, 4 December 1877, 22 May 1883; Brooks, DRA, 23 July 1888.

73. Drummond, DRA, 25 January 1882, 3 May 1884, 19 October 1885. The ignorance issue was raised in a case of an Italian fruit seller who claimed not to understand the American system of coinage.

74. These figures are based on the 100 percent sample of local cases found in a survey of the Daily Reports of Agents covering the period from

1875 to 1899 for the New York district. In the national (10 percent) sample, 32 percent of all cases brought to trial resulted in convictions.

75. Franklin, RMR, September 1866; Newcomb, RMR, December 1866; Downs, RMR, June 1867.

76. Copy of "Circular to All Agents," 1 September 1870, and Whitley, "General Order," 7 February 1871, both in Letters Sent from Headquarters; Whitley, *Circular of Instructions*, 13.

77. The format of the series *Description and Information of Criminals* changed dramatically beginning with volume 4, the first volume dating from Washburn's period as chief of the Service.

78. Drummond, DRA, 16, 26 and 28 April 1875, 18 May 1875, 19 October 1875; Curtis, DRA, 23 December 1878; Brooks, DRA, 23 and 24 May 1889, 22 October 1890, 11 and 22 December 1890, 25 May 1891.

79. William P. Hazen, DRA, 10 January 1899, 11 March 1899.

80. House Executive Document 179, 40th Cong., 2d sess., 1339, pp. 10 and 23, listed 125 pardons, mostly for counterfeiting, in 1866.

81. Drummond, DRA, 17 October 1877, 4 and 8 April 1878, and 10 August 1878 chronicle efforts to forge pardon documents for two convicted counterfeiters.

82. Wood supported two pardons among those listed in House Executive Document 179; for examples of opposition to pardons, see Downs, RMR, January 1867; John Byrne, RMR, May 1869; William P. Hazen, DRA, 23 September 1899.

83. Brooks to Solicitor Alexander McCue, 30 November 1887, in Letters Received from the Secret Service.

CHAPTER 7
CRIME AND POWER

1. *The Congressional Globe*, 37th Cong., 3d sess. (10 February 1863), 843.

2. For an analysis of the problems of traditional criminal cultures coping with new policing methods in England, see V. A. C. Gatrell, "The Decline of Theft and Violence in Victorian and Edwardian England," *Crime and the Law: The Social History of Crime in Europe since 1500*, ed. V. A. C. Gatrell, Bruce Lenman, and Geoffrey Parker (London: Europa Publications Limited, 1980), 261–64

3. I am indebted to Professor Woodruff Smith for this observation.

4. For example, Henry Curtis, DRA, 9 November 1877, 10 August 1878, 13 May 1879; Andrew Drummond, DRA, 3 June 1885; John Brooks, DRA, 21, 28, and 30 April 1888, 5 May 1888, 17 July 1888.

5. These complaints had become so common by 1890 that I decided to

record them only every third year to determine the overall trend. In each of the sample years I recorded every complaint, with the following result: 1890, 46 complaints; 1893, 45; 1896, 29; 1899, 56. My conclusions about the backgrounds of the complainants is based on comments that Secret Service operatives made in their reports of these incidents.

6. On dismissals for possession of a single counterfeit, see Drummond, DRA, 8 April 1880, 3 May 1880, 12 March 1884; Brooks, DRA, 6 May 1889.

7. Prior to the late 1880s, operatives merely advised victims to file a formal complaint. The willingness to mediate these cases began to emerge in New York when John Brooks became chief operative, and may reflect a personal decision on his part. However, subsequent operatives continued the policy. On Brooks, see DRA, 7, 9, 15, and 25 October 1889, 8 and 20 November 1889, 10 December 1889. The samples I compiled on citizen complaints for 1890, 1893, 1896, and 1899 illustrated the continuation of this policy.

8. Brooks, DRA, 9 November 1889.

9. *The Congressional Globe* (10 February 1863), 843.

10. See, inter alia, Curtis, DRA, 15 May 1877; Drummond, DRA, 14 and 15 May 1877, 22 to 24 September 1881, 16 to 26 May 1882, 10 and 14 July 1882, 12 May 1883.

11. James Brooks to Solicitor Henry S. Neal, 17 November 1884, in Solicitor of the Treasury, Letters Received from the Secret Service, Record Group 206, National Archives, Washington, D.C.; Curtis, DRA, 4 January 1879; Drummond, DRA, 25 and 30 August 1881, 18 September 1881, 16 June 1882, 14 March 1884; John Wilkie to J. M. Dinwiddie, 22 December 1906, in Letters Sent, 1899–1914, U.S. Secret Service, Record Group 87, National Archives, Washington, D.C.

12. Drummond, DRA, 9, 10, 19, 22, and 25 August 1881, 12 and 15 October 1881, 5 November 1881.

13. Brooks, DRA, 3 March 1891; William P. Hazen, DRA, 13 September 1898.

14. Drummond, DRA, 17 February 1886.

15. *Chicago Daily News*, 22 November 1894. All newspaper citations in this discussion are from the Service's Scrapbooks, 1894–1912, U.S. Secret Service, Record Group 87, National Archives, Washington, D.C. Although a few newspaper clippings antedate 1894 in the archival records (see Newspaper Clippings, 1880–1930), the creation of the Scrapbooks under Hazen represent the first time that a chief had paid systematic attention to the Service's public image.

16. See newspaper articles collected in the Scrapbooks for July and August 1897.

17. *New York Evening Sun*, 21 April 1899; *Philadelphia Telegram*, 20 April 1899; for other editorials see Scrapbooks, April and May 1899.

18. Israel Stolberg, Philadelphia, to President Theodore Roosevelt, 19 December 1904; E. W. Kinesey, Claypool, Indiana, to the Secret Service Department, 20 December 1904; Harry W. Stephenson, New Haven, Pennsylvania, to Chief of Detectives, U.S. Secret Service, 9 January 1905; Sheriff Joseph G. Francis, Morris, Illinois, to Chief of Secret Service, 14 January 1905, in General Correspondence, 1894–1918.

INDEX